FAIRIES IN NINETEENTH
ART AND LITERA~

Although fairies are now banished to the realm of childhood, these diminutive figures were central to the work of many nineteenth-century painters, novelists, poets and even scientists. It would be no exaggeration to say that the Victorians were obsessed with fairies: yet this obsession has hitherto received little scholarly attention. Nicola Bown reminds us of the importance of fairies in Victorian culture. In the figure of the fairy, the Victorians crystallised contemporary anxieties about the effects of industrialisation, the remoteness of the past, the value of culture and the way in which science threatened to undermine religion and spirituality. Above all, the fairy symbolised disenchantment with the irresistible forces of progress and modernity. As these forces stripped the world of its wonder, the Victorians consoled themselves by dreaming of a place and a people suffused with the enchantment that was disappearing from their own lives.

NICOLA BOWN is a lecturer in the Department of English at Birkbeck College, University of London. She has published articles in *Textual Practice*, *Women: A Cultural Review* and the *Journal of Victorian Culture*, and worked for the Royal Academy on their *Victorian Fairy Painting* show. This is her first book.

CAMBRIDGE STUDIES IN NINETEENTH-CENTURY
LITERATURE AND CULTURE

General editor
Gillian Beer, *University of Cambridge*

Editorial board
Isobel Armstrong, *Birkbeck College, London*
Leonore Davidoff, *University of Essex*
Terry Eagleton, *University of Oxford*
Catherine Gallagher, *University of California, Berkeley*
D. A. Miller, *Columbia University*
J. Hillis Miller, *University of California, Irvine*
Mary Poovey, *New York University*
Elaine Showalter, *Princeton University*

Nineteenth-century British literature and culture have been rich fields for inter-disciplinary studies. Since the turn of the twentieth century, scholars and critics have tracked the intersections and tensions between Victorian literature and the visual arts, politics, social organisation, economic life, technical innovations, scientific thought – in short, culture in its broadest sense. In recent years, theoretical challenges and historiographical shifts have unsettled the assumptions of previous scholarly synthesis and called into question the terms of older debates. Whereas the tendency in much past literary critical interpretation was to use the metaphor of culture as 'background', feminist, Foucauldian, and other analyses have employed more dynamic models that raise questions of power and of circulation. Such developments have reanimated the field.

This series aims to accommodate and promote the most interesting work being undertaken on the frontiers of the field of nineteenth-century literary studies: work which intersects fruitfully with other fields of study such as history, or literary theory, or the history of science. Comparative as well as interdisciplinary approaches are welcomed.

A complete list of titles published will be found at the end of the book.

FAIRIES IN NINETEENTH-CENTURY ART AND LITERATURE

NICOLA BOWN

CAMBRIDGE
UNIVERSITY PRESS

CAMBRIDGE UNIVERSITY PRESS
Cambridge, New York, Melbourne, Madrid, Cape Town, Singapore, São Paulo

Cambridge University Press
The Edinburgh Building, Cambridge CB2 2RU, UK

Published in the United States of America by Cambridge University Press, New York

www.cambridge.org
Information on this title: www.cambridge.org/9780521793155

First published 2001
This digitally printed first paperback version 2006

A catalogue record for this publication is available from the British Library

Library of Congress Cataloguing in Publication data
Bown, Nicola.
Fairies in Nineteenth-century Art and Literature / Nicola Bown.
p.   cm. – (Cambridge Studies in Nineteenth-century
Literature and Culture; 33)
Includes bibliographical references and index.
ISBN 0 521 79315 7
1. Fairies in art.   2. Arts, Victorian – Themes, motives.
I. Title.   II. Series.
NX652.F34 B69   2001
700′.475 – dc21   2001025773

ISBN-13 978-0-521-79315-5 hardback
ISBN-10 0-521-79315-7 hardback

ISBN-13 978-0-521-02550-8 paperback
ISBN-10 0-521-02550-8 paperback

O happy, happy season,
Ere bright Fancy bent to Reason;
When the spirit of our stories
Filled the mind with unseen glories;
Told of creatures of the air,
Spirits, fairies, goblins rare,
Guarding man with tenderest care;
When before the blazing hearth,
Listening to the tale of mirth,
Sons and daughters, mother, sire,
Neighbours all drew round the fire;
Lending open ear and faith
To what some learned gossip saith!
    But the fays and all are gone,
Reason, reason reigns alone;
Every grace and charm is fled,
All by dulness banished;
Thus we ponder, slow and sad,
After Truth the world is mad;
Ah! believe me, Error too
Hath its charms, nor small, nor few.
    Epigraph to J. C. and W. C. Grimm,
        German Popular Stories, 1824

Contents

List of illustrations   *page* x
Acknowledgements   xii

Introduction. Small enchantments   1

1   Fancies of Fairies and spirits and nonsense   12

2   Queen Mab among the steam engines   39

3   A few fragments of fairyology, shewing its
    connection with natural history   98

4   A broken heart and a pocket full of ashes   163

Notes   198
Bibliography   220
Index   230

Illustrations

1 J. M. W. Turner, *Queen Mab's Cave* (Tate Gallery, London 2000)   *page* 7

2 Henry Fuseli, *Titania and Bottom* (Tate Gallery, London 2000)   19

3 J. Parker after Henry Fuseli, *Puck* (Photograph: Witt Library, Courtauld Institute, London)   25

4 Edward Hopley, *Puck and a Moth (Pre-Raffaelite Version)* (Private Collection)   42

5 Thomas Stothard, *Frontispiece to Canto III, The Rape of the Lock* (By Permission of the Syndics, Cambridge University Library)   46

6 David Scott, *Puck Fleeing Before the Dawn* (National Gallery of Scotland)   59

7 David Scott, *Ariel and Caliban* (National Gallery of Scotland)   61

8 Daniel Maclise, *Scene from 'Undine'* (Royal Collection)   71

9 Robert Huskisson, *The Midsummer Night's Fairies* (Tate Gallery, London 2000)   76

10 Richard Dadd, *Puck* (Private Collection, Photograph: Photographic Survey, Courtauld Institute, London)   79

11 Richard Dadd, *Come Unto These Yellow Sands* (Private Collection, Photograph: Witt Library, Courtauld Institute, London)   81

12 Joseph Noel Paton, *The Quarrel of Oberon and Titania* (National Gallery of Scotland)   92

13 Joseph Noel Paton, *The Reconciliation of Oberon and Titania* (National Gallery of Scotland)   93

14 John Everett Millais, *Ferdinand Lured by Ariel* (Makins Collection, Photograph: Bridgeman Art Library)   111

15 John Anster Fitzgerald, *Cock Robin Defending his Nest*
(Private Collection, Photograph: Birmingham Museums
and Art Gallery)   112

16 John Anster Fitzgerald, *Who Killed Cock Robin?* (Private
Collection, Photograph: Birmingham Museums
and Art Gallery)   113

17 John Anster Fitzgerald, *Fairies Sleeping in a Bird's Nest*
(Maas Gallery, London)   114

18 Plate IV, Phillip Henry Gosse, *Actinologia Britannica*
(By Permission of the Syndics of Cambridge
University Library)   121

19 'Insects at Work', Jules Michelet, *The Insect* (By Permission
of the Syndics of Cambridge University Library)   126

20 'The Fresh Water Siren', 'Acheta Domestica', *Episodes of Insect
Life* (Shelf-mark 1258.f.10–12, British Library, London)   130

21 Frontispiece, Ernest Van Bruyssel, *The Population of an Old Pear
Tree* (By Permission of the Syndics of Cambridge University
Library)   134

22 Frontispiece, *The Comical Creatures from Wurtemberg*
(Shelf-mark Rec.e.209, Bodleian Library, Oxford)   138

23 Walter Potter, *The Death of Cock Robin* (Walter Potter's
Museum of Curiosities, Cornwall, Photograph: P. A. Morris)   139

24 Richard Dadd, *The Fairy Feller's Master-Stroke* (Tate Gallery,
London 2000)   151

25 Richard Dadd, *Songe de la Fantaisie* (Fitzwilliam Museum,
Cambridge)   152

26 Herbert James Draper, *The Kelpie* (National Museums and
Galleries on Merseyside, Lady Lever Art Gallery)   178

27 Estella Canziani, *The Piper of Dreams* (Private Collection,
reproduced courtesy of the Medici Society, Photograph:
Maas Gallery, London)   185

28 Elsie Wright, *Frances and the Fairies* (Brotherton Collection,
Leeds University Library)   188

29 Elsie Wright, *Frances and the Leaping Fairy* (Brotherton
Collection, Leeds University Library)   189

30 Frances Griffiths, *Fairy Offering a Posy to Elsie*
(Brotherton Collection, Leeds University Library)   190

Acknowledgements

My sincere thanks are due to the museums, libraries and private owners who granted permission to reproduce the illustrations in this book, many of whom did so either free of charge or for a considerably reduced fee. I am especially grateful to Rupert Maas of the Maas Gallery for his help in locating paintings. Parts of chapters 1, 3 and 4 have previously been published in *Women: A Cultural Review* (vol. 10, 1999), *Journal of Victorian Culture* (vol. 8, 2000), *Textual Practice* (vol. 10, 1996) and *Victorian Culture and the Idea of the Grotesque* edited by David Amigoni, Paul Barlow and Colin Trodd (1998). I am also grateful to staff at the British Library and Cambridge University Library, whose work made this book possible.

I have been lucky to have had a lot of help with writing this book; the more so as it has taken rather a long time to write. It is not an understatement to say that it would not have been written without the encouragement and interest of friends and colleagues to sustain me during the difficult business of thinking and writing, and I cannot hope, without embarrassment or fatigue to the reader, fully to describe my obligations. I owe an especial debt to Lindsay Smith, who supervised the book in its first incarnation as a thesis (dread words!): her interest in the interweaving of word and image in the Victorian period was a formative influence on my work, and the originality of her thinking an inspiration. My mother, Leslie Tomlinson, has been unfailingly supportive, even though she must have doubted the book would ever get finished. The book owes much of its present shape and substance to conversations with among others Gillian Beer, Claire Buck, Carolyn Burdett, Patrick Curry, Erica Fudge, Danielle Fuller, David Hemsoll, Sam Inglis, David Jarrett, Sarah Meer, Mary Peace, Leah Price, Barbara Rosenbaum, Charlotte Sleigh, Jenny Bourne Taylor, Pamela Thurschwell and Sue Wiseman. I talked through many of the central ideas in the book with Wendy Wheeler, and owe a great deal to her bold intelligence. I have also benefited from the comments of audiences at conferences and seminars where I have talked about fairies, and from lively conversations with my students. Whatever I am able to convey to my readers of my curiosity about and love for my subject, and the extent to which this book escapes being dry and pedantic, are due in large measure to the influence of those named here. In particular, I would like to thank David Booth and Caroline Howlett. My last thanks, for everything else that matters, go to Sam: not all of our riches belong to the past.

Introduction. Small enchantments

This book is about magic and enchantment, but it is also about disillusion and fear. It is about the wonderful yet appalling modern world the Victorians made, and why they consoled themselves for their disquiet at it by dreaming of fairies. The Victorians thought of themselves as makers and masters of the modern world: that is the self-image they were most anxious to pass on to posterity. But they also felt oppressed by their responsibilities, fearful of the future and doubtful of the unalloyed benefits of progress. Fear, anxiety, doubt and pessimism cannot be magicked away, it is true, but they can be given an enchanted form. The Victorians dreamed of fairies, who worked a small enchantment for them, and gave them back the wonder and mystery modernity had taken away from the world. They made the fairies into imaginary versions of themselves, and imagined fairyland as a version of the world they themselves inhabited. They consoled themselves by looking at their worst fears and greatest worries for themselves and their world in a magical, enchanted form. By looking at and reading about fairies, the Victorians could imagine themselves as being still in the world they had given up for modernity. They shaped fairyland into the negative image of their own disenchanted world, and saw their own disappointed forms transfigured in the shape of the fairy.

Fairies were everywhere in nineteenth-century culture: in the nursery, certainly, but also in the parlour or drawing room, on the stage and on the walls of annual exhibitions. Fairies were not just for children, nor even mostly for children. Adults fell under their spell freely, and indulged a taste for escapist fantasy in visions and descriptions of fairies and fairyland. The fascination with fairies which is the subject of this book emerged in the late eighteenth century, and the fairy was a pervasive cultural figure for more than a hundred years. Indeed, so many and various were the forms that the captivation with fairies took that in this book I look at only a few of them. Hundreds of fairy operas and operettas, plays, songs and ballets were produced in the nineteenth century, too many for me to deal with here. The same goes for the enormous numbers of fairy tales, traditional and literary, which were published during the period. In this book I concentrate on fairies in paintings, poetry and non-fictional prose. These genres interest me because they allowed the Victorians, most of all grown-up ones, an outlet for their regressive and escapist fantasies. When I first became interested in nineteenth-century fairies I was startled by the mixture of strangeness and sentimentality I encountered. This book is about that combination of strangeness and sentimentality, and in it I argue that understanding the Victorians' enchantment with fairyland is central to understanding their emotional responses to their own world.

The Victorians were fascinated by the supernatural: by ghosts and vampires, by spirits of the dead, by angels, by the gods of other cultures. Their interest in fairies differed from that in other forms of the supernatural, though some themes were constant. In an age of widespread religious doubt, it is not surprising that people's thoughts should have turned to the persistence of the dead and to occult methods of communicating with them. Though Victorian society was acutely conscious of its own modernity, the lure of the past and its beliefs was felt by many. The influence of the empire and its diversity of faiths and gods also prompted many to search beyond Christian traditions for enlightenment. All of these factors affected the interest in fairies. But fairies differ from ghosts and spirits in that they are not manifestations of the dead; fairies have nothing of the ghastly power of the dead awakened. They are local rather than exotic, and many saw them as peculiarly British, part of a national culture. And they lack the powers of the gods, for fairies are small, and work only minor magics. The gods inspire awe; they are omnipotent, omniscient and omnipresent. Though sometimes malicious, fairies are more often mischievous; generally they are nice rather than nasty. Finally, and most importantly, belief in fairies was not required in order for them to act as a consolation for modernity. Most Victorians who dallied with the fairies did not believe in them, though many thought that their forebears had so believed, and they found the conditions of this credence fascinating. Unlike heaven, hell or the 'other side', the idea of fairyland could be entertained *as if* one believed in it without actually doing so. In a period when many were tormented by religious doubt, such 'as if' belief in supernatural beings whom one knew perfectly well did not exist must itself have been a consolation.

The book begins in the eighteenth century and ends in the early twentieth century, and so spans a long nineteenth century. The awakening of interest in fairies I discuss in chapter 1 created the conditions for the flowering of fairy painting and poetry in the nineteenth century. The Victorian period is the focus of chapters 2 and 3, which cover the decades between 1830 and 1870. These two chapters discuss the preoccupation with fairies at its fullest extent and development: it was the Victorians who were the real connoisseurs of the fairy. Chapter 4 mirrors the first by tracing the disappearance of the Victorian fascination with fairies and discussing the reasons why it ended. The content of each chapter is delineated thematically as well as chronologically. The first chapter focuses on the way that changing values accorded to the imagination and to tradition led to the emergence of the fairy as a significant cultural figure. I argue that the interest in fairies is part of a wider rejection of the values of the Enlightenment which found its fullest expression in Romanticism. I also argue that it was these factors which meant that while men were fascinated by fairies, women were largely indifferent to them. In the second chapter, I discuss some of the ways in which fairies represented the modern world. I focus on three issues: the invention of the hot air balloon, the effect on ideas of scale of the development of the steam engine and the factory system, and the idea of Arcadia in the industrial age. I argue that representations of fairies were shaped by reactions to these aspects of modernity, even though fairyland initially seems a long way away from modern technology and industry. The third chapter looks at the ways in which Victorian ideas about science were refracted through representations of fairies. I argue that the figure of the fairy was a potent metaphor for both optimistic and anxious reactions to the scientific developments of the mid-nineteenth century, and that representations of fairies show the emotional effects on the Victorians of scientific ideas such as the theory of evolution by natural selection. The final chapter argues that by the end of the Victorian period the relation of the past and present had become an urgent problem, and that laments for the disappearance of the fairies were a nostalgic expression of this problem. The book ends with a discussion of the way World War One dispelled the enchantments the fairy had been able to offer the Victorians.

There are always other ways in which one might write a book, and this is no exception. Rather than attempting a comprehensive survey of either fairy painting or poetry, instead I discuss them together in order to shed light on wider cultural preoccupations. This means that I have selected only a few of the hundreds of fairy paintings exhibited in the nineteenth century and only a sample of the poems and other writings about fairies published during the period. I have excluded fairy stories written for children in order to concentrate on why grown-ups were interested in them, and this means that for the most part I have also left aside book illustration. A question I have not taken up is the connection between the Victorian interest in fairies and nationalism. Nationalism, particularly in relation to Scotland and Ireland, was an important political and social issue during the period, and the representation of fairies was much affected by nationalist ideas. At its most extreme, the dialogue about Irish home rule could become an argument about who had the better fairies: England or Ireland. To a certain extent this topic is dealt with in Carole Silver's *Strange and Secret Peoples*, but it deserves an extended discussion.[1] Yet another topic I have left aside is the role of the fairy in working-class culture, a subject that receives some attention in *Troublesome Things* by Diane Purkiss.[2]

Painting and poetry are notoriously middle-class interests, and the other debates and texts to which I have referred can be assumed to have circulated mainly among the educated middle class. The interests and tastes of the educated middle class are by no means the beginning and end of Victorian culture; however, because of its economic, social and cultural dominance, the concerns of this class loom largest over this period as a whole. And anxiety, wherever one finds it, is still anxiety. In fact, my interest centres largely, though implicitly, on the emotional lives of middle-class men and women. However, it is notable that virtually all the representations of fairies I discuss were produced by men. Rather than retelling the familiar story of how Victorian men idealised and infantilised women, something which might also be said about the way they pictured fairies, I consider other reasons why men should be so interested in the figure of the fairy. To look at the costs to Victorian men of always having to be 'grown up' is not to belittle the struggles of Victorian women to free themselves from the ways in which they were made to be childlike. Dreaming about fairies and fairyland was one of the ways in which middle-class men tried to ease the burden of their privilege and escape from the pressures and anxieties of authority.

In this book I bring together literary texts, paintings, scientific and sociological writings, folklore, philosophy and journalism. One of the most remarkable things about fairies in the nineteenth century is the huge variety of contexts in which they occur. There is almost no discourse in which one might not come upon a mention of the fairy, even in such an apparently insignificant way as a synonym for 'small' or 'delicate' or 'wonderful'. Indeed, these small mentions form a large part of the evidence that is the basis for the argument I make in this book. It is because fairies appear in these very diverse contexts that I have chosen to bring different genres and media together. Fairy painting originated in the illustration of literary texts, and the use of the fairy as a metaphor in non-literary writings is part of a wider mutual influence between literature and other discourses. Though it is true that words and images do not work in the same way and that they are in some ways antithetical, Victorian culture generally is marked by a close association between word and image. Though literature and the visual arts have their own traditions and formal properties, in this period they often mirrored each other very closely. Literary texts and paintings refer back and forth to one another; they work through the same cultural preoccupations, and they imagine the world in very similar terms. The representation of fairies in both paintings and literary and other kinds of texts is shaped by this close association of word and image, even though they also envision fairies very differently. Therefore, in each of the chapters I discuss paintings alongside literary and other texts, often using images of fairies as the focus of my argument.

The fairies in nineteenth-century art and literature came from many sources. In part, they originated in the goblins, brownies, white women, pixies, nixies and Robin Goodfellows of folk belief. From the late eighteenth century onwards, these legends were ardently collected, collated and compiled into increasingly sophisticated systems of fairy belief. It was widely thought that the way of life that had sustained this rich fairy lore was dying out, and enthusiasts hurried to record such stories as they might before they were all forgotten. At first these collectors thought of themselves as antiquaries, but by the middle of the nineteenth century they styled themselves folklorists. The change of name signalled a change of emphasis: instead of being learned in arcane knowledge, they were studying the culture of the common people and helping to preserve it for posterity. The results of their endeavours were published widely, in scholarly and popular books, in learned journals and in mass-market periodicals. Even if the urban population had discarded its superstitions and forgotten the fairies when people moved from the country to the town, the wide dispersal of folktales and legends was there to remind people of the beliefs and sayings of their forebears. In many respects the widespread fascination with folklore shaped the way that fairies appeared in art and literature in this period. But there were other influences at work: for example, the Shakespeare revival of the eighteenth century was also responsible for awakening the interest in fairies. The great reverence in which Shakespeare was held, and the increasing number of productions of his plays, stimulated interest in the supernatural beings who appear in them. In particular, Boydell's Shakespeare Gallery, which sponsored the first of many projects to illustrate Shakespeare's works, prompted artists to give visual form to the fairies.

These two sources came together in Romanticism. Romantic poets and artists not only revered Shakespeare (as well as Spenser and medieval romances), they were also interested in popular culture. They were attracted by the misty world of superstition and enchantment which lay behind the legends collected by Romantic writers such as Walter Scott. Nearly all the Romantic poets wrote at least one fairy poem, but rarely are the fairies in these poems taken from either a purely literary or legendary source. Shelley's early epic, *Queen Mab* (1813), for example, takes a figure who occurs both in folklore and in Shakespeare, yet his fairy resembles neither of these. When Blake has a fairy sit upon his table and dictate *Europe: A Prophecy* (1794), the fairy is neither purely legendary nor purely literary. He catches the fairy in his hat and, as with a leprechaun, having caught him can command him; the fairy answers him, however, in words far removed from those of legendary fairies: 'I will write a book on leaves of flowers. / If you will feed me on love-thoughts, and give me now and then / A cup of sparkling poetic fancies.'[3]

The Romantic fairy is a figure associated with nature, with magic and with romance; it is tiny and beautiful and possesses butterfly wings. This is the kind of fairy which, for the most part, populated the Victorian imagination, and which is the subject of this book. Although it has a family resemblance to Puck, Ariel and the other Shakespearean fairies, and to the supernatural beings of popular superstition, in most respects it is a very different creature. Even when nineteenth-century artists and writers refer to *A Midsummer Night's Dream* or *The Tempest*, or draw upon stories of leprechauns, hobgoblins or kelpies, the fairy they have in mind is not the 'original', 'authentic' fairy of the source, but this creature of the Romantic imagination. A good example of the mixed character of

Figure 1. J. M. W. Turner, *Queen Mab's Cave*.

the Romantic fairy is J. M. W. Turner's *Queen Mab's Cave* (1846; fig. 1). The title of this painting alludes to Shakespeare's *Romeo and Juliet* and to Shelley, yet it illustrates neither; nor does it refer to any folklore source. Neither of its apparent literary sources seems to have much relation to the picture.

Though hard to make out, the picture seems to be a cliff scene, with a flooded cave in the centre; high, receding cliffs to either side; and on the top of the cliffs, a ruin that alternately resembles Tintagel and the Parthenon. In Turner's late manner, the sea, cliffs and ruin fade into one another: we see looming masses, shadows, and areas of luminosity, but it is impossible to tell where land ends and sea begins, or what is rock and what is ruin. The fairies partake of the same uncertainty. They emerge from the shimmering surface of the water, some seeming to hover above it and some to be swimming in it; some misty figures flicker in and out of focus in the rocky headland, and it is difficult to say definitely whether they are there or not. The fairies one can see clearly are nymph-like; to the right, one is being lifted out of the water by a swan, in a seeming reference to Leda; but those on the rock are red, and may well refer to the iconography of demons. This picture brings together fragments of the past and references to various kinds of supernatural beings, and sets them on the shore, where land and sea meet in a play of light and colour which makes it impossible to discern which is illusion and which is reality. In its review of this painting, the *Art-Union* called it 'vague, illusive and fanciful ... a gorgeous daylight dream'.[4] Turner painted only one picture of fairies, yet he encapsulated the Romantic conception of fairies and fairyland perfectly in this one image: creatures on the border between illusion and reality, in a place not of one time but of many. In this picture fairyland is not just an imaginary country peopled with imaginary beings: it is a metaphor for the imagination, the faculty that blurs the boundary between illusion and reality, and turns them into a 'gorgeous daylight dream'.

The other way in which Romanticism shaped the fairy and fairyland was by making them melancholy. Fairies in Shakespeare are amorous, quarrelsome and lyrical; the fairies of legend are sometimes mischievous, sometimes malicious, and even when they are on good terms with humans, must always be propitiated. Romantic fairies, by contrast, are often plaintive and sorrowful. Keats envisioned the creative imagination as 'Charm'd magic casements, opening on the foam / Of faery lands forlorn', setting the pattern for a nostalgic view of fairyland receding into the golden past, a magic country to which we can return only in wistful imaginings.[5] This mood found its most potent expression in one of the most popular of Victorian poems, Tennyson's 'Bugle Song' from *The Princess* (1847):

> O hark, O hear! how thin and clear,
>   And thinner, clearer, farther going!
> O sweet and far from cliff and scar
>   The horns of Elfland faintly blowing!
> Blow, let us hear the purple glens replying:
> Blow, bugle; answer, echoes, dying, dying, dying.[6]

Representations of fairies took on this melancholy hue because fairies were associated with yesterday, with past glories, lost worlds and times that can never come again. And because they were also imaginary creatures, ideas about fairies were coloured by the terrible paradox of the Romantic imagination: strive as one might to create another reality or to transfigure the world through the creative power of the imagination, in the end that effort must end in failure. As Letitia Landon put it in her poem 'Fantasies', if fairies are real, they are as real only as dreams:

I

I'm weary, I'm weary, – this cold world of ours;
I will go dwell far, with fairies and flowers.
Farewell to the festal, the hall of the dance,
Where each step is a study, a falsehood each glance;
Where the vain are displaying, the vapid are yawning;
Where the beauty of night, the glory of dawning,
Are wasted, as Fashion, that tyrant, at will
Makes war on sweet nature, and exiles her still.

II

I'm weary, I'm weary, – I'm off with the wind:
Can I find a worse fate than the one left behind?
– Fair beings of moonlight, gay dwellers in air,
O show me your kingdom! O let me dwell there!
I see them, I see them! – how sweet it must be
To sleep in yon lily! – is there room in't for me?
I have flung my clay fetters; and now I but wear
A shadowy seeming, a likeness of air.

III

Go harness my chariot, the leaf of an oak;
A butterfly stud, and a tendril my yoke.
Go swing me a hammock, the poles mignonette;
I'll rock with its scent in the gossamer net.
Go fetch me a courser: yon reed is but slight,
Yet far is the distance 'twill bear me tonight.
I must have a throne, – ay, yon mushroom may stay,
It has sprung in a night, 'twill be gathered next day:
And fit is such throne for my brief fairy reign;
For alas! I'm but dreaming, and dreams are but vain.[7]

Dreams of escape, of endless play, of lightness, of being tiny in a miniature world, of a magically beautiful nature: these dreams recur again and again in nineteenth-century images of and writings about fairies. But who is to say that dreams are in vain? In the nineteenth century, and for the Victorians, in particular, such melancholy dreams were a consolation for their disappointment and weariness at their own, all too real, world.

This book is a sympathetic study of one of the less admirable aspects of Victorian culture, the regressive longings and escapist fantasies that shaped its fascination with the supernatural. It is easy to condemn the

Victorians for succumbing to the lure of an idyllic world which never existed, and for making such a sentimental figure as the fairy so important to their fantasy lives. But such judgements carry their own burden, for they sentence both the Victorians and ourselves to that hard discipline formulated by the Victorians' Modernist children which demands that dreams must always be of the future, must always be progressive, and can understand the desire to escape from the present and return imaginatively to the past only as reactionary. Nevertheless, anyone who takes Victorian fairies seriously must risk becoming implicated in the sentimentality of the Victorians' dreams and longings. Nowadays we counter our lapses into regression with irony, distancing ourselves from the charge of sentimentality with our own knowingness about it. This is the alibi that allows me to have a sparkly snow dome with a flower fairy inside it on my desk. But the Victorians were entirely without irony in their enjoyment of fairies: they took them quite seriously, and their pleasure was unmixed with ironic knowingness. So to speak, they liked their sentiment straight.

Towards the close of his meditation on sentimentality, Michael Tanner elegantly sums up the charges against it by terming it a 'disease of the feelings' in which huge, unfocused emotions are called up seemingly out of nowhere or in response to 'virtually random, or alternatively direly predictable stimuli'.[8] Sentimental feelings are out of proportion to their objects, where there is an object, and the objects are ignoble compared to the floods of feelings in which the sentimentalist indulges. He continues, 'a further feature of sentimental feelings is that analysis of them – placing them in relation to their objects, positioning them in relation to other terms in one's emotional economy – shows that they are "easy", easy to come and easy to go, parts of "undisciplined squads of emotions".'[9] Compared to the hard discipline of emotional integrity, the ease with which sentimental emotions are conjured up makes them suspect, if not downright ignoble. Yet Tanner concludes that there is a worse disease than sentimentality: the sterile, arid desert he finds depicted in T. S. Eliot's *The Waste Land*, in which emotion has dried up altogether. Better too much and too easy than none at all.

This warning is central to a sympathetic understanding of Victorian sentimentality. As Wendy Wheeler has argued, the rationality of the Enlightenment, its pursuit of truth and progress and mastery, was itself a disease which had dire consequences.[10] In the nineteenth century the widespread adoption of extreme forms of rationality, such as utilitarian philosophy, the factory system and laissez-faire economics, brought with them the threat of a deathly lack of feeling and a view of human beings as little more than living machines driven by a finite number of calculable desires. Carlyle's warning about the effects of this extreme rationality is only barely hyperbole: ' then may we hope to comprehend the infinitudes of man's soul under formulas of Profit and Loss; and rule over this too, as over a patent engine, by checks, and valves, and balances'.[11] The terrible threat such developments posed to the humanity of human beings is summed up in Carlyle's image of the soul regulated by an engine.

The Victorians' recourse to sentimentality in the face of the brutal and deadening rationalism of modern forms of thought, technology and social organisation was an extreme response to an extreme situation. Confronted with the vast, even overwhelming, power of modernity, they escaped into the past and took comfort by dreaming of fairies who were tiny. The excess of feeling for which the Victorians sought an outlet found a perfect vehicle in fairyland, precisely because it was such a trivial object for these emotions. The small, inauthentic, inadequate fairy was the perfect figure to conjure up dreams of escape from the intolerable present and a perfect vehicle for longings for the past, because it was a smaller, more fragile, more magical version of themselves; they found in fairyland, a land that never was, the perfect escape from their own situation because, like a landscape in a dream, it resembled their own country. Though sentimental, the magic of the fairy was not easy magic, because what it stood for was the difficulty of being human. Fairies probably never helped the Victorians make important moral, political, economic or religious decisions; they never sprinkled fairy dust over poverty, disease, oppression, cruelty or neglect; there is neither call nor need in fairyland for empire or reform. Nonetheless, a little wonder and mystery could make bearable the fact that these things did have to be faced. Fairies could work only small enchantments; but for the Victorians, small enchantments were better than none.

CHAPTER I

Fancies of fairies and spirits and nonsense

'Whose is that?' 'Fuseli's' – 'La! What a frightful thing! I hate his fancies of fairies and spirits and nonsense. One can't understand them.... It's foolish to paint things which nobody ever saw, for how is one to know if they're ever right?'[1]

This snatch of conversation was overheard by the critic T. G. Wainewright in front of pictures exhibited by Henry Fuseli at the annual exhibition of the Royal Academy in 1821.[2] At least, Wainewright claimed he heard it; he may have made it up, since his aim was a jibe against the frivolous and fashionable crowd who failed to appreciate Fuseli's work. The chief carper at Fuseli is a woman: her coquettish tone underlines the superficiality of her feminine judgement. Nevertheless, her comment is worth taking seriously, whether it is genuine or not, because the terms in which she dismisses Fuseli's work are, by implication, the qualities admired by connoisseurs such as Wainewright. He has a taste for 'fancies of fairies and spirits and nonsense', she does not; she complains that we can never know if imaginary beings are 'right' compared with real things, while he, we infer, realises that 'things which nobody ever saw' have their own reality. Wainewright's larger purpose in this satire is to draw attention to the contempt with which the public view the noblest and highest genre of art, history painting, and to ridicule the public's shallow, populist taste. (Whether an elevated taste had ever been general is debatable; certainly by 1821 the cause of history painting was as good as lost.) It is not surprising that for the purposes of Wainewright's invective the public takes on a feminine face. What is surprising is that the dispute in taste, and its submerged political and social meanings, should be framed in terms of a masculine interest in and feminine distaste for fairies.

Interest in the supernatural has recently come to be seen as an important aspect of late eighteenth-century culture. In *The Female Thermometer*

(1995) Terry Castle explores the persistence of the dead in spectral forms which troubles the 'explained supernatural' in the fictions of Anne Radcliffe, and argues that this is symptomatic of a new, modern tendency to regard others as themselves spectral and to 'supernaturalise' the mind. E. J. Clery, in *The Rise of Supernatural Fiction 1762–1800* (1995), connects the ghosts which populate the eighteenth-century literary and popular imagination to Adam Smith's ghostly 'hidden hand of the market'. She argues that the popularity of supernatural fiction should be understood as an effect of the growth of a market in culture, but also as a symptom of the social and psychic effects of market capitalism. Clery and Castle connect the supernatural with aspects of modernity, and see the rationality of Enlightenment as producing a barely repressed, ghostly shadow. Both are interested in the special connections between women and the supernatural in the literature of the period but, because they limit their attention to ghosts and spectres, neither examines the interest in fairies which paralleled the fascination with ghosts which they investigate; and they fail to notice the marked fascination of men, and women's equally marked distaste, for fairies.

Among the hundreds of artists and writers who wrote about or painted fairies between the end of the eighteenth and the beginning of the twentieth centuries, only a very few were women. Among women who wrote for an adult audience, only Charlotte Brontë often used the fairy as a motif in her novels; Letitia Landon, Felicia Hemans, Rosamund Marriott Watson and a small number of others wrote fairy poetry; the obscure Amy Sawyer (none of whose works survives) and Eleanor Fortescue Brickdale were among the few women artists to depict fairies. Though Christina Rossetti's *Goblin Market* (1862) is an apparent exception to women writers' and artists' general indifference to fairy subjects, in fact her goblins are not at all fairy-like, and have little in common with fairies as they are generally represented in Victorian literature and art. In *Goblin Market* the goblins are most frequently referred to as 'little men', but they are also given animal characteristics: 'One had a cat's face, / One whisked a tail . . . One like a wombat prowled obtuse and furry, / One like a ratel tumbled hurry skurry.'[3] During the 1850s and 1860s fairies were very often identified with insects, but Rossetti's furry goblins are quite different from insect-fairies with antennae and iridescent wings.[4] In the late eighteenth and the nineteenth centuries, then, it was overwhelmingly men who were interested in fairies, who wrote about and painted them; women were largely indifferent.

The masculine taste and feminine distaste for fairies can be explained simply. Fairies, one tends to think, are mostly female, tiny and beautiful; the word 'fairy-like' seems a perfect epithet for that ideal of Victorian femininity which required that women be diminutive in relation to men, magical in their unavailability, of delicate constitution, playful rather than earnest. Why should women be interested in a figure which offered them only an image of a femininity from which so many were struggling to escape? Women's ambivalence about this form of femininity is amply demonstrated in Mary Braddon's *Lady Audley's Secret* (1863), in which the child- or doll-like Lucy Audley uses her femininity as a screen for her ruthless manipulation of the men around her. But the deceptiveness of her charm is signalled to the reader from early on in the novel by the contrast between Lucy Audley's super-femininity and the candour and assertiveness of Alicia Audley. Significantly, descriptions of Lucy Audley frequently allude to fairies: her boudoir filled with jewels and satins is 'fairy-like'; so is the handwriting in the note to Alicia which proves the fateful link between Lucy Audley and Helen Talboys. And at the crisis of the narrative, when Lucy Audley decides to attempt to murder Robert Audley, the narrator asks: 'Did she remember the day in which the fairy dower of beauty had first taught her to be selfish and cruel, indifferent to the joys and sorrows of others, cold hearted and capricious, greedy of admiration, with that petty woman's tyranny which is the worst of despotisms?'[5] The epithets 'fairy-like' and 'fairy dower' carry the weight of Braddon's (and by implication, her readers') disapproval of this extreme form of femininity.

But this is only part of the reason for women's indifference to fairies in the face of men's interest in them. Their dislike of fairies originated at the same time as men's fascination with them was born, in the late eighteenth century. Women were not simply rejecting what had become a female stereotype, but were responding to exactly those meanings of the fairy which attracted men in the first place, only one of which was the fairy's use as a caricature of femininity. As we shall see, these meanings have a great deal to do with the comment that 'fancies of fairies and spirits and nonsense', which 'nobody ever saw', 'can't be known to be right'.

Thomas Keightley's *The Fairy Mythology* was the first attempt systematically to catalogue fairy belief in the British Isles, Europe and beyond. Studies of fairy lore were numerous enough by 1826 that Keightley could draw upon a wide variety of scholarly works for his information. In his introduction he proffered a theory of the origins of fairy belief commonly held by scholars and antiquarians:

> If, as some assert, all the ancient systems of heathen religion were devised by philosophers for the instruction of rude tribes by appeals to their senses, we might suppose that the minds which peopled the skies with their thousands and tens of thousands of divinities gave birth also to the inhabitants of field and flood, and that the numerous tales of their exploits and adventures are the productions of poetic fiction or rude invention. It may further be observed, that not unfrequently a change of religious faith has invested with dark and malignant attributes beings once the subject of confidence and veneration.[6]

The fairies are, in small and local forms, the vestiges of ancient deities, viewed by Keightley from an Enlightened perspective as consoling fictions for the common people. Once upon a time, these gods were venerated because they animated the world; now they are diminished into the subject of fireside tales of mischievous 'exploits and adventures'.

Another connoisseur of fairy lore, John Black, suggested a slightly different explanation of fairy belief. Black maintained that fairies fill up the gaps in the common people's empirical knowledge of the natural world. Instead of seeking proper scientific explanations of natural phenomena, superstitious folk think of the world as inhabited and animated by the supernatural:

> In such cases, where the ideas are few, fancy is ever busy to fill up the void which the uniformity of external objects leaves in the mind. The imagination blends itself with the reality, the wonderful with the natural, the false with the true. The ideas acquire strength, and mingle in such a manner with external impressions as hardly to be distinguished from them. And the laws of nature are yet unknown, the problem of probability is unlimited, and fancy grows familiar with chimeras which pass for truth.[7]

Though different, the two theories of fairy origins have much in common. Whether fairies were survivals of ancient deities or supernatural explanations for natural phenomena, both theories suppose that fairies originated in an un-Enlightened age: before knowledge of true religion, before the truth of the world was revealed by science.

The study of fairies is a child of the Enlightenment in several senses. It can be seen as part of the Enlightenment's drive to make knowledge systematic, and the consequent establishment of scholarly disciplines, of which folklore was to become one. More importantly, the impetus behind the study of fairies came from what Isaiah Berlin has called the 'counter-Enlightenment'.[8] The Enlightenment sought universal, rational laws based on a conception of human nature as unchanging, and fought against prejudice, tradition and superstition as impediments to the discovery of demonstrable truths. The 'counter-Enlightenment' opposed these aims by arguing for relativist and historicist views of human society, human knowledge and human nature. Instead of pursuing general truths which would reveal immanent laws governing the functioning of the universe, 'counter-Enlightenment' thinkers sought knowledge in the myriad and changing and equally valuable particulars of human existence.

Berlin identifies Johann Gottfried Herder as one of these thinkers. Herder 'believed that to understand anything was to understand it in its individuality and development, and that this required a capacity which he called *Einfühlung* ('feeling into') the outlook, the individual character of an artistic tradition, a literature, a social organisation, a people, a culture, a period of history.'[9] For Herder the lives of individuals, works of art, stories and religions must be understood as the creation of particular societies at particular times: the *Iliad*, for example, was the creation and expressed the nature of the savage, heroic phase of Greek culture; likewise the Scandinavian sagas and the lays of Ossian drew their special beauty and character from the people from whose lives and character they sprang. Nothing could be more stupid than the Enlightenment's rejection of tradition, its insistence on universal standards and rules, and its assumption that history should be seen as the progressive development of a single culture. Instead, 'indissoluble and impalpable ties of common language, historical memory, habit, tradition and feeling' bound peoples into a plurality of national cultures.[10] A nation had to cherish its culture and traditions in order to understand its own character.

One of the most important fruits of Herder's influence on his contemporaries and successors was the impetus to collect national traditions such as stories, songs, customs and superstitions. The Grimms' folktale collection *Kinder und Hausmärchen* (1812) was an indirect result of Herder's championship of tradition, for he saw national cultures as the creation of the whole of the people, not merely the educated few. And if the great myth cycles and sagas are the most glorious monuments of tradition, even its smallest creations were perceived to be valuable, hence the interest in fairies. In fact, as scholars of traditional stories and beliefs frequently remarked, the fairies were one of the most widespread and 'poetical' of all superstitions.

The 'counter-Enlightenment' and later the Romantic interest in fairies was a criticism of the Enlightenment, a sense that the latter had destroyed, or would destroy, the cultures which fostered the fairies. Fairy beliefs had to be collected lest they be lost, for the traditions of the common people were fast being forgotten. Industrialisation, urbanisation, new forms of social life, news, novels: as these encroached on the life of the common people they displaced the stories and customs which had been handed down as tradition through generations.

It is the association between fairies and the attack on the Enlightenment which underlies men's fascination with fairies and women's lack of interest in them. In general, the claim of reason's supremacy which is at the Enlightenment's centre had little new to give to men (at least, not to the middle-class men who were interested in fairies), for they were already established as the reasoning sex. Enlightenment thinkers sought to ground the universal rules which would guarantee human happiness and build the good society on ideas of paternity and fraternity which were already in place.[11] By contrast, it was women who were associated with those things which the Enlightenment wished to discard or destroy as enemies to reason, or obstacles to the discovery of truth: ignorance, superstition, prejudice, tradition, fantasy, and, most of all, unreasoning emotion.

The 'counter-Enlightenment' wished to rescue tradition, emotion, fantasy, prejudice and so on because, as Gadamer says in *Truth and Method* (1965):

In contrast to the Enlightenment's belief in perfection, which thinks in terms of the freedom from 'superstition' and the prejudices of the past, we now find that olden times, the world of myth, unreflective life, not yet analysed by consciousness, in a society 'close to nature', the world of Christian chivalry, all these acquire a romantic magic, even a priority of truth.[12]

But, he goes on to argue, this reaction to the Enlightenment takes place wholly within its own terms: 'the romantic reversal of this criterion of the Enlightenment [the 'prejudice against prejudice'] actually perpetuates the abstract contrast between myth and reason'.[13] The Enlightenment's declaration of the autonomy of reason is the precondition and ground of the 'counter-Enlightenment's' rediscovery of the irrational. In this sense, it was because men were already in possession of reason, were already sovereign subjects, that they could turn to the 'dark side' of Enlightenment: to myth, unreason, tradition, superstition and emotion. Because the language of progress had installed them at its centre, men could turn back to the 'unreflective life' of the past, and seek out its denizens: the fairies.

The 'dark side' is, of course, also the feminine side. When the Grimm brothers went looking for traditional stories, they asked women to tell them fairy tales.[14] Women are the bearers of tradition, the adherents to superstition (as the phrase 'old wives' tale' suggests), the gossips and witches; and, of course, they think with their hearts rather than their heads. The wearisomely familiar idea that women have no access to reason, and therefore cannot be fully educated, become political subjects or citizens, or escape from the guidance of fathers and brothers, was repeated in the eighteenth century across a whole range of discourses from political theory to the novel. Early feminism had to make the claim for women's access to reason, and therefrom to education, independence and political subjecthood; indeed, women's claim to rationality was feminism's most important, foundational assertion.

That assertion had its costs, because reason had to be claimed at the expense of emotion, tradition, superstition and so on. The association between women and what Gadamer calls the 'unreflective life' of myth and unreason had to be broken in order to secure for women an equal stake in Enlightenment modernity. That is why the 'counter-Enlightenment' could not appeal to women in the same way as to men; why the world of the past imbued with poetry and enchantment held little nostalgia for them; and why women, by and large, did not turn in their writing and art to the figure of the fairy. It was, in a sense, a metaphor for all that feminism was struggling to rescue women from.

Feminism in the late eighteenth century is almost synonymous with the name of Mary Wollstonecraft, and this characterisation of feminism is, broadly, that of Wollstonecraft's *A Vindication of the Rights of Woman* (1792). In order to show how and why men's and women's attitudes to fairies differed, I shall compare the meanings of fairies for Henry Fuseli, the Swiss painter who became Keeper of the Royal Academy, one of the most important and influential exponents of history painting in the English art establishment of the late eighteenth century, and for Wollstonecraft and a few of her female contemporaries. Fairies were central to Fuseli's art precisely because they symbolise unreason and tradition, although, as we shall see, he renders the association between femininity and unreason pathological; in contrast, Wollstonecraft's dismissive reference to fairies shows them to be utterly bound up with her general repression of the claims of unreason and emotion.

Figure 2. Henry Fuseli, *Titania and Bottom*.

Henry Fuseli's pair of paintings *Titania and Bottom* (fig. 2) and *The Awakening of Titania* (Winterthur: Kunstmuseum) were made in the late 1780s, about ten years after his arrival in London following a protracted stay in Rome, during which he taught himself to draw and paint by copying the classical and Renaissance masters. The paintings were later bought by Josiah Boydell for display in his Shakespeare Gallery, which opened in 1792 on Pall Mall. The aim of the Shakespeare Gallery was to collect together the work of the leading British artists of the day, each of whom would illustrate scenes from the greatest of British playwrights. Among the contributors were Sir Joshua Reynolds, President of the Royal Academy, and other leading Academicians. However, Fuseli's paintings went beyond the gallery's purpose of providing saleable illustrations of well-known passages from Shakespeare, for he used his *A Midsummer Night's Dream* paintings to explore wider concerns about the effects of the imagination on the human mind. As Petra Maisak has argued, Fuseli 'was not concerned at all with merely illustrating a text (in the sense of illuminating or embellishing it); he wanted, instead, to interpret and stage it anew from a subjective point of view'.[15]

Fuseli's illustrations of scenes from *A Midsummer Night's Dream* were very favourably received. *The Public Advertiser* wrote that 'if Shakespeare had been a painter, he would perhaps have given somewhat of a similar picture', and opined that when Fuseli rendered 'those objects, which being formed by fancy, are not fettered by rules', he was almost always successful; another praised Fuseli's 'wild and extravagant luxuriance of fancy'.[16] It is clear that contemporary reactions to the pictures centred on their expression of and appeal to the fancy or imagination. One further review will make clear how central this notion is to these paintings. This time the commentator is Fuseli himself, in an unsigned article published in May 1789 in the *Analytical Review*. This is his description of *Titania and Bottom*:

This is the creation of a poetic painter, and the scene is peculiarly his own; a glowing harmony of tone pervades the whole; and instead of being amused by mere humour, an assemblage calculated to delight the simple correct taste bursts in on us to relax the features without exciting loud laughter. The moment chosen by the painter, when the queen, with soft languor, caresses Bottom, who humorously addresses her attendant, gave him licence to create the fanciful yet not grotesque group, which he has so judiciously contrasted as not to disturb the pleasurable emotions the whole must ever convey to a mind alive to the wild but enchanting graces of poetry. The elegant familiar attendants seem to be buoyed up by the sweet surrounding atmosphere, and the fragrant nosegay bound together with careless art, yet so light, that the rude wind might disperse the insubstantial pageant. The soft and insinuating beauty, the playful graces here displayed, would, without reflection, scarcely be expected from the daring pencil that appears ever on the stretch to reach the upmost boundary of nature.[17]

On one level, of course, Fuseli is taking the opportunity to talk up his work, including the forthcoming engravings of the pictures, to the middle-class readers of the *Analytical Review* who might be expected to be patrons of the Boydell venture. The reader is instructed how to view the pictures: '. . . the assemblage . . . bursts in on us to relax the features without exciting loud laughter'; at the same time he is flattered on his connoisseurship: the picture is 'calculated to delight the simple correct taste'. On another level, the terms in which Fuseli describes his picture are extremely telling. In particular, the phrases 'poetic painter' and 'insubstantial pageant', and the description of a composition which 'gave him licence to create the fanciful yet not grotesque group' that will especially appeal to 'a mind alive to the wild but enchanting graces of poetry', together work to frame the painting's attraction almost wholly in terms of its appeal to, and representation of, the imagination. It is this appeal to the imagination which links Fuseli's work to the 'counter-Enlightenment'.

As a young man, Fuseli had come within the orbit of German thinkers like Bodmer and Klopstock, who contributed to the trend in German thought which led to Herder and to Romanticism. Up to the mid-1770s he was reading Herder's and Goethe's latest works, sent to him by his friend Lavater. One of the works he read was Herder's essay on Shakespeare, one of a number by contemporaries arguing against what they saw as the pernicious influence of French neo-classicism, and in favour of an authentic, 'northern' poetic drama such as that to be found in the genius of Shakespeare. For Fuseli, Shakespeare was, together with Milton, the greatest of writers (notwithstanding his familiarity with and respect for the classical authors), and his two major projects of the years 1780–1800 were the Shakespeare Gallery (which he later claimed as his original idea) and his own Milton Gallery.[18]

Herder's essay on Shakespeare, published in 1773 as part of a pamphlet entitled *On the German Character and Art*, attacks the doctrine of the classical unities and defends Shakespeare on the grounds of the power of his imagination to conjure up places and times, to move the reader, in imagination, to a different world:

Have you never perceived how in dreams space and time vanish? What insignificant things they are, what shadows they must be in comparison with action, with the working of the soul? Have you never observed how the soul creates its own space, world and tempo as and where it will? . . . And is it not the first and sole duty of every genius, every poet, above all of the dramatic poet, to carry you off into such a dream?[19]

Just as Shakespeare carries the reader off into a dream, Fuseli intends his Boydell pictures to have a similar effect on the viewer. The mind of the spectator 'alive to the wild but enchanting graces of poetry' will be carried to fairyland, an imaginary dream-world where 'space and time vanish', and where pleasure, not reason, holds sway.

If we look closely at Titania and Bottom we can see, however, that the sway that pleasure holds is an ambiguous and perhaps even dangerous one. The lovers are shown attended by Titania's train, just before they fall into the sleep from which they will wake disenchanted. The composition is circular, centring around the figures of Titania and Bottom. The light, however, which comes from the left, highlights the ring of fairies who encircle them while at the same time casting their shadows on Bottom, who thus recedes into the dark background. This arrangement of figures into a highlighted circle around Titania is emphasised by the wand she holds in her raised hand, as if she has just used it to describe the circle which encloses the composition. Because Titania's wand is positioned in such a way as to imply that the scene is within its compass, it seems as if Titania, rather than Oberon, has the power of enchantment in this scene. This suggestion is strengthened by the fairy above Bottom's head, whose arms and body imply a semicircle which is carried on through the figures to the right-hand side of the picture. This fairy's outstretched arm meets the end of Titania's wand, thus closing the circle of enchantment over Bottom's head.[20] Although it is Oberon who has cast the spell which the painting illustrates, its composition suggests instead that Titania is the one wielding powers of enchantment.

The most prominent figures in this picture are all female. The largest of the fairies are female, and Cobweb, Peaseblossom and Moth, all male fairies, are indistinguishable as individuals. Though the largest figure in the painting is Bottom, all the other male figures – for example, the three male fairies to be found along the left, centre and right of a horizontal line running though the centre of the composition – are considerably smaller than the painting's female figures. Overall, the difference between the full-sized and smaller fairies, those on Titania's left and the smaller ones at their feet, for instance, seems less marked than the difference in size between female and male fairies. This is accentuated by the relative prominence or obscurity of the female and male fairies, and the degree to which they are lit; in general the female fairies are larger, more prominent and highlighted, compared to small, insignificant or shadowed males. And the dominant femininity that these compositional features embody is also present thematically. The most prominent fairy on the right-hand side holds on a leash a bearded male fairy many times smaller than herself, and this figure of female dominance is repeated in the hooded figure to her right who holds a small male fairy on her lap, and the female fairy to the left-hand side who clutches a small male fairy as if he were a baby. In the background a row of female fairies is arranged as if in parody of a rank of (male) angels or seraphim.

The relationship of Titania and Bottom is central to the picture. Bottom is the largest figure of all, which should be predictable given the convention that fairies are miniature versions of humans. However, the size of the painting (215.9 × 274.3 cm) works to naturalise Titania's size rather than Bottom's because she is life-size, even though in the scale of the picture she is smaller in relation to him than a woman would be to a man. The effect of this is that he appears gigantic, unwieldy and perhaps even gross. Although it is true that in *A Midsummer Night's Dream* Bottom is never intended to be a fine figure of a man, nevertheless the transformation of Man into beast worked upon him by Oberon's (Titania's) enchantment is figured less importantly in this painting by the ass's head than by the distortion of scale between fairy and human, male and female. As if to underline this point, Bottom, whose pose is partly drawn from Michelangelo's Florence and Palestrina *Pietàs*, stares down at a tiny, Michelangelesque figure in the palm of his hand. For Fuseli, Michelangelo's work was the embodiment of the heroic ideal, the noblest achievement of European art, and its closest attempt at picturing the bodily perfection of human virtue. (On the other hand Raphael, from whose painting of Eve in the Vatican Loggias Titania is derived, is associated in Fuseli's writings with the expression of character through emotion.[21] The values Fuseli attaches to these painters are thus implicitly gendered.) Bottom is hardly Christ-like; the figure in his hand is no divinity or hero, but a fairy.

Bottom's gigantic grossness in relation to Titania, the dominance of the female fairies, and the tiny figure at whom Bottom gazes are all examples of a distortion of scale which signifies a disturbance in the stature and centrality of man. The reversal of male by female dominance is thus linked to a reversal of the relation between fairy and human; the human is displaced from its central position only to have that centre occupied by the fairy; the figure of the fairy mocks the human by reference to the ideal beauty which, in neo-classical aesthetics, represents the perfection of the human form. The figure which most nearly corresponds to the most fully achieved realisation of this ideal is the smallest figure in the painting, a figure which graphically represents the displacement of the male by a perversely dominant femininity, and is evidence of how closely the masculine and the human are intertwined in the concept of the ideal. The degradation of the one and the displacement of the other are represented by their grossness or miniaturisation. Titania's flirtatious glance at the two figures confirms whose body is to be considered both beautiful and powerful in this scene, and reminds us just how far this female body is from the virtuous ideal.

In this painting, and indeed throughout Fuseli's work, there is a clash between neo-classical and Romantic aesthetics, Enlightenment and 'counter-Enlightenment' values. At a theoretical level Fuseli espoused the neo-classical theory of the ideal, expounded at length in his *Lectures on Painting* (1806–31), and this is central to the representation of the body in his work. But his subject matter, both in the Boydell pictures and elsewhere (he painted many subjects from northern myths as well as dream and nightmare subjects), is drawn from 'counter-Enlightenment' or Romantic interests. This is due to Fuseli's pessimism about progress and the perfectibility of human nature: he believed in neither. He had no faith in reason to counter the excesses of appetite, and thought that great art was inevitably the production of excess and barbarity. Eudo C. Mason comments of him that

nearly all along the line Fuseli is in conflict with the cherished beliefs, hopes and ideals prevailing amongst the advanced minds of his day. He not only fails to share their optimistic faith in civilisation and its power; he does not even want to share it ... He was content that the absolute, ineradicable, tragic imperfection of all things human should bear witness to the splendour of the perfect as an unattainable ideal.[22]

The depravity of human beings changes according to historical circumstances; in this sense Fuseli is perfectly in accord with Herder that art is an expression of a people at a particular moment. But Fuseli takes this one step further to imply, both in this picture and in his writings, that the present age is the most depraved of all.[23]

This is expressed in a number of ways, for example in his comments on the French Revolution. But most relevant to this painting are his comments on women. 'In an age of luxury,' he wrote in one of his aphorisms, 'women have taste, decide and dictate; for in an age of luxury woman aspires to the function of man, and man slides into the offices of woman. The epoch of eunuchs was ever the epoch of viragos.'[24] In this painting, the fairies stand for a vision of human nature in the late eighteenth century, an age of feminist viragos in which the imagination has been allowed to run wild and overturn the relation between men and women – and indeed to make men effeminate. The erotic charms of Titania cover over the castrating effects of the free play of the unbounded fancy; the dominance she exercises over the scene represents the tyranny of an imperious, emasculating imagination disguised as an erotic fantasy. If such a scene is pleasurable, at least to the male spectator, it can only be perversely so. It is only because they are imaginary and not human that the fairies can represent in a pleasurable form a vision about the depths to which the human might sink.

Fuseli's pessimism about human nature and his ambivalent attitude to the imagination can also be seen in the Boydell *Puck* (1790; fig. 3).

Figure 3. J. Parker after Henry Fuseli, *Puck*.

In this image Puck flies (or rather, seems to stride) purposefully through the air on his exploits in a wood rather stormy than dreamy; there are no Titania and Bottom swooning here, but instead a horse and rider splashing through the stream, and on the left fairies running or flying through the undergrowth. The composition, full of movement, serves to foreground the figure of Puck himself, as he rushes towards the viewer, backlit by moonlight, and with the streamer he holds circling around him as a kind of decorative emphasis. In particular, the shape, features and contours of Puck's body are emphasised by these means, and it is this that forms the compositional and thematic centre of the image.

The disposition of Puck's limbs, with the streamer and the patch of moonlight that together imply a circle enclosing the figure, recalls William Blake's famous print *Albion Rose* (1794). *Albion Rose* is derived from a version of Vitruvian Man from Scamozzi's *Idea dell' Architettura Universale* (1615), which attempts to realise the proportions of man in terms of the golden mean and to picture a geometrically perfect human form, and it is very possible that *Puck* is derived from the same source.[25] Puck's wings are positioned just as the arms are in Scamozzi's engraving and his limbs are arranged in such a way as to gesture to the perimeter of the Vitruvian circle, partly sketched by the streamer. The allusion Fuseli makes to the Vitruvian man implicates the figure of Puck in the discourse of the ideal, central to the neo-classical theories of art which dominated the teaching (if not the practice) of the Royal Academy. The theory of the ideal was drawn from Renaissance writings on art, and was invariably illustrated by recourse to examples of Antique sculpture and Renaissance painting. Both Fuseli's own writings on the ideal and those of Joshua Reynolds, first President of the Royal Academy and the most influential exponent of the theory in this period, concentrate on the representation of the human body: indeed, the human figure is the only example of the practice of the ideal which is fully elaborated either in Reynolds's *Discourses on Art* (1778) or Fuseli's *Lectures on Painting*.

For Reynolds, the essential of the ideal is the elevation of the particular over the general, an 'abstract idea of ... forms more perfect than any one original', and it is only in these abstract ideas that can be found 'the perfect state of nature'.[26] The pursuit of the ideal consists in the observation of nature in order to reject what is particular and select only what is general and thus truly beautiful: 'Deformity is not nature, but an accidental deviation from her accustomed practice. This general idea therefore ought to be called Nature, and nothing else, correctly speaking, has a right to that name.'[27] The artist must learn to distinguish Nature from deformity in order to give pictorial form to ideal beauty, which is Nature in its highest state. In particular, the artist is to depict the human body in its highest, ideal form, and to portray 'the heroick arts and more dignified passions of man' in order to exemplify virtue. Art should lead the spectator to venerate virtue, for 'the nobility or elevation of virtue itself, consists in adopting this enlarged and comprehensive idea'.[28] The ideal, therefore, is both an aesthetic and a moral term, so that the perfection of the depicted human body is inextricably bound up with the perfection of human nature.

Puck, however, falls far short of ideal beauty and perfect proportion as envisaged in the Vitruvian man. His limbs, for example, are too short in proportion to his body. Both they and his torso are over-muscled, with the contours of the body emphasised through the use of chiaroscuro. The pectorals seem especially enlarged, and this draws attention to the very prominent nipples. Even without the wings it is clear that Puck's body is a grotesque rather than ideal body, a perverse parody of Vitruvian man: it is out of proportion and excessive, representing bestial deformity rather than ideal perfection. Though not much is visible of Puck's face because of the angle of the head, what can be seen appears to follow the conventions for representing the African face: curly hair, heavy-lidded eyes, a broad nose and thick lips. The apparently African, exaggerated features of Puck's face must be linked to the black of his wings, and suggests that for Fuseli the grotesque had a racial dimension. (It is striking that in his illustration of *The Tempest* for Boydell, Fuseli makes Caliban, Prospero's 'thing of darkness', look very similar to Puck.[29]) This in turn is correlated with a suggestion of goat-like characteristics: the separation of the toes of the right foot, and the twin tufts of hair on his chin. Having no iconography to follow in representing fairy wings, Fuseli has given Puck bat's rather than insect's wings, and this adds yet another sinister connotation to those suggested by his body. The bat's wings imply that Puck's ability to fly itself carries with it something unnatural or even evil. Even before the appearance of the vampire in the early nineteenth century the bat was associated in popular superstition with witchcraft and black magic. This implication may also be reinforced by the sign Puck makes with his left, sinister hand. Not only has he a grotesque, bestial, racialised figure; he is also linked with dangerous forms of femininity through the implied association with witchcraft. As Puck rushes threateningly towards the spectator he draws a train of sinister figures behind him. Particularly significant are the moth (symbol of sleep), and the horse (a night-mare?) rearing with its rider clutching onto it. The latter's closed eyes suggest that this is an enchanted sleep-rider. These elements, which relate to the spell Puck puts on the human characters in the play, indicate that Puck's enchantments are far from innocent, and are instead dark and dangerous ones. Giving him bat's wings is perfectly consonant with a representation of the 'merry wanderer of night'[30] which uses every aspect of the body to show just how far from the ideal Puck really is.

Both in its composition and its subject this picture parodies the moral ideal and replaces it with a figure which is deformed and grotesque in ways which strongly suggest that the anti-ideal is a figure not of austere virtue but of dangerous, possibly erotic, fantasy. Such a painting undoubtedly makes its appeal to the spectator on the basis that it represents a fancy or fantasy for the spectator's pleasure. Like *Titania and Bottom*, *Puck* represents the effects upon the human subject of an unbound, dangerous fancy. It shows that what humans who have allowed their fancy free play might really look like is equivalent to the anti-ideal. The other side of Fuseli's 'counter-Enlightenment' interests is his dependence on the neo-classical theory of the ideal which forms the basis of his *Lectures on Painting* (1806-31), and which informs the values attached to the representation of the body in his work. His treatment of the allegorical relation between the human and the ideal in his lectures shows how he conceived the connection between the dangerous imagination and the anti-ideal embodied in the figure of Puck.

Fuseli's lectures to the Royal Academy students were given over twenty-five years and do not consistently maintain one coherent theoretical position. They are also composed in the convoluted style that contemporary observers noted was characteristic of his English. However, a theme Fuseli returned to several times is the role of metaphor in relation to the ideal. Although fairies could not be part of the ideal for Fuseli, they could stand metaphorically for humans, but this made the way in which the ideal could be said to represent human qualities very problematic. Fuseli solves this problem by suggesting that fairies and other supernatural creatures can be allegorical figures only in certain circumstances. He approaches the problem in the two lectures on 'Invention', where he suggests (almost in passing, *à propos* of his wider scheme of producing a hierarchy of genres within the grand style) his idea of the metaphorical relation of the ideal to the human. In the second of the two, Lecture Four, in a discussion of the types of subjects appropriate to Fuseli's three classes of grand-style painting (epic, dramatic and historic), Fuseli makes a long digression on allegory.

Allegory, or the personification of invisible physic and metaphysic ideas, though not banished from the regions of invention, is equally inadmissible in pure epic, dramatic and historic plans, because, wherever it enters, it must rule the whole . . . the epic, dramatic and historic embellish with poetry or delineate with truth what either was or is supposed to be real; they must therefore conduct their plans by personal and substantial agency if they mean to excite that credibility, without which it is not in their power to create an interest in the spectator or reader. The great principle, the necessity of a moral tendency or of some doctrine useful to mankind in the *whole* of an epic performance, admitted, are we therefore to lose that credibility which *alone* can impress us with the importance of that maxim that dictated to the poet narration and to the artist imagery? Are the agents sometimes to be real beings and sometimes to be abstract ideas? . . . What becomes of the interest the poet and artist mean to excite in us, if in the moment of reading or contemplating, we do not believe in what the one tells and the other shows?[31]

Allegory is inadmissible in the highest genres of painting because their moral importance lies in their credibility. Fuseli seems here to be ground-ing the moral claims of art in a kind of aesthetic realism. Unless Zeus appears as himself, that is, as a deity rather than a personification of might or justice, the maxim or principle he embodies is lost because he is not believable. Mythical or superhuman figures must be given some kind of realism to 'work' both morally and aesthetically: 'When Minerva, by her weight, makes the chariot of Diomede groan, and Mars wounded, roars with the voice of ten thousand, are they nothing but the symbol of the battle's roar?'[32] To be credible, mythical deities must be more than simply the metaphorical representations of human qualities, be-cause it is their imagined autonomous existence that invests them with precisely the qualities which they are being used to show in the plan of the picture.

The theory of the ideal is central to the problem Fuseli is tussling with in this passage. In the highest genres of painting it would be impossible not to represent Zeus, Minerva or Mars in idealised forms, since the whole notion of the ideal is derived from classical representations of just such personages, and it derives its moral importance from secular rein-terpretations of them as personifications of justice, wisdom, war and so on. Fuseli implies here that the ideal works morally only if its metaphori-cal bonds with the human are loosened or even broken. The gods, who are ideal, must be different from men, who are not. Significant, too, is the way in which this moral function of the ideal is also an aesthetic func-tion. To communicate the maxim, the picture must 'excite' the viewer, and the verisimilitude of the painting produces a magical effect on the viewer which enables the moral lesson to be communicated: 'It is that magic which places on the same basis of existence, and amalgamates the mythic or the superhuman, and the human parts of the Ilias, of Paradise Lost, and of the Sistine Chapel, that enraptures, agitates and whirls us along as readers or spectators.'[33] It is only when the difference between man and the gods is represented realistically or credibly that the viewer is enabled to perceive the relations between them through the aesthetic experience of viewing the picture. The ideal can only function if it is not metaphorically secured to the human.

In contrast to this position, a passage from the preceding lecture out-lines (in the midst of a general introduction to invention and a discussion of its limits) in what way the supernatural, be it mythical or legendary, might be understood in relation to the human:

Such were the limits set to invention by the ancients . . . guarded by these, their mythology scattered its metamorphoses, made every element its tributary, and transmitted the privilege to us, on equal conditions. Their Scylla and the Portress of Hell, their daemons and our spectres, the shade of Patroclus and the ghost of Hamlet, their naiads, nymphs and oreads and our sylphs, gnomes and fairies, their furies and our witches, differ less in essence than in local, temporary and social modifications. Their common origin was in fancy, operating on the materials of nature, assisted by the legendary tradition and the curiosity implanted in us of divining into the invisible; and they are suffered or invited to mix with or superintend real agency, in proportion of the analogy which we discover between them and ourselves.[34]

Here Fuseli seems to be suggesting that the supernatural can be rep-resented within the same scenes as human beings only on the basis of allegory; the supernatural must stand for some aspect of the human – 'the analogy which we discover between them and ourselves' – in order to be considered credible, 'suffered or invited to mix with or superintend real agency'. Indeed, representations of the supernatural can be credible in serious works of art or literature (rather than 'tales too gross to be believed in a dream') only if such 'imaginary creations' are 'connected with the reality of nature and human passions': 'Without this, the fiction of the poet and the painter will leave us stupefied rather by its insolence, than impressed by its power; it will be considered only as a superior kind of legerdemain, an exertion of ingenuity to no adequate end.'[35]

In apparent contradiction to the view developed in Lecture Four, in this passage Fuseli promotes allegory as being both more credible than, and morally superior to, simple verisimilitude. However, the examples used there, Zeus, Minerva and Mars, among other classical deities, are very different from the kinds of supernatural being cited here. While it would be impossible to think of Zeus being represented in any terms but the ideal, the opposite is true of the examples in this passage. Indeed, such figures as Scylla and the Portress of Hell, furies and witches, daemons and spectres, might call for an anti-ideal in which the horrid and ghastly would find their most perfect representation. Though the shade of Patroclus and the ghost of Hamlet seem a long way from such frightful phenomena, they are presumably included because of their fearful and weird aspect. By their inclusion in this list, sylphs, naiads, nymphs, gnomes and fairies are classed among those subjects which are inappropriate candidates for the ideal body. Even though they are not perhaps horrid or terrifying, still they cannot be beautiful; nor, because they cannot be beautiful, can they be invested with the moral qualities of the ideal. It is these aspects of the supernatural, and only these, therefore, which can function allegorically in painting, and which can be understood in a programmatic way as representing the human: not the human in its most exalted, but in its most degraded, least general and most particular form.

The fairies in *Puck* and *Titania and Bottom* are anti-ideals which represent the debauched condition of modern humanity. Fuseli's fairy paintings are not merely erotic fantasies freed from historical context, but on the contrary comment on the nature of the human, as Fuseli understood it. Indeed, if they are erotic fantasies, it is in this mode that they engage most urgently and comment most stringently on what it is to be human. Viewed as allegories, they show the vitiating effects of an unbound fancy on the human body – and by a further allegorical extension, on the social body. If Fuseli's lectures appear contradictory on this point, this is because its implications are imperative yet disturbing: the troubling implications are 'hidden' by the labyrinthine complexities of Fuseli's style and his attempts in the passage from Lecture Four to draw back from the point he has made in Lecture Three. In a similar way, the disturbing quality of the representation of fancy in the paintings is concealed beneath what Fuseli himself calls their pleasing, poetic and playful qualities. Yet again it is precisely these qualities that provide a clue to the simultaneous presence of a dire warning about the workings of fancy.

It would be wrong to see as merely personal to Fuseli this vision of fairies as a representation of human nature debased by the imagination. His fairy paintings attracted comment, both admiring and detracting, precisely because they intersected with a general anxiety about the effects of the imagination circulating in late eighteenth-century culture. This has several sources, in particular the campaign against an unbridled imagination waged by women, most notably by Mary Wollstonecraft, in their attempt to claim rationality for the female mind. The latter is especially important given the link made in Fuseli's work between the imagination and a powerful, erotically charged and emasculating femininity.

In his famous and often-reprinted essay from *The Spectator*, 'The Pleasures of Imagination' (1712), Joseph Addison makes a link between fairies and the imagination which was to form the pattern for representations of fairies throughout the period:

> There is a kind of Writing, wherein the Poet quite loses sight of Nature, and entertains his Reader's Imagination with the Characters and Actions of such Persons as have many of them no Existence, but what he bestows on them. Such are Fairies, Witches, Magicians, Demons, and departed Spirits. This Mr *Dryden* calls the *Fairy Way of Writing*, which is, indeed, more difficult than any other that depends on the Poet's fancy, because he has no pattern to follow in it, and must work altogether out of his own invention.[36]

The kind of imagination, or fancy, which is able to conjure up fairies is, in contrast to other varieties of the imagination described in Addison's essay, un-Enlightened, uncontrolled by reason and untempered by judgement. Descriptions of fairies 'raise a pleasing Kind of Horrour in the Mind of the Reader . . . [and] bring up into our Memory the Stories we have heard in our Childhood, and favour those secret Terrours and Apprehensions to which the Mind of Man is naturally subject'.[37] The kind of imagination that pictures fairies is primitive, in that it harks back both to childhood and to the darkness between ancient and modern Enlightenments: an imagination unregulated by 'Learning and Philosophy'. The English (and foremost among them, that most imaginative of poets, Shakespeare) are especially liable to this kind of fancy, and thus produce the best 'fairy writing', 'for the English are naturally Fanciful . . . [and disposed] to many wild notions and visions, to which others are not so liable'.[38]

It is significant that Addison names this wild and unregulated imagination which creates fairies, fancy. During the eighteenth century the terms imagination and fancy gradually diverged, the term imagination becoming associated with a capacity tempered by judgement which tended to unify and idealise. It was strongly connected with the aesthetic sphere, partly because the imagination was seen as the origin of the poetic impulse, but also because the aesthetic was increasingly seen as the only space in which ideal unity could be achieved. In contrast to the imagination, which was a cultivated faculty of the Enlightened mind, the word 'fancy' gradually came to name a wilder capacity of the mind. As Jochen Schulte-Sasse has argued, those aspects of the imagination which escaped from the realm of the aesthetic were increasingly seen as dangerous and called 'the fancy'.[39] In other words, imagination was bound by reason into the realm of the aesthetic, a regulated space allowed for the free play of the human mind; fancy, on the other hand, became attached to the propensity of the imagination to escape such a boundary. For Addison, the fancy was the faculty which conjured up the fairies, which themselves harked back to and were a reminder of the darkness of the un-Enlightened mind; the preponderance of the fancy in the work of England's most celebrated poet can be taken as a symptom of a disturbing darkness in what, towards the end of the eighteenth century, came to be thought of as the 'national culture'.

During the eighteenth century the pleasures and dangers of the imagination were considered by writers across a range of discourses. However, while they consistently draw a distinction between fancy and imagination, they value these terms very differently. On the one hand there are those who welcome the imagination only so long as it is regulated; on the other, there are those who celebrate the wild and unbounded fancy. The former emphasise the importance of reason, and stress that the cultivation of reason is central to all human endeavours, from the just administration of the social order to the creation of art. The latter group, on the other hand, see emotion as the origin of action and the force that binds humans into social groups. They value tradition as the store of creative imaginings through which a people or nation can know itself. These two positions are roughly equivalent to the terms Enlightenment and 'counter-Enlightenment'.

In his *Essay on Genius* (1774), Alexander Gerard makes a distinction between an imagination guided by reason and one allowed to roam freely which exactly replicates the difference between imagination and fancy. He argues that

a fine imagination left to itself, will break out into bold sallies and wild extravagance, and overleap the bounds of truth or probability; but when it is put under management of sound judgement, it leads to solid and useful invention, without having its natural sprightliness in the least impaired. It is the union of an extensive imagination with an accurate judgement, that has accomplished the great geniuses of all ages.[40]

In Gerard's view imagination tempered by judgement is essential to the 'accomplishment of great genius', but without the control of reason, the fancy will, because of its nature, 'overleap the bounds of truth or probability' and lead to 'wild caprice or extravagance', or unreasoning emotion.[41] Johnson's discussion of the imagination in *Rasselas* (1759) shows how this dangerous fancy was thought of as having social costs: unbound by reason, the fancy was an uncontrollable force that might very well lead to mental, bodily or social disorder:

No man will be found in whose mind airy notions do not sometimes tyrannise, and force him to hope or fear beyond the limits of sober probability. All power of fancy over reason is a degree of insanity . . . it is not pronounced madness but when it becomes ungovernable, and apparently influences speech or action. By degrees the reign of fancy is confirmed; she grows first imperious, and in time despotic. Then fictions begin to operate as realities, false opinions fasten upon the mind, and life passes in dreams of rapture or anguish.[42]

Johnson's telling metaphor of the mind as a state rendered ungovernable by an insurgent fancy which eventually becomes tyrannous underlines the importance attached by Enlightenment thinkers to the regulation of the imagination, and the danger they perceived in an unregulated, unbound fancy.

By contrast, writers associated with 'counter-Enlightenment' tendencies tended to present the fancy more sympathetically and, significantly, followed Addison in linking the fancy with fairies. The final invocation of Taliesin in Thomas Gray's 'The Bard' (1757) celebrates the ability of poetry to stir the emotions of the people. The emotive power of poetry is ascribed to its combination of reason with a wild imagination:

> The verse adorn again
> Fierce war and faithful love,
> And truth severe, by fairy fiction dressed.
> In buskined measures move
> Pale grief and pleasing Pain,
> With Horror, tyrant of the throbbing breast.[43]

And in 'An Ode on the Popular Superstitions of the Highlands of Scotland, Considered as the Subject of Poetry' (1788), William Collins presents the wildness of fancy not only as an alternative source of poetic subject matter but as the source of the poetic impulse:

> Fresh to that soil thou turn'st, whose ev'ry vale
>   Shall prompt the poet, and his song demand:
> To thee thy copious subjects ne'er shall fail;
>   Thou need'st but take the pencil to thy hand,
> And paint what all believe who own thy genial land.

> There must thou wake perforce thy Doric quill,
>   'Tis fancy's land to which thou sett'st thy feet;
>   Where still, 'tis said, the fairy people meet
> Beneath each birken shade, on mead or hill.[44]

The rest of the poem accomplishes what Collins in these lines suggests, that poetry can and should be made of the sayings, legends and superstitions of the common people concerning witches, kelpies, will-o'-the-wisps and fairies. The 'fairy way of writing' is truly a national way of writing, because poetry comes out of the store of tradition that makes up the nation's identity. But it is only through fancy that the poet can turn such materials to good account, because the creations of tradition are animated by the same fancy which is the origin of the poetic impulse. And instead of the well-governed imagination of the Enlightenment, the fancy that Collins entertains is the wild fancy which, in Addison's words, raises a 'pleasing Kind of Horrour in the Mind of the Reader'. The national culture, and with it the untamed fancy, lead to the 'dark side' of the Enlightenment where poetry and the fairies live.

It is this dark, unregulated imagination, the fancy that sees pictures of fairies, which women were particularly concerned to argue against, and Wollstonecraft and other women writers consistently use the term 'fancy' in their denigrations of the imagination. Mary Wollstonecraft seems generally to have regarded the imagination as a degenerative faculty. In her writings those who indulge their imagination descend into folly or vice, and may at last risk their bodily or mental health. Even the great poets (significantly, she singles out Shakespeare), in other respects so unlike the 'ignorant women . . . [who] allow their imagination to revel in the unnatural and meretricious scenes sketched by the novel writers of the day', may, unless of unusual virility, suffer the deleterious effects of this faculty:

Considering the thoughtless manner in which they have lavished their strength . . . when, lost in poetic dreams, fancy has peopled the scene, and the soul has been disturbed, till it shook the constitution, by the passions that meditation had raised; whose objects, the baseless fabric of a vision, faded before the exhausted eye, they must have had iron frames.[45]

Wollstonecraft associates the unbounded fancy with emasculation, and locates its vitiating effects in the effeminisation of men who give way to it. Her condemnation of its effects on women, who are more prone to wild imaginings because less used to cultivate reason, and who, one supposes, do not have the requisite 'iron frames' to resist the fancy's blandishments, is characteristically severe.

In this quotation from *Maria* (1798), the novel that in fictional form presents Wollstonecraft's strongest criticisms of sensibility in women, the imagination is viewed as the delusive power of erotic fantasy through which women are led astray and ultimately doomed to be nothing more than creatures of feeling, nothing more than women.[46] Here, Maria languishes in her cell, dreaming of her lover Darnford, who will eventually prove her downfall:

A magic lamp now seemed to be suspended in Maria's prison, and fairy landscapes flitted round the gloomy walls, late so blank. Rushing from the depth of despair, on the seraph wings of hope, she found herself happy. – She was beloved, and every emotion was rapturous.[47]

The disastrous outcome of this relationship only serves to confirm what is hinted at here, that the 'magic lamp' of fancy, which gives rise to the 'fairy landscapes' of indulged sensibility, is both delusive and disordering. Wollstonecraft connects the association between fancy and fairies, inherited from Addison, to a critique of femininity in which the effects of over-feminisation, including the cultivation of the fancy to which women are particularly susceptible, are made responsible for women's acceptance of their subordinate position in relation to men. The fairy is a metaphor for the imagination, which is purely delusive; by indulging it, women exclude themselves from rationality, education, independence and political subjecthood. Barbara Taylor has suggested for Wollstonecraft the erotic imagination brings women into being as (only) women, but that it nevertheless forms an important, if dangerous, current in her thought.[48] Wollstonecraft's dismissive reference to the fairies symbolises a powerful erotic imagination which had to be repressed, even though at great cost, in the service of feminism's strategic goals.

Two further examples will, I think, indicate how urgent this problem seemed to women at the end of the century. Mary Hays's cautionary novel *The Memoirs of Emma Courtney* (1796) contains a warning about the imagination similar to Wollstonecraft's in *Maria*, this time in the context of the necessity for properly guided, rational education for the female mind, for the eponymous heroine's 'imagination had been left to wander unrestrained in the fairy fields of fiction . . . of historical facts and the science of the world I was entirely ignorant'.[49] There is no space for fancies of fairies in 'historical facts and the science of the world', and it is to the latter that women must devote (or perhaps discipline) themselves if they are to be rational, Enlightened beings. Similarly, Mary Robinson's 'Ode to the Muse' (1791) invokes the imagination, and with it, fancies of fairies, only insofar as it remains bounded by reason; it is better not to be a poet than to be caught up by the fancy and to give way to it in transports of feeling:

> Then, FANCY, on her wing sublime,
> Shall waft me to the sacred clime
> Where my enlighten'd sense shall view,
> Thro' ether realms of azure hue . . .
> The dapper fairies frisk and play
> About some cowslip's golden bell;
> And in their wanton frolic mirth,
> Pluck the young daisies from the earth . . .
>   But if thy magic powers impart
> One soft sensation to my heart,
> If thy warm precepts can dispense
> One thrilling transport o'er my sense;
> Oh! keep thy gifts, and let me fly,
> In APATHY's cold arms to die.[50]

To imagine fairies, to cultivate the fancy, is safe only within the bounds of reason, where its pictures are perceived by the 'enlighten'd sense'. But should the fancy lead the female poet astray into 'fairy fields' in which sense, or reason, is overwhelmed by 'thrilling transports' of sensibility, of femininity that is, then not only poetry but, in a hyperbolic gesture, life itself must be renounced.

In her *British Synonymy* (1794), Hester Thrale Piozzi identified the fancy as commonly associated with femininity, giving the following as an example of its usage:

> Sure in this shadowy nook, this green resort,
> IMAGINATION holds *his* airy court;
> Bright FANCY fans *him* with *her* airy wings,
> And to *his* sight *her* varying pleasures brings.[51]

Such varying pleasures as this distinctively feminine, disordered and vitiating imagination had to offer must indeed have been specialised. Whether the effects of an unbounded fancy are represented as a threat to the position and masculinity of men, as in Fuseli's work, or as a threat to the precarious grasp of reason on the female mind, as it is for Wollstonecraft, Hays and Robinson, the fancy, and with it the fairy, is always bound up with a degradation of the human which is thought of in gendered terms. The fancy brings nearer an emasculated or over-feminised state of the human, repeatedly represented, in the late eighteenth century, in the figure of the fairy. Fancies of fairies and spirits and nonsense, to recall Wainewright's jibe at women, do, after all, turn out to be 'terrible things'.

Fairies are not always nice; their enchanted world is not a comfortable place. If the fairies are descended from gods once loved and venerated, as Thomas Keightley argued, these have turned into beings 'invested with dark and malignant attributes'. In traditional tales fairies are malicious and mischievous as often as they work magic and marvels. Literary fairies, such as those in *A Midsummer Night's Dream*, toy with mortals for their own purposes. But the negative connotations with which fairies were invested by Henry Fuseli and Mary Wollstonecraft say less about the fairies themselves than what they were required to symbolise: the human subject shaped by the conflicting claims of imagination and reason, tradition and progress, past and future. Fairies look towards the past: that is their appeal as a consolation for Enlightenment modernity. That is why, at the end of the eighteenth century, fairies peopled the imaginings of men, and why, at the same time, they failed to cast their enchantments over women.

CHAPTER 2

Queen Mab among the steam engines

It is a little-known fact that the industrial revolution caused the extinction of the fairies. That the coming of the factories should have coincided with the departure of the fairies was no accident: so much is attested by Elizabeth Gaskell in her *Life of Charlotte Brontë*, in which she declares that Tabby

had known the 'bottom', or valley, in those primitive days when the fairies frequented the margin of the 'beck' on moonlight nights, and had known folk who had seen them. But that was when there were no mills in the valleys; and when all the woolspinning was done by hand in the farmhouses around. 'It wur the factories as had driven 'em away,' she said.[1]

Tabby's voice (even reported second-hand) is authoritative: she is, we are asked to accept, a 'true believer' in fairies who bears witness, even at second hand, to their former presence.

But numerous others testify similarly that the fairies left the country in the last quarter of the eighteenth century, just when factories and mills were beginning to be prominent features of valleys all over the North and Midlands. Michael Aislabie Denham was an antiquary with a special interest in folklore, and especially the supernatural, who published a number of pamphlets on the customs and superstitions of the north of England. In *To All and Singular Ghosts, Hobgoblins and Phantasms of the United Kingdom of Great Britain and Ireland* (1851), he noted that those born on Christmas Eve could not see spirits:

What a happiness this must have been seventy or eighty years ago and upwards, to those chosen few who had the good luck to be born on the eve of this festival of all festivals; when the whole earth was so overrun that there was not a village in England that had not its own peculiar ghost. Nay, every lone tenement, castle or mansion-house which could boast of any antiquity had its bogle, its spectre or its knocker . . . Every common had its circle of fairies belonging to it. And there was scarcely a shepherd to be met with who had not seen a spirit![2]

39

The brownies, hobhoulards, kit-a-can-sticks, pictrees, gringes, nickies, whitewomen and jinny-burnt-tails (to name a few of the two hundred varieties of supernatural being Denham listed) have disappeared, utterly vanished from the houses, churchyards, green lanes and commons they used to inhabit until 'seventy or eighty years ago', that is, until around 1770 or 1780. One would, Denham implies, be lucky nowadays to meet a shepherd who had been unlucky enough to have encountered the fairies.

Similarly, the geologist Hugh Miller tells a story of the departure of the fairies which happened around the same time. He describes how two children, truanting from church

on a Sabbath morning, nearly sixty years ago . . . saw a long cavalcade ascending out of the ravine through the wooded hollow . . . The horses were shaggy, diminutive things, speckled dun and gray; the riders, stunted, misgrown ugly creatures, attired in antique jerkins of plaid, long gray cloaks, and little red caps, from under which their wild uncombed locks shot out over their cheeks and foreheads.[3]

One of the children asks the last rider, 'What are ye, little mannie? and where are ye going?' To the first question the creature (who is, of course, a fairy) replies, 'Not of the race of Adam,' and to the second, 'the People of Peace shall never more be seen in Scotland'.[4] Writing in 1841, Miller takes this as incontrovertible empirical proof ('quite as conclusive as the case admits') that the fairies left the country in the 1780s.[5]

In his late lecture, 'Fairyland', one of a series on English art given in 1884, Ruskin pronounced on the case conclusively. Ruskin made use of the fairy as a metaphor throughout his writings, and some of his early efforts at poetry have fairy subjects, including a lament for 'The Emigration of the Sprites'. In his encomium on fanciful and imaginative landscapes (mainly aimed at children), which he takes to be representations of fairyland, he thunders at his audience:

There are no railroads in it, to carry the children away with, are there? no tunnel or pit mouths to swallow them up, no league-long viaducts – no blinkered iron bridges? There are only winding brooks, wooden foot-bridges, and grassy hills without any holes cut into them! . . . And more wonderful still, – there are no gasworks! no waterworks, no mowing machines, no sewing machines, no telegraph poles, no vestiges, in fact, of science, civilization, economical arrangements, or commercial enterprise!!![6]

Railroads, gasworks, mowing machines, telegraph poles; science, civilisation, economical arrangements, commercial enterprise: these are the effluvia of modernity which despoil the landscape of fairyland and which drive away the fairies, along with everything that is 'decent and orderly, beautiful and pure'.[7] Ruskin's despairing rage against the despoliation

of the countryside infused his attack on the human effects of industrialisation in such works as *Unto This Last* (1860). The departure of the
fairies was only one metaphor in Ruskin's arsenal for the human and
environmental damage wrought by industrial modernity. Yet the idea
that the factories had driven away the fairies was a powerful one which
resonated widely in Victorian culture.

The fairies whose departure was recounted in tales such as Tabby told
were what might be called 'real fairies'; that is, their existence was real
to those who believed in them, and formed part of the store of beliefs,
stories, customs and sayings of their locality, inherited from elders and
handed on to the next generation. It was these fairies whose exploits
the burgeoning numbers of folklorists were so anxious to catalogue.[8] As
soon as their disappearance from commons, hollow hills and villages
began to be recorded and their habits and their doings began to be
collected; as soon as their usual or occasional presence ceased to form
part of the daily life, conversations and beliefs of those to whom they
had previously been a reality; then, the fairies emerged, multiplied,
in quite another sphere. 'Real fairies', the fairies who had left, were
identified by the Victorians with an older, rural world which was being
destroyed by industrial modernity. It was the rural labouring class who
believed in fairies; Carole Silver suggests that fairy belief may even have
lingered as a 'sort of secret learning, a knowledge they controlled and
did not have to share with class, governmental, or religious oppressors'.[9]
But the fairies which populate the Victorian middle-class imagination
are urban creatures: their habitat is the West End stage, the annual art
exhibition and the parlour or drawing room. Though real fairies might
have been driven away by industrialisation, the modern world that
industrialisation created welcomed the fairies back in another form.

A good example of the persistence of fairies in the imaginary landscape of industrial modernity is *Puck and a Moth* (1854; fig. 4) by
Edward Hopley. Originally this was exhibited as one of a pair exem-
plifying Hopley's views on the 'absurdity' of Pre-Raphaelitism. The
'Pre-Raffaelite' and 'Post-Raffaelite' versions treat the same subject
according to what Hopley imagined to be the traditional, academic mode
of composing subject-pictures and the dogmas of Pre-Raphaelitism. His
ideas were explained in a *Letter on Pre-Raffaelitism*, published at the same
time, which argued that in Pre-Raphaelite paintings 'the moral of the
picture must necessarily suffer when struggling against "irresistible lit-
tleness and indubitable cobwebs and caterpillars"'.[10] Hopley condemns
the too-literal transcription of nature, in which moral truths and considerations of beauty (represented in the 'Post-Raffaelite' version by the

Figure 4. Edward Hopley, *Puck and a Moth (Pre-Raffaelite Version)*.

atmospheric lighting and the dark background of indistinct ferns contrasting with Puck's figure) are overwhelmed by the shocking particularity of botanical and entomological detail. In the 'Pre-Raffaelite' version, the bright, overall lighting enables the viewer to identify the details of the vegetation surrounding Puck as well as those of the far background.

Looking at the 'Pre-Raffaelite' *Puck and a Moth*, the eye lights first on the figure of the fairy in the centre of the foreground. Then, however, the eye is drawn by the strong contrast between the dark foreground and the light background to the fields, church and houses, and to a railway train that runs along a track which exactly demarcates the foreground and background. The railway train was widely taken as the epitome of modernity. In her account of her first railway journey, Fanny Kemble exclaimed that 'no fairy tale was ever half so wonderful' as the sights she saw from the train: the magic of fairy tales was outmoded by the capabilities of modern technology.[11] The train and railway line, then, are signs that this scene is a modern one. And the way the picture's composition requires the spectator to view it emphasises its depiction of modernity. The leap the eye makes between foreground and background, between hallucinatory close-up and minutely detailed distance, forces it to cross and recross the railway line at exactly the point where the engine has been arrested. The engine and the church directly behind it imply a diagonal that, carried into the foreground, reaches the fairy. The diagonal connects the fairy and the church, both of which stand metonymically for the ideas of tradition, the persistence of the past in the present, and the presence of the supernatural in the everyday world. Between them the train, the sign of modernity, works as a kind of pivot, the point at which the eye passes and repasses the railway line, the line of modernity. The organisation of the composition around a pivot is in sharp contrast to more traditional landscapes, where central objects stabilise the composition. In Constable's *The Cornfield* (1826; London: National Gallery), for example, the church is a central organising highlight which holds together both the composition of the landscape and its symbolic meanings.

Whilst the fairy is the centre of *Puck and a Moth*, the railway separates foreground and background at the same time as linking them through the train's pivotal position. The foreground and background of the picture cannot be taken in together, and the whole can be understood as one scene only by connecting near and far through the presence of the train and its track through the picture. *Puck and a Moth* presents the spectator with an image that can be understood only by looking at its component parts and working to fit together the fairy, the train, the moth, the church and so on. This fragmentation of the visual field is characteristic of Pre-Raphaelite painting. While academic subject-pictures and landscapes provide an impression of unity for the spectator, a composition in which the whole can be taken in at one glance, Pre-Raphaelite paintings baffle the spectator with their minute delineation of details which the viewer must work to make sense of. The two versions of *Puck and a Moth* exemplify this difference: the 'Post-Raffaelite' version has no background except the sky, so that the spectator is free to focus upon the fairy as the unproblematic centre of the picture, in contrast to the 'Pre-Raffaelite' version. W. F. Axton links this kind of dislocation of perspectives to a number of other instances of fragmentation in mid-Victorian culture: the development of an architecture of details and oblique angles, the multiplication of narrative voices within the novel, the proliferation of voices and perspectives in the dramatic monologue.[12] More generally, Axton links the fragmentation of perspectives to modernity, suggesting that what he calls 'the modern temper' necessitates the relinquishing of a unified viewpoint for the multiple, shifting, contingent viewpoints that he argues are characteristic of Pre-Raphaelite landscape painting: 'In the landscape paintings of the Pre-Raphaelites and their followers, one artistic manifestation of [the modern] temper, the enigmatic artifact whose status vis-à-vis the spectator is in radical doubt, but whose complex ambivalences may yield to multiple perspectival decodings, is much in evidence.'[13]

In *Puck and a Moth* Hopley parodies Millais's *Ferdinand Lured by Ariel* (1849; fig. 14) with the intention of showing that Pre-Raphaelitism robs landscape of 'moral meaning' and produces an unacceptably modern representation of the world. It appears that Hopley's aim is to show, through two views of Puck, that representing a figure associated with tradition in a modern manner is absurd, although ironically the 'Pre-Raffaelite' version is undoubtedly the more successful and visually arresting of the two pictures. Putting the fairy into a modern context and depicting him in a modern manner not only highlights the contrast between the fairy and his modern surroundings, but also draws attention to the ways in which modernity has shaped the world. But though the presence of the railway train organises the picture, it does not dominate it, for the presence of the fairy provides a counterweight to that of the train. While the church recedes fuzzily into the distance, Puck looks at home in the foreground. Hopley's picture shows that in the presence of encroaching modernity the world is still animated by the supernatural, even if the compositional and symbolic stability traditionally associated with the presence of the church is dwindling.

Puck and a Moth is not unusual in bringing together fairies and the modern world. In this chapter I will argue that the fairy was a constant presence in Victorian culture because it provided a relief from and a consolation for the Victorians' overwhelming consciousness of the modernity of their world. Modern developments such as the railway, the hot-air balloon and the steam-driven engine allowed humans to exceed their natural strength and made them capable of feats previously unimaginable. But progress always has its costs, and optimism is always shadowed by anxiety. The Victorians could visualise both their new capabilities and their fears in the form of the fairy; dreaming of fairies allowed them imaginatively to escape from their world while at the same time picturing it in a magical form. In this chapter I will look at three kinds of imaginary responses the Victorians made to the modern world through the figure of the fairy. First I will look at the ideas of flight made possible by the invention of the hot-air balloon, and argue that the winged, flying fairy represents ideas about the transcendence of materiality and the superhuman capabilities of the human body. In the next section I will argue that industrialisation distorted natural ideas about the scale of human beings in relation to God and to the world, and look at how the figure of the fairy both represents and compensates for this distortion. Finally, I will argue that fairyland is an Arcadia for the industrial age, and that the fairies who populate it are dream-images of the factory workers whose condition worried so many Victorians. Each of these discussions will focus upon pictures of fairies, and will show how images which seem to have little to do with the grimy reality of modernity do indeed represent it. Our dreams and fantasies are shaped by the very things from which we seek imaginative escape.

DREAMS OF FLIGHT AND FAIRY WINGS

Once upon a time, fairies had no wings. The fairies of legend, whose exploits folklorists have collected and catalogued, do not fly, and people who claim to have seen them never report that they have wings. In their long literary history, from the medieval romance through to Shakespeare and Drayton, fairies do not have wings, even though, like Puck, they can sometimes move through the air. Pope's mock-epic 'The Rape of the Lock' (1714), has the first winged fairies, airy sylphs derived

Canto II.

Thos Stothard R.A. del.^t   Anker Smith A. Sculp.^t

Belinda smil'd, and all the world was gay.

All but the sylph. ——

Published 1.st November, 1798, by F.I Du Roveray, London.

Figure 5. Thomas Stothard, *Frontispiece to Canto III, The Rape of the Lock.*

from Paracelsus' theory of elemental spirits; Pope uses them to parody
the machinery of the Olympian gods in the epic. Pictures of winged
fairies appeared at the end of the eighteenth century: the first example is
Fuseli's *Puck* (1790), who has bat's wings. Thomas Stothard's illustrations
for a 1798 edition of *The Rape of the Lock* were the first to give fairies
butterfly wings, and these established the convention for nineteenth-
century artists. As the frontispiece to Canto III (fig. 5) shows, Stothard's
fairies are clearly derived from *putti* and are generally drawn from
Raphael and Murillo, yet he has also followed the textual source, both
in giving them insect wings and in making them invisible, as described
in these lines from Canto II:

> Some to the sun their insect wings unfold,
> Waft on the breeze or sink in clouds of gold;
> Transparent forms, too fine for mortal sight,
> Their fluid bodies half dissolved in light.

In this sense both poem and illustration place the sprites halfway
between angels (invisible, disembodied) and fairies (visible, embodied).[14]
Fairies gained their wings in the 1790s, and by the beginning of the
nineteenth century they had, so to speak, taken off. But there is nothing
new in images of winged beings, for angels in art have a long history.
So what is the difference between fairies and angels? Why should fairies
suddenly develop the power of flight and wings to go with it?

Like their bodies, the wings of angels are symbolic. Theologically
speaking, angels are composed entirely of spirit, and the bodies and wings
which clothe them in pictures represent the spiritual qualities of angelic
nature. A late nineteenth-century discussion of angels in art noted:
'Wings are the distinctive angelic symbol, and are emblematic of spirit,
power, and swiftness. Seraphim and cherubim are usually represented
by heads with one, two, or three pairs of wings, which symbolize pure
spirit, informed by love and intelligence.'[15] We should not be troubled
by the question of how their tiny wings keep the chubby bodies of the
putti in seventeenth-century paintings in the air, for the flight of angels
is not to be understood as literal flight: rather, the angel's wings are a
sign of its ability to move between heaven and earth. The angel comes
down from the firmament to deliver his divine message, but his flight
through the ether is not imagined. The light and airy quality that we
associate with depictions of angels such as those by Reni or Murillo signifies not a real ability to fly through the air, but the spiritual nature of
angels.

Describing the frescoes of the Arena Chapel in Padua, Ruskin comments of the depiction of angels:

Modern science has told us that a wing cannot be anatomically joined to a shoulder; and, in proportion as painters approach more and more to the scientific, as distinguished from the contemplative state of mind, they put their wings on more timidly, and dwell with greater emphasis on the human form, with less upon the wings, until these last become a species of decorative appendage, – a mere *sign* of an angel.[16]

Ruskin is here drawing a distinction between Renaissance painters, for whom the conventions of the angel's wings were sufficient to convey its spiritual nature, and later artists, for whom the symbolic nature of the angel's wings is fully apparent. He contrasts the age of faith with the modern age of science, and regrets the consciousness of the sign that modernity brings with it. Looking at representations of angels contemporary with Ruskin's comment, it is clear that his distinction is a perceptive one. The revival of religious art in the Victorian period produced a number of angels, such as Rossetti's *The Girlhood of the Virgin Mary* (1848; London: Tate Gallery) and *Ecce Ancilla Domini!* (1849; London: Tate Gallery) and Burne-Jones's *The Flower of God* (1863; Private Collection). But the angels in these pictures are static, and their wings, when they possess them, are clearly not used for flight. When they do try to fly, they are prevented by other means. Other winged figures, such as Love in Simeon Solomon's *Love in Autumn* (1866; Private Collection) are similarly earthbound and immobile. In earlier eras, wings represented the ability of supernatural beings to move between different realities, but by the time of Ruskin's comment, the flight of angels had become embarrassing, the symbolic nature of the convention too evident to evoke belief.

In contrast, the wings of Victorian fairies are meant for flight, and the fairies are often depicted in mid-air. A good example is David Scott's pair of paintings, *Puck Fleeing Before the Dawn* and *Ariel and Caliban*, both of which represent a flying body which is not heavenly but terrestrial: going up, as it were, rather than coming down. Scott's pictures of fairies could only have been painted once humans were themselves able to fly, because human flight enabled a new way of imagining flying, one which would have been impossible before the invention of the hot-air balloon. It is a truism that the imagination enables us to escape the confines of the body and to picture what we cannot physically see or do. Nevertheless, inventions which dramatically change human capabilities, such as the air balloon, also transform our imaginary visions: flights of fancy take on a different, and in some ways more literal, cast. In particular, the way in which the supernatural is pictured in relation to the human was transfigured by the invention of flying. The delights and terrors of human flight were given imaginary form in pictures such as Scott's which showed supernatural beings with butterfly wings and human bodies leaving the earth and rising into the realm of angels.

Some of the most pleasurable of all dreams are dreams of flying. In contrast to earth-bound nightmares, in which one struggles to run with leaden feet, in dreams of flight one feels a sense of euphoria as the feet leave the ground and one soars up into the air, looking downwards as the ground and the people left behind recede, or upwards as one rises effortlessly higher and higher. Such dream-images of the weary trudge of walking and the delirious excitement of leaving the ground also have their counterparts in waking life. Though walking is in many places described as satisfying, perhaps even spiritually fulfilling, it is equally an activity in which the physical limitations of the body are always evident in footsoreness, exhaustion, blisters and aching bones. John Clare describes this acutely in his painful account of his walk back to Northamptonshire from Epping Forest, where he had been confined to a lunatic asylum:

I remember passing through Buckden and going a length of road afterwards but I dont reccolect the name of any place untill I came to stilton where I was compleatly foot foundered and broke down I started quite refreshed only my feet was more crippled than ever I could scarcely make a walk of it over the stones and being half ashamed to sit down in the street I forced to keep on the move.[17]

Just to describe the putting down of one foot after the other emphasises the bodily endurance involved in walking. In contrast to the insistent physicality of the walk, images of flight gesture towards a transcendence of the physical world, even when they convey not lightness of heart but heaviness of spirit, as in this passage from Coleridge's notebooks:

Friday evening. The immoveableness of all things through which so many men were moving – a harsh contrast with the universal motion, the harmonious system of motions in the country, and everywhere in Nature. In the dim light London appeared to be a huge place of sepulchres through which hosts of spirits were gliding. Soon after this I saw Starlings in vast Flights, borne along like Smoke, mist, like a body unendued with voluntary Power . . . then oblongated into a Balloon with the Car suspended, now a concave semicircle, still expanding, or contracting, thinning or condensing, now glimmering or shivering, now thickening, deepening, blackening![18]

The grim materiality of the city, the 'huge place of sepulchres', makes men seem ghostly and disembodied, and this spectral aspect of the human in relation to the 'immoveableness of all things' is linked metaphorically to the vast flights of starlings, wheeling about in formless, evanescent clouds. Both men and birds are disincarnated, the men transformed into ghosts gliding in and out of the tomb-like structures of the city, the birds 'borne along like Smoke, mist, like a body unendued with voluntary Power'.

The image of the flock of starlings shaped like a hot-air balloon is a striking and unusual one; it is significant because it was only after the invention of the balloon by the Montgolfier brothers in 1783 that dreams of human flight, and especially the imagined flight of the mind's eye, could be measured against an experience of what it was actually like to leave the ground. Before this epoch, as Anne D. Wallace notes, imagined flights in literature are literally 'flights of fancy', in which the imagination itself is thought of as performing the flight, not the human being in which the imagination resides: 'Typically, the eighteenth-century flight of fancy resembles not a continuous fly-by but rather a series of glances from a single landing point or from a number of landings unconnected by reports of physical flight.'[19] So, for example, in this passage from Thomson's *The Seasons* (1726–8), the idea of fancy's flight is used to suggest the transcendental power of the imagination, its ability to go where no mere body could:

> To me be Nature's volume broad displayed;
> And to peruse its all-instructing page,
> Or, haply catching inspiration thence,
> My sole delight, as through the falling glooms
> Pensive I stray, or with the rising dawn
> On fancy's eagle-wing excursive soar.[20]

The distinction here is between the earth-bound walker and his 'soaring' imagination: it is clear that it is only in the imagination that the narrator can fly, only the fancy which can be thought of as having wings.

In contrast, Shelley's 'Ode to the West Wind' (1819), which was written after the invention of the balloon, imagines not only the view from the sky, but also what it would be like actually to be there:

> Thou on whose stream, 'mid the steep sky's commotion,
>   Loose clouds like earth's decaying leaves are shed,
> Shook from the tangled boughs of heaven and ocean.

Angels of rain and lightning! there are spread
On the blue surface of thine airy surge,
    Like the bright hair uplifted from the head

Of some fierce Maenad, even from the dim verge
    Of the horizon to the zenith's height,
The locks of the approaching storm.

If I were a dead leaf thou mightest bear;
    If I were a swift cloud to fly with thee;
A wave to pant beneath thy power, and share

    The impulse of thy strength, only less free
Than thou, O uncontrollable! if even
    I were as in my boyhood, and could be

The comrade of thy wanderings over heaven,
    As then, when to outstrip thy skiey speed
Scarce seem'd a vision.[21]

The wind here not only looks down on the earth, but has a new and intimate view of the sky. The sky is seen not as it appears to the earth-bound, to the purely human, but as it might appear to the wind itself: the view to the horizon is not to the last landmark that can be discerned by the eye from its terrestrial viewpoint, but instead to the 'dim verge' where the curve of the earth appears, from the 'zenith's height'. And instead of remaining below while his imagination soars above, the speaker desires to be lifted bodily above the earth, like a leaf, like a cloud, to fly with and be borne by the wind – just like a passenger in a balloon.

After the first display of a balloon flight in 1783, ballooning swiftly entered the popular imagination. Numerous broadsheets and pamphlets gave accounts of the Montgolfiers' and others' ascents, and they were followed by parodies, skits, poems and plays using the balloon as a theme: for example, *The Air Balloon, or Flying Mortal* by Mary Alcock (1794); *The Mogul Tale; or the Descent of the Balloon* (1796) by Elizabeth Inchbold; and the anonymous *The Modern Atalantis, or Devil in an Air Balloon* of 1786.[22] Balloon literature continued to be prolific until the mid-1830s, with numerous accounts by early balloonists, propositions for flying machines and parachutes based on the balloon, and opportunistic uses of the balloon for publicity purposes. Accounts of balloon flight and stories about ballooning were readily available and, judging from the number of reprints of works such as Alcock's and Inchbold's, highly popular.

Balloons were a thoroughly modern phenomenon. As Simon Schama points out, their first flights were distinctively modern spectacles, cutting through the protocols enshrining the appearances of the monarch and his court, and putting instead the commoner at the centre of public attention, in the middle of a vast crowd in which all ranks were mixed together. An anonymous French painting, *The Montgolfier Balloon at Lyon* (Eighteenth Century; Le Bourget: Musée de l'Air et de l'Espace) shows high and low ranks watching the balloon ascend. While aristocratic boys blow bubbles in the foreground, their bourgeois counterparts play with a toy windmill: both ranks are equally fascinated by the phenomenon of flight. Balloons were also a very modern kind of invention, for the Montgolfier brothers were not gentlemen-scientists but paper manufacturers, 'a new type of citizen-hero: Franklins of the stratosphere'.[23] The balloon also enabled a new perspective on the earth which was itself modern. Schama cites a satirist who wondered if 'to future generations, the Assumption of the Virgin would no longer seem miraculous': that is, whether the capacity of humans to mount into the air undid the divine or semi-divine nature of those who traditionally had been able to do so.[24] This point is also made in Robert Darnton's discussion of ballooning:

A group of peasants, for example, reportedly greeted a balloon landing in a field by shouting, 'Are you men or gods?' And at the other extreme of French society, a well-born balloon enthusiast imagined seeing 'the gods of antiquity carried on clouds; myths have come to life in the marvels of physics.' Science had made man a god.[25]

The ascent into the air puts the human being into the space of the divine, into God's habitation in the heavens. A tract published in 1789 warned that those who became entranced by balloons would forget the real purpose of looking up to heaven, and recounts a fable of a child who forgets to say her prayers for the first time after a balloon passes over her village.[26] This theme was reiterated in the poem *The Air Balloon Spiritualized* (1823) by the Rev. R. S. Medley. It explains that the sinner appears to rise in his 'glittering tinsel and his gaudy pride', but will eventually 'fall and sink to hell'. The Christian, on the other hand, stays on the ground while his soul rises up to heaven: 'Up to God his meditations rise, / His best affections soar above the skies.' The poem concludes: 'Thus the *True Christian* will be proved soon / The very contrast to an *Air Balloon*.'[27] These opponents of ballooning connected the evident allure of human flight with its potential to unsettle traditional ideas about the place of man in the cosmos.

In addition to allowing humans to mount into the heavens, balloon flight also permits to them a God's-eye view of the world: for the first time, humans looked down upon the earth and saw its landscapes, people and their works from the perspective of God. As one writer put it, when the balloon ascends, 'the whole world appear[s] to be receding from us into the dim vista of infinite space'.[28] Such a perspective must necessarily unsettle traditional assumptions about the place of humanity within the world. On the one hand, to assume the God's-eye view from the car of the balloon is to assume a position of perspectival and conceptual mastery; on the other hand, what one sees from the car of the balloon is that man and his works are very small indeed. This perception is neatly summarised by Henry Mayhew in his account of a balloon trip over London:

> The little mites of men, crossing the bridges, seemed to have no more motion in them than the animalcules in cheese; while the streets appeared more like cracks in the soil than highways, and the tiny steamers on the river were only to be distinguished by the thin black thread of smoke trailing after them . . . it was a most wonderful sight . . . to look down upon the whole [of London] as the birds of the air look down upon it, and see it dwindled into a mere rubbish heap – to contemplate from afar that strange conglomeration of vice, avarice and low cunning, of noble aspirations and humble heroism, and to grasp it in the eye, in all its incongruous integrity, at one single glance.[29]

But the balloon also permits an escape from the world into the new physical and imaginative realm imagined in 'Ode to the West Wind', in which one might leave the body behind, freeing oneself from earth-bound constraints and the materiality of the body. For instance, one ballooning enthusiast of the 1830s describes the difference between the ascent and descent of the balloon as the difference between enchantment and pain:

> . . . the descent to the ground is alone unpleasant: it affords a metaphorical picture of human life, in which we mount enchanted by the new objects which arise in succession in the horizon, involve our heads in the clouds in an endeavour to strike the stars, and descend again to our mother mould, as in the final passage to the grave, annoyed by difficult respiration and diminished sensibility.[30]

The euphoria of the ascent and the depression of the descent are associated with the release from and the return to the burdens of the body, and with the freedom of being above and away from terrestrial humanity. When high in the air, the balloonist imagines himself to be among the ethereal creatures who inhabit (or used to inhabit) the sky in the popular or poetic imagination. He becomes, for a moment, ethereal himself:

On first rising we seem amidst thousands of faces, to be central to the directed gaze of oceans of human countenances, forming a crowd which seems to swell like waves of the sea . . . then the silent and agreeable calm which succeeds, when in a region elevated above the restless currents which sweep the face of the earth, we seem to have ascended into the habitations of ethereal spirits . . . when we lean over the car, suspended as it were between Earth and Heaven, the mind indulges in a thousand romantic reveries; and we could almost stretch out our hand to stay the chariot of some goddess drawn by peacocks, or to catch a few of those fairy phantoms of the air which fable acting on credulity built up in the imagination during the season of curious childhood.[31]

Such sensations were far from unusual. In his *History of the Balloon from its Discovery to the Present Time* (1839), Robert Beavan states that the euphoria of the ascent and the sensations of peace and calmness in the air were universally experienced by balloonists: 'This happy state is in no wise restricted to solitary cases, or dependent in any way on the physical or mental constitution of the parties.'[32] He also alludes to the difficulty of the descent and 'the fatigue and depression of the muscular power produced by the accomplishment of [the] journey.'[33] Another account confirms that while suspended in the air the balloonist is particularly susceptible to visions and daydreams: 'there might one revel in all the delights of the imagination, with not the ruffling of a butterfly's wing to put your fancies to flight'.[34] Leaving the ground was accompanied by the dream-like sensation of leaving the body behind; to convey this feeling, balloonists turned to images of wings, butterflies, phantoms and fairies.

However, ballooning is not the only way of escaping the body's confines for, even if one does not actually leave the ground, the new imaginative possibilities offered by balloon flight mean that 'flights of fancy' concentrate much more on the (imagined) sensation of flying. An example of the prevalence of metaphors of actual flight in works concerning fairies can be found in George Darley's verse drama *Sylvia, or the May Queen* (1827), a pastoral romance with a cast of mortals and fairies. The hero Romanzo and Sylvia (who is not only beloved of the fairies, but is constantly described as a fairy-like being) meet and fall in love, and, in their lovers' idyll, Romanzo addresses Sylvia thus:

> Oh, I could follow you
> To the world's bound! o'er unsupporting seas
> And snows as infirm as light! Methinks I could
> Fleet across bottomless gulfs on the thick air,

And scale cliffs that nought but sunbeams climb,
Borne up by aspiration towards your beauty.
     I have oft dreamed
Of gliding by long leaps o'er the green ground
In breathless ecstasy: through plashy lanes
Tree-sided; and down sloping esplanades
Battening in sunlight; along valleys dim,
High-terraced rivers and wild meadow-lands,
Bending my easy way: by will alone,
And inward heaving, rais'd, I seem to flee,
With pleasant dread of touching the near grass
That brushes at my feet.[35]

To dream of flying is like dreaming of love: a pure, ardent, spiritual love in which one leaves the ground, gliding over the earth in pure ecstasy. When Romanzo is captured by evil spirits, they torture him by making him heavy: 'Though my feet do move, / Weights, huge as millstones, seem to clog their steps, / Locking me to this gaol.'[36] The nightmare is to be imprisoned in the body, to walk with leaden feet; the dream is to leave the earth, to soar upwards and to leave the body's confines behind. Dreams of earthbound heaviness and blissful flight are not themselves characteristically modern, for they have a long history; but in modern times such dreams are given a new and literal referent by the ability of humans to fly in the balloon.

Early experiments in flight generated a huge amount of publicity: large numbers of accounts by balloonists, as well as poems, plays, popular prints and tracts on the theme, were published in the first two decades or so after the Montgolfier balloon was invented. After that, interest was periodically sparked by new developments or spectacular occurrences, such as the death of M. Garnerin in 1812 in a ballooning accident near Bordeaux. The mid-1830s saw a resurgence of 'balloon-fever' associated with two notable events: the first cross-channel balloon flight in 1837, and the highly popular Vauxhall balloon, installed in 1836. The latter was a fixed balloon, tethered at Vauxhall, in which, for a small fee, the public could make an ascent and view the panorama of London. The Vauxhall balloon made flight available to the moderately well-off; the poorer simply made an ascent, whilst those with more money could hire the balloon for a flight across London. Both the experience and spectacle of the balloon were enormously successful. The accounts of the intrepid cross-channel balloonists from the following year emphasised the spectacular nature of the experience of flight: they described flying at night as being like moving in a vault of solid black marble which dissolved in front of the balloon and hardened behind.[37] These two events brought the balloon and the idea of flight into the centre of popular consciousness, and it is no surprise that the accession of Queen Victoria prompted a proposal for a *New National Anthem Sung in the Aerial Regions* (1838), which had first been declaimed from the car of a hot-air balloon.[38]

It is in this context that David Scott's pictures of flying fairies were painted and exhibited. Though prints and paintings of balloons were fairly common, the reflections about the human body in flight contained in writings on ballooning lack visual equivalents. One of the very few paintings to represent the human body in flight is Paul Landon's *Daedalus and Icarus* from 1789 (Alençon: Musée de Beaux-arts). Instead of depicting the moment of Icarus' fall, as is usual, Landon shows Icarus stepping off the cliff and into flight. The endeavour of flight is at the centre of the picture, which pays great attention to the human, corporeal quality of Icarus' body. There are few other images of a body in flight, until Scott's *Puck Fleeing before the Dawn* and *Ariel and Caliban*. Scott's abiding interest in the human body and in materiality and its transcendence found perfect expression in the ideas about flight connected with hot-air balloons that were circulating in the mid-1830s. His pictures of flying fairies represent visually the ideas about human flight which ballooning inspired, and render very powerfully both the optimistic and pessimistic reflections about the nature of humans and their relationship to God associated with the invention of human flight.

David Scott regarded himself as, and indeed was, the lone exponent in the Edinburgh of his day of the very grandest manner of history painting. The son of an engraver, his first essays in art were copies of Blake's illustrations of Robert Blair's *The Grave* (1805–7) and of engravings after Fuseli's illustrations of Milton. Like both Blake and Fuseli, Scott esteemed Michelangelo above all other artists; his work bears the distinct imprint of his 1833–4 visit to Rome where he attentively studied Michelangelo, as well as the earlier influence of Blake and Fuseli. (Throughout his writings on art, these two are the only modern artists mentioned.) Comparing David Scott to Michelangelo, William Bell Scott wrote in his memoir that his brother was one of the

powerfully conscious and reflective order of thinkers. With them the poetic mind is the potter, and nature but the clay. Exploring the roots of life in religion, metaphysics, and science, they come out into the world of action as directors and instructors; and in taking upon them the office of the artists, they transcend knowledge by imagination, and subjugate the universe to their imperial sway.[39]

Though the comparison is hyperbole, William Bell Scott's recognition of the highly intellectual nature of his brother's art is important. It is clear from his writings that David Scott had read widely, and the writings contain speculations on metaphysics, religion, science and art. His closest friend was Samuel Brown, a speculative chemist; his inclusion in the Hill-Adamson album and the list of friends he asked to write for a planned almanac show that he was connected with a wide circle of Edinburgh's artistic and intellectual elite. Though his pictures were routinely met with indifference or baffled incomprehension by newspaper critics and the public, many of his works were bought by influential admirers or by subscription, and have found their way into public collections.

Puck Fleeing Before the Dawn (1837; fig. 6) and *Ariel and Caliban* (1837; fig. 7) are good examples. They were badly reviewed when exhibited at the Royal Scottish Academy in 1838: 'Caliban is a caricature of the "human face divine"', wrote one critic, 'and what merit, we may ask, can there be in the delineation of mere deformity? Nor does Ariel realize our ideas of this spirit.'[40] Both works were nevertheless bought by the Society for the Promotion of Fine Art, and were subsequently donated to the National Gallery of Scotland in Edinburgh. They were produced at the high point of Scott's limited success, the year after his illustrations to Coleridge's *The Rime of the Ancient Mariner* were published, and shortly before the most acclaimed work exhibited in his lifetime, *Vasco da Gama Encountering the Spirit of the Cape*.

Throughout his short career, Scott was preoccupied with ideas of the materiality of the body and its transcendence. Contemplating himself at the age of thirty, he wrote that the Greeks represented heroes as being no more than that age; gods – save the celestial gods like Zeus – the same; those associated with the flesh as middle-aged; and Cupid as a boy. 'What may be inferred from this? That they considered man as progressing *into* materiality, and at last, it may be said, dying into it, to be regenerated.'[41] Of his paintings, *Philoctetes left in the Island of Lemnos* (1839; Edinburgh: National Gallery of Scotland) concentrates on the materiality of the body of the hero, excluding almost everything else from the image, and posing his body so that it is stretched out for the viewer's contemplation. His disastrously received *magnum opus*, *The Agony of Discord: or the Household Gods Destroyed* (1834; now lost), similarly focused on the materiality of the body, placing the father of the house (modelled on the central figure of the *Laocoön*) at the centre of a mass of struggling bodies.[42]

On the other hand, Scott also repeatedly represented the spirit world and themes of bodily transcendence in his work. His most critically successful work, *Vasco da Gama Encountering the Spirit of the Cape* (1842; Leith: Trinity House[43]), shows the spirit given the form of a roughly human-shaped gathering of storm clouds and lightning, described by his friend Samuel Brown as 'a vast, vague, half-visible and fearful colossus, conjured out of the palpable darkness of the distance'.[44] The illustrations to *The Rime of the Ancient Mariner* (1836) show even more clearly Scott's fascination with the relation between body and spirit, materiality and its transcendence. *The Spectre-bark Shoots off* clearly foreshadows *Vasco da Gama*, and *While Spirits of Peace Descend* plays on an opposition between the airy immateriality of the spirits and the bodily heaviness of the dying sailor. In *The Spirit of the South Departs* we see not a body chained to the ground by its material nature, like *Philoctetes*, but a spirit leaping up into the air in the ultimate transcendence of the body: flight.

Scott's last project was a series of allegorical illustrations for J. P. Nichol's *The Architecture of the Heavens* (1850), a serious work of popular astronomy. An undated fragment which may be related to this project gives an account of the disembodied soul's journey through life. The metaphysical speculations of this fragment make sense of the allegorical nature of the illustrations, in which an astronomer holds a star, and a comet is represented by a curled-up, projectile human body:

It was night, and a new human soul was born. Gradually it comes out into consciousness, through the struggling senses; through pain, and striving many ways, it feels the upward longing desire, as if it needed to find the sun. Looking up into the firmament, through the night in which it was born, it sees the shining of many lights. To one of these it bends its course ... flies to a further circle ... hastens on to the bounds of the starry sphere, then hither and thither in search of the brightest, still unsatisfied. At last it sees the earth it has left below lying in the starlight, and returns; experiences the solidity and the earthiness, united with all good, which it has elsewhere met. And here it lives until the day breaks, and it dies away into the absorption of the mighty radiance.[45]

The mysticism of this fragment is underlined by the metaphor of flight used to figure the soul's journey. The disembodiment of the soul, after it passes through pain and the 'struggling senses' and flies from one star to another, and its embodiment as it returns to earth, where it experiences 'solidity and earthiness', depend upon a metaphor of flight which is itself underpinned with the literal experience. It is no accident that this passage strongly recalls the impressions of ethereality and embodiment experienced by the balloonist as he ascended and descended. The 'flight through the stars' was made imaginable by the real experience, readily available at second hand through accounts by balloonists, of flying in a hot-air balloon.

Figure 6. David Scott, *Puck Fleeing Before the Dawn.*

Puck fleeing before the Dawn and *Ariel and Caliban*, then, are consonant with preoccupations which lasted the duration of Scott's career, for they clearly allude to his themes of materiality and transcendence of the body. Yet they are also distinguished from his other works, which are characterised by an absolute distinction between body and soul, matter and spirit, human and supernatural. This distinction finds its visual expression in the diaphanousness of the spirits and the exaggerated musculature of the human bodies. Puck and Ariel, however, occupy an ambiguous, half-way position between matter and spirit. As fairies, they are terrestrial creatures who fly, rather than disembodied spirits who simply appear as if from nowhere; they need wings in order to take to the air and their flight is awkward, yet at the centre of the pictures; their bodies are carefully modelled so as to emphasise their embodiment or materiality rather than their spiritual nature. In short, fairies are supernatural beings closer to humans than to angels or spirits, for they are earthly, bodily creatures who can with difficulty raise themselves off the ground, just like humans. The difference is that they use their wings rather than a hot-air balloon. They represent a modern version of the myth of Daedalus and Icarus: a dream of flight, an escape from the nightmare of being trapped in the body.

Each picture has something to tell us about dreams of flight. Puck stands out from the sketchy background, the modelling of his limbs in strong contrast to the flat, almost monochromatic fairies who fly lazily on

their backs, and to the small figure of Oberon, whose drapery is confused
with the bodies of the fairies next to him, and whose face is blurry and
obscured. This appears to bring Puck forward to the bounds of the plane
of the picture's surface, and this is in keeping with the painting's subject:
by 'fleeing', the viewer is meant to understand that Puck is moving fast to
the ends of the earth, and certainly beyond the edge of the picture. Puck
is curled up to such an extent and his head is at such an angle to his body
that it would have to be improbably plastic: a body that could achieve
anything. Yet at the same time his pose seems an anxious, self-protective
one, as if what is before him holds some danger which neither Puck nor
the spectator of the painting can see, perhaps signified by the clouds
emerging from the right-hand side of the picture. The contrast here is
between the fairies in the background, at their ease, in their element,
and the anxious figure of Puck: rather than flying gracefully in the
background, he is driven into the foreground and out of the picture,
as if into embodiment. Puck seems on the verge of bursting into the
three-dimensional world of the spectator and out of the dream-world of
the fairy; away even, perhaps, from the wings which keep him suspended
in the hostile sky with its looming clouds. And the flashes which highlight
his eyes: are they sparkles or tears? Is Puck mischievous or anxious,
gleeful or fearful? Far from being the 'merry wanderer of the night' of
the painting's textual source, who boasts that he will 'put a girdle round
about the earth in forty minutes', this Puck is a much more ambiguous
figure: a fairy whose tiny, insubstantial body is about to be swallowed
up by the darkness before him and turned into a wholly material body
just like that of the human spectator.[46] Crouched before the future and
straining back towards the past, he looks back to the dream of being a
fairy, like those beings whose sketchy flatness emphasizes their unreality,
their likeness to figures in a dream. In this, Puck resembles the dreaming
figure of the painting's spectator. If only one might float at one's ease,
instead of being earth-bound; fly off towards the dawn, instead of into
the dark clouds; if only we were fairies, rather than humans.

　　Ariel and Caliban was described by William Bell Scott as representing
'the two poles of human nature; the ascending and descending forces of
mind and matter'.[47] Ariel lolls at his ease in the air, one foot lazily trailing
Caliban's head as if to emphasise the contrast between Ariel's immateriality and Caliban's brute physicality. The girlish face, long blonde ringlets
and graceful though un-rounded limbs which make up Ariel's androgy-
nous beauty contrast with the hugeness and physical strength of Caliban,
who casually holds a snake powerless in the vast grip of his reptilian claws.

Figure 7. David Scott, *Ariel and Caliban.*

If Ariel, like the butterfly which hovers above him, signifies ease and lightness, Caliban conversely signifies heaviness and toil, connoted by the bundle of faggots he holds under one arm. The toad beside him, the butterfly's counterpart, stands as a metaphor for all that is earthly and ugly, for leap as they may, toads never will fly. Ariel and Caliban are dream and nightmare: the dream of escape from the earth's confines and of unearthly beauty, of a body without sex which will never know the pains of corporeality; the nightmare of a brute, toiling, earth-bound body which will never know anything else, and can only gaze upwards with helpless longing.

The opposition between earthiness and aerial lightness which Caliban and Ariel symbolise parallels that between Ariel's blonde whiteness and Caliban's dark skin and 'African' features. In this respect the two figures look like a crude expression of ideas of European superiority over Africans, and this reading is given emphasis by recalling Prospero's statement about Caliban, 'this thing of darkness I acknowledge mine'.[48] Slavery in British dominions had only recently been abolished in 1833 after a prolonged campaign, and anti-slavery iconography, often showing a kneeling African with the motto 'Am I not a man and a brother?' had been widespread. Scott moved in liberal circles in Edinburgh, and it is hard to believe that he would not have seen such images and shared the sentiments of the anti-slavery campaigners.[49]

Blake's influence on Scott offers another way of interpreting the image. It is possible that Scott knew Blake's *Songs of Innocence* (1789), which includes 'The Little Black Boy'. In opposition to racist ideas of Africans and Europeans as fundamentally different, Blake offers a radical view of racial differences as 'clouds' which mask the underlying identity of all humans:

> When I from black and he from white cloud free
> And round the tent of God like lambs we joy,
>
> I'll shade him from the heat till he can bear
> To lean in joy upon our father's knee;
> And then I'll stand and stroke his silver hair,
> And be like him, and he will then love me.[50]

The notion of the body as a cloud which will be discarded in the afterlife, allowing the essential similarity of human beings to become apparent, has a clear affinity with Scott's ideas of embodiment and disembodiment. Caliban's yearning gaze up at airborne Ariel signifies not that he is inferior but that he longs for the immateriality which is the hope of mortal men: Ariel and Caliban are essentially the same but at different stages in the 'soul's journey' from materiality to disembodiment. The representation of racial difference in the picture is therefore overdetermined by the ideas connoted by the image of the flying and the earthbound human body.

In this painting the spectator can see, in metaphorical form, two versions of what the human being might be: mind and matter; transcendence of the earthbound body or entrapment within it. The two figures are linked – they touch one another, they gaze into one another's eyes – because they are counterparts of each other. In the forms of dream and nightmare they represent a metaphor for the human being only imaginable in modern times. Caliban represents the nightmare of being forever chained to the earth, of being only a body; Ariel offers the dream of escape, of being nothing more than a disembodied soul, or a balloonist who never has to return to earth, or a beautiful, winged fairy who, like Puck, might flee before the burdens and cares of the modern world.

Henry Mayhew claimed that 'there is an innate desire in all men to view the earth and its cities and plains from "exceeding high places", to look down and see the world from the heavens'.[51] But although balloon flight made a perfect vision from above possible, it was physically painful, reminding the balloonist of his fragile, mortal body. It was morally painful too, as Mayhew also recognised: 'To take, as it were, an angel's view of that huge town where, perhaps, there is more virtue and more iniquity, more wealth and more want, brought together into one dense focus than any other part of the earth . . . such is the scene we behold, and such the thoughts that stir the brain on contemplating London from the car of a balloon.'[52] Though flying brought joyful release and thrilling, transcendent vision, it also brought new burdens, for to transcend the limits of the human body is also perhaps to overstep the limits of human power and knowledge. Not for nothing did peasants call out to the balloonists on landing, 'Are you men or gods?' The figure of the flying fairy is coeval with the air balloon because in a metaphorical form it could represent the pleasures and dangers of human flight. At the same time it also stood as a metaphor for a new, modern condition of humanity released from its terrestrial bondage into the possibility of an all-seeing, heavenly gaze; but what this gaze showed was that humanity had been dwarfed by its own works. The cities, factories and machines of industrial modernity had rendered humans tiny, scaled them down to the size of a fairy.

HOW LARGE ARE FAIRIES?

In Robert Howlett's famous photograph taken on board the steamer, the *Great Eastern*, Isambard Kingdom Brunel stands in front of a reel on which is wound a huge chain. The juxtaposition of Brunel and the chain is normally understood metonymically: the chain is a metonym for the grandeur and enormity of Brunel's work, which in turn stands for the grandeur and enormity of Brunel's stature as an engineer and a man. But the photograph can be read otherwise. The hugeness of the chain poses the question of who could wind the chain round the reel, and draws attention to Brunel's diminutiveness in relation to his works: no-one but a giant, nothing but a machine, could lift or wind that chain. The photograph bears witness to a paradox of scale which is central to the industrial world, for at the same time as the image celebrates the vastness of human achievements, it simultaneously shows that human beings are dwarfed by them, and that the power upon which the modern world depends is achieved in despite of human weakness. In the industrial world the human being is both large and small, strong and weak, gigantic and miniature. Humans can be understood as big and strong only if the human being and the machine are thought of as in some sense the same, if they are linked in a metonymic relation of creator and servant. The machine must be thought of as a gigantic pair of human hands in order to magnify the human being.

But in the factory the role of the human operative is to be the machine's servant, reversing the two roles; there the humans appear diminished to tiny, weak, miniature beings dwarfed by the machines they tend. This perception is shared by both propagandists for and opponents of the factory system. Andrew Ure's *The Philosophy of Manufactures* (1835) is on the one hand a technical yet popular explanation of the processes of mechanised cotton spinning and weaving; on the other it provides an optimistic, utilitarian justification of the factory system as the system best adapted both to the efficient production of goods and to the happiness and well-being of the working population. Of the invention of the factory system he says:

The main difficulty did not, to my apprehension, lie so much in the invention of a proper self-acting mechanism, for drawing out and twisting cotton into a continuous thread, as the distribution of the different members of the apparatus into one co-operative body, in impelling each organ with its appropriate delicacy and speed, and above all, in training human beings to renounce their desultory habits of work, and identify themselves with the unvarying regularity of the complex automaton. To devise and administer a successful code of factory discipline, suited to the necessities of factory diligence, was the Herculean enterprise, the noble achievement of Arkwright.[53]

Two things are significant here: first, that each mechanism in the spinning process has been joined into one 'co-operative body', the organic metaphor implying that the machine has taken on a life of its own; second, that the system requires and is predicated upon the subordination of the human to the body of the machine. As Ure tellingly puts it, the identification of the human with the machine is required, so that the human being becomes both identical with the machine (that is, mechanised), and takes from the machine his identity (that is, thinks of himself as a machine). The 'Herculean', superhuman enterprise of the factory system is thus the subjugation of human beings to the machine.

Ure's controversial work was attacked by Peter Gaskell, a physician, in *Artisans and Machinery* (1835). Gaskell concentrates his polemic on the effects of mechanisation on the human being in all its aspects: physical, social, moral and spiritual. Though Gaskell is forced to acknowledge the wider economic benefits of industrialisation, he argues fervently and compellingly that the factory system in fact achieves the opposite of what proselytisers like Ure claim for it: that mechanised industrial production in itself achieves a happy, prosperous and contented workforce. Rebutting Ure's claims, he argues:

The universal application of steam power as an agent for producing motion in machinery has closely assimilated all the branches of manufacturing industry, both in their moral and physical relations. In all, it destroys domestic labour; in all, it congregates labourers into towns, or families; and in all, it lessens the demand for human strength, reducing man to a mere watcher or feeder of his mighty assistant, which toils and labours with a pertinacity and unvarying continuance requiring constant and sedulous attention.[54]

Ure sees the relationship between man and machine as an essentially benevolent one between the 'benignant power of steam' and its 'myriads of willing menials'. The 'gigantic arm' and 'gentle docility' of the power loom require only 'attention and dexterity on the part of the worker'.[55] Gaskell, however, is at pains to stress that the worker is no longer an artisan employing his skill, strength and labour, but the 'mere watcher and feeder' of the 'mighty assistant' which completely subsumes him.

Both writers emphasise the relative sizes of the machine and the factory worker, even though their views of mechanised labour are entirely opposed. Their recourse to the idea of the giant to convey the power of steam-driven machinery implies the corollary that humans are dwarfed, even if, like Arkwright, they also have superhuman stature. These descriptions of the factory system underline what Howlett's photograph of Brunel as an industrial giant shows: that the role of master makes the human being gigantic; the role of servant makes it miniature.

The double effect of this photograph, simultaneously to magnify and to diminish, is a typical effect of scale which most discussions of the miniature ignore. For example, writing of the manipulation of scale in the microphotograph (a photograph designed to be viewed through a microscope, so that its image is greatly magnified and tiny details become visible to the eye), Marina Benjamin argues:

The microphotographic universe, though elastic, was fundamentally stable; within it things could expand or shrink, but they preserved their identity. Its effect on the observer was reassuring. This is what Carroll's Alice learns from her adventures – however big or small she is, she is still Alice; even when she is growing in the house she retains her composure.[56]

Elasticity of scale is reassuring for Benjamin because it implies no concomitant uncertainty about the nature or identity of the human subject. Other things might shrink or grow, and humans might imagine themselves shrinking and growing, but in the end the Victorians knew what size they were. For Gaston Bachelard, on the other hand, the wondrous simultaneity of the miniature and the gigantic draws attention to their identity:

When we have followed Supervielle's entire poem . . . we perceive that the familiar world assumes the new relief of the dazzling cosmic miniature. We did not know that the familiar world was so large. The poet has shown us that large is not incompatible with small . . . tiny and immense are compatible . . . If a poet looks through a microscope or a telescope, he always sees the same thing.[57]

Magnification and miniaturisation are the same thing because they show us anew the familiar in a wondrous form. For Bachelard, Blake's 'Heaven in a grain of sand' is equally a handful of sand in the myriad stars of the night sky. But what about the uneasy moment when scale shifts, when the viewer is conscious not just of the identity of small and large, but of an uncertainty about how to tell them apart and, the corollary of this uncertainty, a confusion about how scale might be marked in such a moment of uncertainty? In a world of simultaneous magnification and miniaturisation, where is the 'true scale' to be found? If the thing that shrinks and grows is not something seen in the world (a grain of sand, the night sky) but the human body of the viewer, this shifting in scale will tend to undo a stable sense of the self, of the place and stature of the human being. When the caterpillar asks Alice who she is, she is unable to answer, 'for I can't understand it myself, to begin with; and being so many sizes in a day is very confusing'.[58] Perhaps Alice is not really so self-assured.

In the pre-industrial world the ratio of scale was God: man. Man was the miniature of God, made in God's image, and to God the world was a vast miniature seen from his celestial, transcendent perspective. The invention of the hot-air balloon granted this perspective to man, allowing humans to see themselves and their works from a new position in which they and their world became miniaturised. The counterpart of the transcendent view from the balloon which miniaturises the world is provided by the microscope and naturalist's hand-lens, which magnify the tiny world of microscopic life forms. Microscopy, which became very widespread in the middle decades of the nineteenth century, provided ample opportunities for its enthusiasts to muse on the abrupt disparities of scale it produced. Here is an example from Phillip Henry Gosse's *The Romance of Natural History* (1860):

Scarcely anything more strikes the mind with wonder than, after having been occupied for hours, perhaps, in watching the movements and marking the forms of these and similar creatures, till one has become quite familiar with them, suddenly to remove the eye from the instrument, and taking the cell from the stage, look at it with the naked eye. Is this what we have been looking at? This quarter inch of specks, is this the field of busy life? are here the scores of active creatures feeding, watching, preying, escaping, creeping, dancing, revolving, breeding? Are they here? Where? Here is nothing, absolutely nothing, but two or three minutest dots which the straining sight just catches now and then in one particular light.[59]

The microscope turns minute specks of dust into very large creatures indeed, for the eyepiece of the instrument excludes everything outside the stage, and the magnification is so great that sometimes the observer can see only part of the creature, thus giving the impression of immense size. In the absence of scale markers the minute becomes the gigantic. But this has a further magnifying effect on the human observer, because in comparison to the tiny life forms inside the microscope he or she is truly enormous. The hot-air balloon and the microscope symbolise the ways in which modern technologies destabilised perceptions of scale in two directions: the human body was made into a miniature, and it was also made gigantic, and sometimes both at once.

Despite such disturbances, the scale relation God: man can remain stable as long as its corollary, creator: creation, also remains undisturbed: that is, as long as man remains the dearest of God's creations, the 'scale marker' for the world. But this relation was unbalanced in the nineteenth century in several ways: by the growing suspicion produced by the study of myth, archaeology and comparative religion that God might in some way be a creation of man; by the progressive unsettling of the biblical account of the world which culminated in Darwin's formulation of the theory of evolution by natural selection; and by the increasing ability of man to exceed his own capabilities, to master the world through the power of the machine.

This is one explanation of the tendency of those writers appalled by the spectacle of industrialisation to describe its phenomena, such as factories, steam engines, furnaces and power-looms, as demonic or satanic. The landscape of industrial modernity is represented as akin to imaginings of hell; industrialisation is thought of as another Fall brought about, like its original, by humanity's ambition to emulate and perhaps even over-reach God in knowledge and power. (Of course, this is a representation of industry which has a long history, going back at least as far as Milton's description of Pandaemonium in *Paradise Lost*.[60]) Thomas Carlyle described his first train journey in terms which combine exhilaration with dread: 'Out of one vehicle into another, snorting, roaring we flew: the likest thing to Faust's flight on the Devil's mantle; or as if some huge steam night-bird had flung you on its back.'[61] In his late lecture, 'The Storm Cloud of the Nineteenth-Century', Ruskin explicitly describes industrialisation as a latter-day Fall:

Blanched Sun, – blighted grass – blinded man. If, in conclusion, you ask me for any conceivable cause or meaning of these things – I can tell you none, according to your modern beliefs; but I can tell you what meaning it would have borne to the men of old time. Remember, for the last twenty years, England, and all foreign nations, either tempting her, or following her, have blasphemed the name of God deliberately and openly; and have done iniquity by proclamation, every man doing as much injustice to his brother as it is in his power to do.[62]

Another way of representing industry was to present it as sublime, to emphasise the glow of the furnaces, the contrast between artificial light and natural darkness, and the immense power of industrial processes. This approach is exemplified by Joseph Wright of Derby's *Arkwright's Cotton Mills by Night* (1782–3; Private Collection) and Phillip de Loutherberg's *Coalbrookedale by Night* (1801; London: Science Museum). Although the imagery of the sublime helped to render the scene of industry heroic, because many of its features were shared with depictions of the apocalypse such imagery also suggested that the industrial landscape was hellish.[63]

Both those representations of the industrial world which emphasise its sublimity and those which see it as satanic are equally concerned with questions of scale. The scene of industry is one in which natural laws have been cast aside, in which human operatives are dwarfed by the vast magnificence of the machinery, rendered obscure by the fiery glow of the furnaces and runnels of liquid metal, or made ant-like in their multitude, and in which the inhuman speed and power of the steam engine is cast as positively demonic. Such comparisons serve to unsettle natural relations of scale, and represent this disturbance in its sublime or satanic aspect. Each of these in itself brings forward questions of scale, on the one hand because the sublime object's vastness, obscurity, or power (to think of the sublime in its Burkean version) always depends on its relation to the small human observer, and on the other because the incomprehensible capaciousness and duration of hell necessitates a conceptual diminution of the damned human spirit to a tiny one among multitudes – as is vividly illustrated in John Martin's *The Last Judgement* (1853; London: Tate Gallery).

Industrial modernity demonstrates human capacities at their most powerful, showing us man the master of nature and creator of the machine. But at the same time it exposes the human being as enfeebled and diminished, no longer the creator but the servitor of the machine, the mere operative in the factory powered by the steam engine, tending the vast mechanical apparatus. Here, then, is a disturbance of scale relations in which a simultaneous magnification and miniaturisation is apparent. Like the moment of unease when the observer cannot discern whether an object is large or small, this must have been profoundly unsettling because it brought into question the nature and status of human beings both in relation to the world and in relation to God. Such elasticity of scale cannot be in any sense reassuring.

How is such a veering between large and small, such an uncertainty about the stature of the human being, to be made good? One way might be for humans to imagine creatures in some ways miniatures of themselves, to re-establish a sense of scale by replicating in miniature the scale relation God: man and turning it into human: fairy. Susan Stewart has argued that miniature worlds, objects and beings tend to be idealised and perfected versions of their human-sized counterparts. She suggests that fairies' bodies are scaled-down human bodies, perfect in every tiny detail:

Whereas the grotesque erupts into a medley of erotogenic zones, of gaps and orifices, the doll/fairy presents a pure, impenetrable surface: proportional within a suitably detailed context . . . The fairies present the animate, human counterpart to the miniature. Unlike the gigantic, which celebrates quantity over quality, the fairies represent minute perfection and a cultured form of nature.[64]

The miniature ideal body of the fairy is static and unchanging, a body that is 'for ever', unlike the bodies in which we live, which do grow and then shrink again as we age: 'the ideal of the body exists within an illusion of stasis, an illusion that the body does not change and that those conditions and contingencies which shape the ideal are transcendent and "classic" as well'.[65] The miniature body of the fairy is not subject to time, nor to the vicissitudes of life and labour; it exists in an absolute and unchanging state of diminution in relation both to the human body and to the world. Because the fairy is a figure from the past, the time before industrial modernity, it also represents permanence: the fairy has always been so.

The figure of the fairy, then, presents the human body in a miniaturised, perfect version from which the appalling power and terrible weakness of the human being have been erased, for fairies live in a state of effortless leisure, sustained by rather than shaping and using the world. The Victorians could take solace in imagining fairies because fairies showed them a perfect version of themselves on a scale small enough to confirm their own dominance in the world. If the Victorians could no longer be certain that they were a miniature of God made in his image, and worried that they might have exceeded the place and powers allotted to them in the creation, they could at least assure themselves that they were the magnification of the fairy which was, in an ideal form, made in their image. But the figure of the fairy occasions a further, paradoxical effect of scale, because it also operates as a miniature version of God – God seen, as it were, through the wrong end of the telescope. Though the fairy was often a consolatory figure through which the Victorians' anxieties about scale could be made good, it must sometimes have reminded them that their stature was gained at the cost of the diminution of God.

During the 1830s and 1840s at least one fairy subject was exhibited every year at the annual exhibitions of both the Royal Academy and British Institution. Some of these works were by artists pre-eminent in other genres, who painted only one fairy subject. *Queen Mab's Cave* (1846; London: Tate Gallery) was one of several paintings on supernatural subjects Turner exhibited towards the end of his career; Landseer's *Titania and Bottom* (1851; Melbourne: National Gallery of Victoria) was commissioned by Isambard Kingdom Brunel for a projected Shakespeare Gallery, and although Landseer is, as usual, more interested in the animals than the humans, his composition shows the influence of Fuseli's paintings for Boydell's Shakespeare Gallery upon which Brunel's project was based. Following the examples of Thomas Stothard and Henry Howard, both protégés of Fuseli, history painters occasionally turned to fairy subjects for paintings which could be both light and serious. A good example is the Irish artist Daniel Maclise. In addition to large pictures on national themes, such as *King Alfred in the Camp of the Danes* (1852; Nottingham Castle Museum), Maclise produced a number of fairy paintings, the most successful of which, *Scene from 'Undine'* (1844; fig. 8), was

Figure 8. Daniel Maclise, *Scene from 'Undine'*.

bought by Victoria and Albert for the Royal Collection.[66] Victoria's taste was splendidly conventional, so her purchase of this picture demonstrates how popular fairy painting was, at least among the middle classes who attended the annual exhibitions and bought the pictures exhibited there, or the engraved versions of them included in new art periodicals like the *Art-Union*. *Scene from 'Undine'* takes its subject from an immensely popular fairy romance by Friedrich de la Motte Fouque (*Undine*, 1811, first English translation 1818), a work which itself draws attention to the metaphorical link between fairies and humans through the multiple transformations between fairy and human its heroine undergoes. In both its composition and style and its subject, *Scene from 'Undine'* bears witness to the influence of German culture on the arts in Britain in the first half of the nineteenth century.[67] Maclise's painting offers a presentation of the human body in which variations of scale are both represented and set in a stable relation between human and non-human, so that disparities of size are displaced, normalised and rendered reassuring.

The painting illustrates a passage in the novel where Undine and her husband, the knight Huldbrand, are riding through an enchanted forest to the town where he lives. They are ambushed on the way by the evil spirit Kuhleborn, who is jealous of the transformation love has effected on Undine in turning her from a fairy into a human. Maclise has set these three characters in the centre of his crowded composition, with Kuhleborn looming over the two mortals. Around the centre of the picture is a 'frame' of intertwined plants and tiny fairies. Here the demonic and the magnified are united in the form of Kuhleborn, whilst at the other end of the scale the fairies are perfect miniature humans. This continuum of scale and the values it represents were noticed by Maclise's biographer, who wrote of this painting:

The composition is entirely in the spirit of German poetry, and is treated in the spirit of German Art. The two principal figures and the horse are surrounded by a kind of framework – Lilliputian beings, entangled among the ferns and wood-plants, in an infinity of attitudes, but all their faces indicative of fear or surprise at the intrusion on their solitude; while Kuhleborn, like an arch-fiend, casts the dark shadow of his presence over the strange fantastic scene, in hideous contrast to the singular beauty, both of nature and of the human and animal form, that prevails all around. There is some wonderful painting in all the details of the picture, which everywhere shows the most ingenious fancy and inventive power.[68]

The 'singular beauty' of the human form is connected metonymically with the Lilliputian perfection of the fairies and set in contrast to the hideousness and gigantic size of the demonic Kuhleborn. The extremes of size represented by the 'arch-fiend' and the fairies serve to naturalise the size of the humans in the composition, whilst the conventional masculine and feminine beauty of the couple emphasises that it is the humans who are at the centre of this represented world. However, this reassuring naturalisation can only take place because the magnification and miniaturisation of the human are both present and displaced: from the centre of the composition, and from the human body. Though the humans are fairy-like in their beauty, they are neither too large nor too small. Scale relations are reassuringly normal, but this normality is conferred only by the presence of the supernatural beings against which the human beings are measured. The reassurance of the painting lies, perhaps precariously, in the compositional space it allots to the human, for this disguises how far it is necessary to go in order to show that the human body is, after all, the right size.

Fairy paintings, moreover, were not the only representations of fairies readily available to the middle-class public, for during the 1830s and 1840s fairies were a common sight on the London stage. In 1832 Marie Taglioni danced *La Sylphide* to wild acclaim, using the *new pointe* technique she had perfected. The ballet, which tells the story of a fairy who falls in love with a mortal man, was a perfect vehicle for this technique, the lightness of which offered the illusion of flight. The vogue for Romantic fairy ballets was continued with *Giselle* in 1841. The fairy extravaganza, a variant of pantomime based on fairy tales and featuring magical set-pieces and transformation scenes, was an annual Christmas event during these decades, the most spectacular being the fairy extravaganzas of J. R. Planché, staged yearly between 1836 and 1856. Planché's collaborator, and the director of many of his extravaganzas, was Madame Vestris who, in 1840, staged an enormously successful production of *A Midsummer Night's Dream* at Covent Garden. Vestris's staging was considered to be the first effective production of the play since the seventeenth century, and though she cut many of the lines and emphasised the scenes with the fairies and the mechanicals, Vestris restored to the repertoire a play hitherto considered unsuitable for theatrical production.[69]

Vestris turned *A Midsummer Night's Dream* into a spectacular theatrical experience, using Mendelssohn's *Overture and Incidental Music* (1826), elements of the Romantic ballet, new developments in stage lighting (such as limelight) and in scenery (such as the panorama), using the Grieve family of stage designers to produce the sets. These developments helped to turn the early Victorian stage, and Vestris's production in particular, into a highly visual experience. Limelight, for example, heightened colours and accentuated the glitter of reflective surfaces, and made it possible to produce dream-like lighting effects by using gauzy panels in front of the lights. The elaborate stage sets and scenery developed by designers such as John Grieve often contained references to or even recreated well-known paintings; theatrical illusion tended more and more to simulate the lifelike.[70] The cuts Madame Vestris made to *A Midsummer Night's Dream* emphasised longer speeches over dialogue (especially that of the lovers), and this worked with the stage design to make the play appear like a succession of vivid, animated pictures – many of them, of course, featuring fairies.

As Michael Booth has argued, Victorian culture was marked by a taste for visual spectacle which extended into all areas of cultural life: ' . . . the world,' he remarks, 'was saturated with pictures'.[71] Entertainments became more visual: printed books and periodicals included ever greater amounts of illustration; gadgets like the stereoscope brought spectacular pleasures into the home; even the streets afforded new visual delights to passers-by in the form of plate glass shop windows filled with alluring wares. 'Peering through a brilliantly lit rectangle of glass into a wonderland of attractive goods for sale was like looking into a peepshow or a stage flooded with light behind a proscenium. The elements of a rectangular frame of vision, a bright light, a viewer, and the varied objects of his view were common to daily life and entertainment as well as the theatre.'[72] The continuum between theatrical spectacle and everyday life was continued into visual art. Not only did the stage bring pictures 'to life', but artists too increasingly recognised a commonality between painting and theatre. Paintings of scenes from plays abounded, with Shakespearean subjects (including, of course, fairy paintings) being only the most popular, and scenes of everyday life, such as William Powell Frith's *Ramsgate Sands (Life at the Seaside)* (1854; Royal Collection), increasingly resembled the staged panoramas so popular in the theatre. In fact, the vivid colours and overall bright lighting which characterise so much Victorian painting, combined with the rectangular frame and the viewer, mean that visual art and theatre appealed to the same taste for gorgeous spectacle. In this context, the popularity of fairy painting and plays among a large (and growing) middle-class public is easily explicable. The success of Madame Vestris's *A Midsummer Night's Dream* and the sale of *Scene from 'Undine'* to Queen Victoria were elements of the same phenomenon.

All fairy paintings must negotiate questions of scale. Those which include both humans and fairies, like *Scene from 'Undine'*, require the artist to have made a decision about the relative sizes of humans and fairies; those which depict fairies alone involve deciding how large the fairies are in relation to their background. Many works complicate these questions by including fairies of different sizes. Similar considerations of scale are involved in the theatre, where stage sets for large scenes are inevitably scaled-down reproductions giving the impression of space and recession by means of theatrical illusions. Such scale models are inevitably disrupted by comparison with the human actors moving about inside them. These problems are intensified in fairy scenes: either the convention that fairies are tiny must be sacrificed, or they must be played by children. Both the spectator in the theatre and the viewer of a painting gaze through the proscenium arch or frame into a scaled-down version of the world they inhabit. The disparities of scale present in the world of the spectator are thus dramatised and intensified in the brightly lit rectangle inside the theatre's arch or the picture frame.

Many fairy paintings from the 1830s and 1840s exemplify both a pre-occupation with scale and a resemblance to the theatre. Francis Danby's *Scene from A Midsummer Night's Dream* (1832; Oldham Art Gallery and Museum) shows the quarrel of a tiny Oberon and Titania dwarfed by enormous grasses, flowers and toadstools. It also mimics the moonlight effects being developed in the spectacular theatre, which used transparent screens and gaslight, later limelight, to achieve a haunting impression of dusk with bright white moonlight.[73] Similar effects can be seen in moonlight scenes by E. T. Parris and John Lamb.[74] However, the combination of theatricality and exaggeration of scale is given its most acute rendering in works by two artists who specialised in the fairy genre: Robert Huskisson and Richard Dadd.

Robert Huskisson enjoyed a brief moment of fame in the late 1840s when he was 'discovered' by the entrepreneur S. C. Hall, editor-proprietor of the *Art-Union*, later the *Art Journal*. Hall bought Huskisson's *The Midsummer Night's Fairies* (fig. 9) from the 1847 Royal Academy exhibition, and it appeared in engraved form in the *Art Journal* in October 1848. Hall also owned (and perhaps commissioned) the painting's pendant, '*Come unto these Yellow Sands*' (1847; Private Collection), and this, too, was engraved for Hall's journal. Few other works by Huskisson are known: *The Mother's Blessing* (1848), which was used for the frontispiece of Anna Maria Hall's *Midsummer Eve: A Fairy Tale of Love* (1848); a copy of Etty's *The Rape of Proserpine* for Lord Northwick; and a subject from Milton's *Comus*, again in the style of Etty, for the Liverpudlian collector, Thomas Miller.[75] Hall, Huskisson's main patron, also sponsored

Figure 9. Robert Huskisson, *The Midsummer Night's Fairies*.

Richard Dadd: Dadd's *Come Unto These Yellow Sands* (1842) was engraved for the *Art Journal,* and he contributed the illustration to 'Robin
Goodfellow' for Hall's *Book of British Ballads* (1842). Hall was indirectly
involved in the theatre through his wife, who wrote several plays, and
was an associate of Charles Dickens, who had many connections in the
theatrical world including a friendship with Tom Taylor, the writer of
pantomimes and burlesques.[76] Hall's interests bring together the visual
arts and the theatre, and his taste for fairy subjects is perfectly consonant
with that of middle-class theatre-goers and the readers of his periodicals.

The conceit of *The Midsummer Night's Fairies* (and Huskisson's *Come
Unto These Yellow Sands*) is that the viewer looks through the invisible
'fourth wall' of a theatre into fairyland. A buff-coloured frame surrounds
the fairy scene, and this contrasting frame is a *trompe-l'œil* resembling
a proscenium arch with low-relief human figures reclining on it. The
scene inside is jewel-coloured and the groups in the foreground (soldiers

fighting a snail) and background (Titania and her attendants) are picked out with dramatic highlights. These colour and light effects resemble those attainable with gaslight on the stage, and the contrast between the neutral arch-like frame and the glowing interior strengthens the illusion that the viewer is gazing into a stage set. But this is not a full-sized theatre: the fuchsia flowers, dew-drops and snail all indicate the miniature scale of the scene. The picture itself is small: only 29 × 34 cm. Indeed, it resembles nothing so much as a toy theatre with a printed paper surround and, instead of cardboard cut-out figures and scenery, real, living supernatural beings. (This association would have been evident to the original viewers of the painting, for in the 1840s toy theatres were at the height of their popularity, and most middle-class homes with children would have possessed one.[77]) The sensation, then, is of looking into a living miniature, a model which has woken up, a toy which has come to life.

The fascination of the living miniature is, however, not entirely comfortable, for it must always recall the size of the human spectator. A link between the viewer and the fairies inside the picture is provided by the figures on the frame-arch, situated between the space of the picture and the space of the viewer. These figures are clearly human rather than supernatural, and this is the source of their ambiguity, for they are the same size as the fairies inside the frame. Should the viewer identify his or her own body with those on the frame, the world inside the picture would become gigantic, the home of monstrous beasts and outsized vegetation. This ambiguity of scale is emphasised by the tiny figures in the foreground which, even within the picture space, make Oberon and Titania appear like giants. Like a gleaming plate-glass shop window or a stage brilliant with gas light, *The Midsummer Night's Fairies* draws the eye to its bright rectangle glowing with colour. Inside its miniature world are the fairies; outside, the human spectators. Between them is a scale relation which is both dramatised and rendered unstable by the way in which the framing device draws attention to the size of the figures. The seductiveness of the image comes partly from its unsettling quality, its pleasurable confusion over how large and small the figures on the inside and outside of the frame are in relation to one another.

Huskisson's figures show the influence of William Etty, the most determined painter of the nude in the 1840s, and of Daniel Maclise. But he also looked very carefully at the work of Richard Dadd, who, in his short public career, was almost entirely identified as a fairy painter.

In its 'Obituary', published in 1843, after Dadd had murdered his father and been committed to Bethlem Hospital for the Criminally Insane, the *Art-Union* wrote: 'He took especial delight in portraying fairies. In 1841, the work which may even now be considered his most successful, "Titania Asleep," was exhibited at the Royal Academy. Next appeared a "Puck," that excited universal admiration at the exhibition of British Artists.'[78] Dadd's work made a considerable impression on the critics, who praised his inventiveness and imagination; the continuing popularity of his early fairy paintings was ensured by their inclusion in the Manchester Art Treasures exhibition in 1857.[79] These, then, were images of fairies which made a considerable appeal to their audience and which helped to form ideas about what fairies looked like and about their demeanour, nature and stature. But if the enchanted fairyland Dadd painted was a popular one, it was also one which allowed uneasy moments of slippage in scale to become visible, and with them anxieties about the nature and stature of the human being.

Dadd's early fairy paintings are strongly theatrical, using framing devices and dramatic lighting. *Titania Sleeping* (1841; Paris: Louvre) has an outer, arched frame of three bats with interlocking wings. Inside this frame is Titania's bower, picked out with a strong central highlight, and framed itself by an arch of tumbling fairies and convolvulus. Titania and her attendants are set inside two successive 'proscenium arches', and the highlight on this group strengthens the theatricality of the concep-tion. The central idea of *Puck* (1841; fig. 10), the child-fairy sitting on a toadstool, is taken from Reynolds's Shakespeare Gallery painting (1790; Private Collection), which inaugurated the fashion for Puck to be played by a child.[80] Again, the lighting in this picture is strongly theatrical. The main source of light is the moon behind Puck, which illuminates him and is reflected off the moony paleness of his skin, and also casts strong shad-ows from the dancing fairies which lead to and are subsumed within the shadowy darkness forming a circle around the bright moonlight at the centre of the painting. The theatricality of this strong contrast between light and shade is further emphasised by the convolvulus flower which hangs directly over Puck's head, and this, with its ring of dew-drops, resembles a chandelier or spotlight, further drawing attention to Puck as the star of the scene. Even the dew-drops hanging from the surround-ing foliage and grasses contribute to the theatricality of the light-effect, since, catching the moonlight, they resemble the lights at the side of the stage. All these devices serve to focus the spectator's eyes on Puck at the centre of the picture and then secondarily on the dancing fairies who

Figure 10. Richard Dadd, *Puck*.

circle the toadstool. This intense luminosity disguises, until one looks closer, the unnerving effects of scale.

The highlights on Puck make him look large, and in comparison to the fairies beneath him, he is. But when compared to the size of the toadstool he sits upon and to the flowers, grasses and foliage surrounding him, he is small, extremely small, and this makes the fairies tiny. Through a trick of scale, Puck is made to look larger than the moon, even though he is very little (the effect is the same when one holds out a hand at arm's length to cover the sun). These disparities of scale are counterpointed by the comparison between the fairies inside the picture and the human figures on the painted spandrels which surround it and form its 'frame'. Like those on the 'proscenium arch' in Huskisson's picture, these figures confuse the viewer's sense of how large he or she is in comparison to the fairies. Furthermore, the reversal of scale between the tiny adult fairies and the larger (though still small) child Puck brings into question the nature of the fairy's body itself. Do fairies, contrary to nature, shrink instead of grow as they become adult, or are there several kinds of fairies? In the latter case, which kind of fairy naturalises the size of human beings? If the human figures are the markers of scale, then everything in the picture, save the adult fairies, is grossly enlarged; if Puck and the natural world are in scale, then the human figures around the frame are greatly reduced. There can be no resolution to these questions, for the slippage of scale between the 'frame' and the picture cannot be anchored in an external referent, except the human body of the viewer. The relationship between picture and viewer is puzzlingly circular, for the questions of scale which the picture dramatises can only be resolved by reference to a scale marker whose size cannot be determined by comparison to the figures in the picture. The *Art-Union*'s reviewer, whilst praising the painting, warned Dadd that he should 'stop short of the boundaries which divide the imagination from the absurd'.[81] The sense of 'absurdity' the painting provokes lies in the way it represents the disruption of scale relations, the elasticity of small and large, gigantic and miniature, that undermines the spectator's certainty about what size and stature belong to the human being.

This effect can also be seen in *Come Unto These Yellow Sands* (1842; fig. 11). Again the problems of scale are not immediately apparent. The eye of the spectator is drawn instead by the theatricality of the lighting and by the decorative qualities of the wreaths of fairies spiralling down from the rock, where a Titania-like figure stands, to the ground, where the procession of fairies dances away out of the left of the picture. It is not until one notices the shell lying in the right foreground that the question of size intrudes itself. The shell acts as a marker of scale which absolutely disrupts the rest of the painting. If it is life-size, then the rock arch is very small indeed, and so are the fairies which are roughly human-size in relation to it. The waves in the background are also rendered out of scale by the shell, for the shore must be much further away than it appears. If, on the other hand, everything in the picture is in scale, then the shell must be gigantic, shed by a monstrous sea creature. The picture can only cohere if one of these possibilities is closed off: either the shell is large, or it is small. The incoherence of scale is uneasy, since it disrupts a stable sense of the size of human beings. The shadowy, looming bulk of the rock arch seems to be roughly the 'right size', that is, the size it would appear to a human being positioned at the same

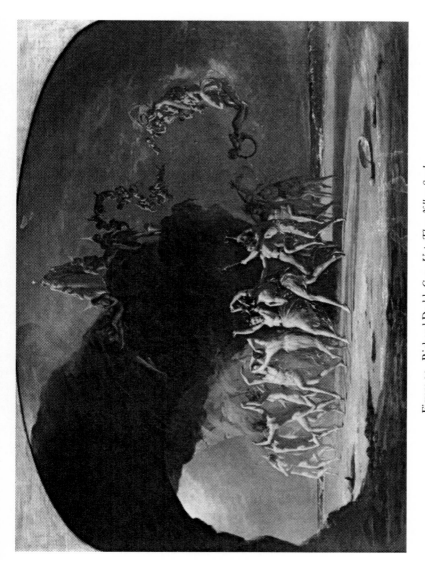

Figure 11. Richard Dadd, *Come Unto These Yellow Sands.*

distance as that implied by the position of the painting's spectator. If this is the case, then the fairies are about the same size as the viewer, and only their supernatural lightness differentiates them from human beings. But if the shell is the 'right size' (and there is nothing else in the composition either to confirm or undermine its scale), then the rock arch, the fairies and, by implication, the human spectator who 'recognises' himself or herself in the fairies' size are all transformed, instantly, into miniatures.

In these pictures persistent uncertainties about the true size of human beings in relation to the world are given a pictorial and metaphorical form. The fairy's body stands in metaphorical relation to the human body: the fairy is a metaphor which projects back human weaknesses and deficiencies in a good, even magical form. The elasticity of the fairy's body, its ability to be at once in and out of scale with its surroundings, represents in a metaphorical form humans' malaise at being both master and servant of the gigantic power of steam-driven machines. But it does so in a reparative way. Though these paintings don't resolve the uncertainty about what size things are and so reassure the spectator that humans are, in the end, the right size, they do provide a consolation. After all, the pictured beings are fairies, not humans. In the enchanted world of the fairy, the body can be both large and small without any of the queasiness the stretching back and forth of scale might engender. To look into this enchanted world, then, is to escape from the oppressive sense of the hugeness of the machine and the dwarfing of the human body beside it. It is also to contemplate the gigantic human achievement of mastering the world that the invention of industrial processes comprises, and to see the fear that man might have overreached himself, might have become too big for his own gigantic boots, temporarily transformed into the dream of a world in which humans are legitimately huge, because its inhabitants are tiny fairies.

FAIRYLAND, AN INDUSTRIAL ARCADIA

Charlotte Brontë's 'industrial' novel, *Shirley* (1849), ends with the story of the departure of the fairies. Once more, they are said to have left at the end of the eighteenth century, and it is factories which are said to have driven them away:

'What was the hollow like then, Martha?' 'Different to what it is now; but I can tell of it clean different again; when there was neither mill, nor cot, nor hall, except Fieldhead, within two miles of it. I can tell, one summer evening, fifty years syne, my mother coming running in just at the edge of dark, almost fleyed out of her wits, saying she had seen a fairish (fairy) in Fieldhead Hollow; and that was the last fairish that ever was seen on this country side (though they've been heard within these forty years). A lonesome spot it was – and a bonnie spot – full of oak and nut trees. It is altered now.' The story is told . . .[82]

The story is told: the factories have come and the fairies have fled; the industrial landscape is no longer a fit home for them. But fairies continued to inhabit the cultural landscape of industrial Britain, even in conjunction with the factories. Describing the factories of Coketown in his 'industrial' novel, *Hard Times* (1854), Charles Dickens uses what may seem a rather inapt metaphor:

The fairy palaces burst into illumination, before pale morning showed the monstrous serpents of smoke trailing themselves over Coketown. A clattering of clogs upon the pavement; a rapid ringing of bells; and all the melancholy-mad elephants, polished and oiled up for the day's monotony, were at their heavy exercise.[83]

Amongst the characteristic grotesqueness of the 'serpents of smoke' and the 'melancholy-mad elephants', the ironic force of the opening metaphor might be missed. Fairy palaces are places of magic and marvels; there one spends who knows how many days and nights in dancing, feasting and love, eating the fairies' enchanted food, only to return to earth aged and grey and forgotten. Surely nothing could be more unlike a visit to a cotton mill or iron foundry.

However, Dickens's choice of metaphor is in fact a judicious one. There is indeed much to connect the grim and ghastly industrial world with the enchanted never-never-land of the fairy, precisely because they are so utterly different from one another. For the middle class, the contemplation of the industrial world they inhabited could not bring unmitigated satisfaction, however much they enjoyed its material, social and political benefits. The devastation of the industrial landscape, sublime though it might have been in some versions, must also have been distressing. The devastating poverty and enfeeblement of industrial workers must (for those who cared to see it) have brought to mind the common humanity shared by observers and observed, employers and workers.

One way for middle-class Victorians to disavow the distress caused by the contemplation of the degradation of the body and spirit both they and industrial workers possessed was to deny it: to exaggerate the differences between 'them' and 'us', and think of the worker and the middle-class observer as different kinds of human being. But another response was to project the distress elsewhere, to escape from it and at the same time to visualise it in another form; to dream of creatures a little like humans, a little unlike, living in a world a little like the one humans inhabit, but at the same time different. For middle-class Victorians, to take to dreaming of fairies in the midst of the horrors of their industrial world was to dream of that world in a good form. In the dream they might escape from their guilt and anxiety about their unlikeness to the vitiated bodies of factory workers and about the despoliation of the countryside. But, as is the paradoxical way of dreams, they also saw in them in reversed and idealised form the factory workers and industrial landscape they wished to escape from.

Everyone knows that the industrial world was an ugly one. The sky became black; spoilheaps, dingy factories and mines disfigured the land-scape; the new industrial towns grew large and squalid slums for the accommodation of factory workers. Contemporary accounts of the in-dustrial landscape emphasise the unnaturalness of the scene, noting the ways in which industrial processes like mining and smelting have per-verted nature: they bring what is inside out, turn night into day, transform white skins into black, and dull the light and heat of the sun with the glare of the furnace. The benefits of industry were gained at the cost of the beauty of nature. A well-known description of the Black Country in 1830 from *James Nasmyth: Engineer* (1883), gives a vivid impression of how such losses were perceived by contemporary observers:

The earth seems to have been turned inside out. Its entrails are strewn about; nearly the entire surface of the ground is covered with cinder-heaps and mounds of scoriae . . . By day and by night the country is glowing with fire, and the smoke of the ironworks hangs over it . . . Workmen covered with smut, and with fierce white eyes, are seen moving about amongst the glowing iron and dull thud of the forge-hammers. Amidst these flaming, smoky, clanging works, I beheld the remains of what had once been happy farmhouses, now ruined and deserted . . . the grass had been parched and killed by the vapours of sulphureous acid thrown out by chimneys; and every herbaceous object was of a ghastly grey – the emblem of vegetable death in its saddest aspect.[84]

Nasmyth saw this scene from the ruins of Dudley Castle, a metonym for an idea of the pre-industrial past in which the natural world was undisturbed and humans lived in harmony with nature. The blasted trees and parched earth remind us that this harmony has been utterly destroyed.

The pre-industrial world was, of course, a world of farms and villages, commons and hollow hills. This was the world where the fairies left footprints from their midnight revels on the village green. The fairy's presence in memories of such landscapes is a sign that they are nostalgic constructions. Thomas Keightley, for example, introduces the section of *The Fairy Mythology* (1826) on Irish fairies by reminiscing about the vanished rural world of his boyhood:

It is pleasing to us, now in the autumn of our life, to return in imagination to where we passed its spring – its most happy spring. As we read and meditate, its mountains and its vales, its verdant fields and lucid streams, objects upon which we probably shall never again gaze, rise up in their primal freshness and beauty before us, and we are once more present, buoyant with youth in the scenes where we first heard the fairy legends of which we are now to treat.[85]

Like many departed and vanished things, fairies are consistently associated with nostalgic yearnings for golden ages, times of stability and simplicity. The destruction of the real fairy's habitat was answered by representations of a fairyland in which nature is magically fruitful and gives up its gifts without labour, without the need for the necessary transformations of the worked landscape. Fairyland is a version of pastoral, in other words, an Arcadia for the industrial age. A good example of this idea is the following description in Phillip James Bailey's 'A Fairy Tale'(1855), in which a mortal child is lured to fairyland:

'Lovely mortal! wilt thou, wilt thou quit with us thy childhood's bowers,
And in our enchanted Eden wander through a world of flowers?
All delights that thou hast dreamed of, gathered there shall be, and thine;
Flowers that fade not, games that end not, skies that always mildliest shine;
Kneaded cates of amber honey, and the rosebud's dewy wine;
Wreaths of jewels, combs of silver, beads and bracelets all of gold,
And a diamond girdle round thee! mine I give thee now, behold!
Bowls of rubies thou shalt sip from, and from crystal tables dine,
And, at eve, on lily leaves, and mingled violets recline;
Wilt thou with me, sweet one, tell me!' 'King,' she answered, 'I am thine.'[86]

This is a particularly *nouveau-riche* fairyland, combining as it does an Arcadian landscape with the accoutrements of an industrialist's mansion. Its lineaments, however, are constantly repeated in fairy poetry and painting. Ruskin's 'The Emigration of the Sprites', from Poems (1850), has the fairies dancing around toadstools under mossy oaks, 'And acorn cups upon the ground, / From which so fine, when fairies dine, / They always drink their dewy wine', and the painter Joseph Noel Paton recycles the topos in his 'Fairy Madrigal':

> While round and round above
> We quaff so merrily,
> From buttercup and harebell blue
> Our nectar-dew,
> Nor lack from lips divine
> Sweeter wine![87]

The exaggerated prettiness of fairyland, all moonlight and roses, bowers, nooks, gossamer and nectar, offers an imagined landscape exactly the reverse of the one to be found in the Black Country and elsewhere. And whereas the industrial landscape bears witness everywhere to the work that has produced it, in fairyland the fairies have nothing more to do than flit from flower to flower. The life of the fairies is one of endless idleness and play, sustained by a natural world which effortlessly supports them in beauty and pleasure.

If the landscape was changed, perverted by the effects of industrial processes, no less so were human beings. As the gradual amelioration of labour conditions by the Factory Acts and other legislation shows, the deleterious effects on human beings of mechanised labour and the factory system were evident enough to those who cared to see them, even if it was easy enough to close one's eyes to the spectacle of industrialisation. Throughout the nineteenth century, sections of the middle class shed sentimental tears and professed righteous indignation over the physical condition of the industrial working class, especially its most vulnerable and pitiable members, labouring children. However, work itself was widely venerated in Victorian culture. Both mental and physical labour were endowed with moral force: through its own kind of technological process work, particularly physical labour, produced virtue not merely for the worker, but for society. Perhaps the most systematic representation of this idea is Ford Madox Brown's *Work* (1853–64; Manchester City Art Gallery). The industrial worker, however, did not use his or her muscles but tended, and became a servant of, the vast powers of steam-driven machinery. This was interpreted by many as a diminution and enfeeblement of the human body; artisanal skills, it was argued, would be made redundant by the ever-increasing power and dexterity of the machine.

This idea is forcibly expressed in *Artisans and Machinery*, Peter Gaskell's attack on Andrew Ure's apologia for the factory system. Arguing that

mechanisation leads to mass unemployment, Gaskell is not only concerned with the economic effects of the redundancy of human labour;
he is equally if not more concerned with the moral and spiritual effects
of this change:

The effects of mechanical production, as far as we have traced them, are, in
the first place, to lower the value of human labour, and, in the next, to destroy
it altogether, except in so far as the hands engaged in machine-making are
concerned: and even these are being encroached upon – machines making
machines. The intermediate step between the two just mentioned, is its effects
upon the higher qualities of the operative, namely, his skill, emulative pride, and
respect for his own position It is, as Dr Ure remarks, the great aim of machinery
to make skill or strength on the part of the workman valueless, and to reduce him
to a mere watcher of, and waiter upon *automata*. The term artisan will shortly
be a misnomer as applied to the operative; he will no longer be a man proud of
his skill and ingenuity, and conscious that he is a valuable member of society; he
will have lost all free agency, and will be as much a part of the machines around
him as the wheels or cranks which communicate motion.[88]

For Gaskell, the humanity of the human labourer (which he thinks of
as identical with the manliness of the working man) is in the process
of being leached away. Without this quality, the labourer will become
a human automaton without free will, social consciousness or moral
agency. His very body will become a 'wheel or crank', an inferior part
of the machines around him.

   Gaskell was not alone in noticing that industrialisation inevitably entailed the reduction and enfeeblement of the human body and spirit.
For example, an editorial in *The Times* announced the mechanisation
of its production in these terms: 'A system of machinery has been de-
vised and arranged which, while it relieves the human frame of its most
laborious efforts in printing, far exceeds all human powers in rapidity
and despatch . . . little remains for man to do than to attend upon and
watch this unconscious agent.'[89] And Robert Southey, writing of a visit
to Robert Owen's experimental industrial community at New Lanark,
poured vitriol on Owen's 'vanity' in believing 'these *human machines* as he
calls them (and literally believes them to be) . . . happy'. He continues that
Owen's system 'tend[s] directly to destroy the individuality of character
and domesticity – in the one of which the strength of men consists, and
in the other, his happiness. The power of human society, and the grace,
would both be annihilated.'[90] A more famous condemnation is that of
Carlyle, whose essay 'Signs of the Times' (1829) concerns itself closely
with the moral and spiritual effects of mechanisation:

It is the Age of Machinery, in every outward and inward sense of that word; the age which, with its whole undivided might, teaches and practises the great art of adapting means to ends. Nothing is now done directly or by hand; all is by rule and calculated contrivance . . . Not the external and physical alone is now managed by machinery, but the internal and spiritual also. Here, too, nothing follows its spontaneous course, nothing is left to be accomplished by old, natural methods. Everything has its cunningly described implements, its preestablished apparatus; it is not done by hand, but by machinery.[91]

Carlyle insists that it is only by understanding that mechanisation has penetrated into the interior of the human being that its pernicious effects can be truly seen: ' . . . then may we hope to comprehend the infinitudes of man's soul under formulas of Profit and Loss; and rule over this too, as over a patent engine; by checks, and valves, and balances'.[92] Conservative attacks on industrialisation, such as Carlyle's, focus on the diminution of the idea of the human which mechanised labour necessitates; they look back to artisanal labour as the model of the proper relation between human being and economic production. But even liberal thinkers such as John Stuart Mill expressed doubts about the mechanisation of the soul and the internal effects of the factory system:

Supposing it were possible to get houses built, corn grown, battles fought, causes tried, and even churches erected and prayers said, by machinery – by automatons in human form – it would be a considerable loss to exchange for these automatons even the men and women who at present inhabit the more civilized parts of the world, and who assuredly are but starved specimens of what nature can and will produce. Human nature is not a machine to be built after a model, and set to do exactly the work prescribed for it, but a tree, which requires to grow and develop itself on all sides, according to the tendency of the inward forces which make it a living thing.[93]

In this famous passage from *On Liberty* (1859), Mill opposes an organic model of human nature to a mechanistic one, reflecting widespread concerns about the influence that industrial processes and working practices might have beyond the factory doors.

No-one was more sensitive to the moral and emotional effects of mechanisation, which he saw spreading beyond the working class and through society as a whole, than Dickens, and this theme permeates his writing from the 1850s. *Hard Times*, for example, is partly about how the internal effects of the 'Age of Machinery' might be recognised and counteracted. The opposite in the novel to the mechanised horrors of the 'fairy palaces', the factories, and their intellectual outpost, Gradgrind's schoolroom, is the circus, which symbolises the capacity to invent for nothing, to make believe, to revel in the free play of the imagination. And it is Sissy Jupe, the clown's child who cannot be prevented from telling fairy tales, who eventually helps to humanise and even to save Thomas Gradgrind: 'He raised his eyes to where she stood, like a good fairy in his house, and said in a tone of softened gratitude and grateful kindness, "It is always you, my child!' "[94] It is in these qualities, which Sissy possesses so abundantly, that humans' moral agency, dignity and spirit ultimately reside. Addressing a prize-giving speech to the Institutional Association of Lancashire and Cheshire (a union of Mechanics' Institutes that organised examinations), he reiterated the theme: 'Do not let us in the midst of the visible objects of nature, whose workings we can tell off in figures, surrounded by machines that can be made to the thousandth part of an inch, acquiring every day knowledge which can be proved upon a slate or demonstrated by a microscope – do not let us, in the laudable pursuit of the facts that surround us – neglect the fancy and imagination.'[95]

Dickens's concerns over industrialisation were frequently voiced in *Household Words*, the journal he edited in the early 1850s, and in which *Hard Times* was serialised. 'Ground in the Mill', an exposé of the horrendous industrial injuries which happened in unregulated factories, appeared in April 1854 alongside part four of the novel. A series of articles appeared with the burden that the imagination was under threat from the forces of industrial modernity. The first was one of Dickens's most famous essays, 'Frauds on the Fairies', which appeared in October 1853, as a response to his erstwhile illustrator George Cruikshank's revision of Cinderella as a temperance tract. 'Everyone who has considered the subject,' he wrote, 'knows full well that a nation without fancy, without some romance, never can, never will, hold a great place under the sun.'[96] Several articles amplified the idea, including 'A Case of Real Distress' (January 1854), which claimed that Queen Mab was under threat from 'Boards, Commissions, and Societies, grimly educating the reason, and binding the fancy in fetters of red tape'.[97] And in an essay which echoed Dickens's own rhetoric, one writer asked: 'What have I done that all the gold and jewels and flowers of Fairyland should have been ground in a mechanical mill and kneaded by you – worthless unimaginative philosophers – into Household Bread of Useful Knowledge administered to me in tough slices at lectures and forced down my throat by convincing experiments?'[98] The writer connects the vanishing world of the past and the weakening link of tradition in order to mount a defence of play and imagination in the face of the mechanisation of human nature through the idea of fairyland. Dickens's own views were sometimes more temperately expressed, and he seems to have thought that the work of the imagination, for which fairies were a symbol, was to moderate the excesses of industrial modernity. In a letter to Henry Cole written while working on the last instalments of *Hard Times*, he wrote:

I often say to Mr Gradgrind that there is reason and good intention in much that he does – but that he overdoes it. Perhaps by dint of his going his way and my going mine, we shall meet at last at some half-way house where there are flowers on the carpets, and a little standing room for Queen Mab's chariot among the steam engines.[99]

   Fairies and fairyland were commonly employed in debates about the less tangible aspects of industrialisation as metaphors for the imagination in its playful, fanciful forms. It is no surprise, then, to find that the image of the fairy should occur in those writings that seek to argue that mechanisation relieves humans of heavy, tiring labour, that factory work is light and pleasant. Andrew Ure's notorious *Philosophy of Manufactures* yields this example. Describing child weavers at their looms, he asserts that:

They seemed to be always cheerful and alert, taking pleasure in the light play of their muscles, – enjoying the mobility natural to their age. The scene of industry, so far from exciting any sad emotions in my mind, was always exhilarating. It was delightful to observe the nimbleness with which they pieced the broken ends, as the mule-carriage began to recede from the fixed roller-beam, and to see them at their leisure, after a few seconds' exercise of their tiny fingers, to amuse themselves in any attitude they chose, till the stretch and winding-on were once more completed. The work of these lively elves seemed to resemble a sport, in which habit gave them a pleasing dexterity.[100]

Searching for an image to convey the lightness and ease of mechanised labour, and to refute the suggestion that factory work transforms children into exhausted drudges, Ure lights on the idea of the fairy: the being who never works, and whose time is spent in idle play. If they are thought of as 'lively elves', the child labourers can be no more than playing, their tasks thus rendered effortless and pleasurable – just as if they were tumbling in and out of flowers, or flying from bower to bower on their gossamer wings. The counterpart to this idea is found in the degraded form of the sexual play which haunts Gaskell's *Artisans and Machinery*. The high temperatures in the factory (which apparently bring on early puberty), the undress of the factory workers, and the unchecked sexual banter between men and women in close proximity, all give rise to an eroticised ambience which corrupts even the pleasure of the human body, rendering it unnatural and perverse, in the image of the industrial landscape.[101]

These parallel images of play – the lewd worker and the lively elves – mirror the parallel between the blasted industrial landscape and the idea of fairyland as Arcadia. Fairyland became especially potent as an imagined landscape of ease and beauty because the factories which polluted the landscape of industrial Britain were thought of as having driven the fairies away. The factories themselves stood for a utilitarian rationality which was opposed to the imagination, for which the fairies were a metaphor. And the fairies could come to represent the factory workers in an imaginary form partly because both were diminutive, and partly because the fairies' life of endless play was both the opposite of the operative's life of seemingly endless drudgery and, at the same time, a metaphor for it. The mirroring process by which fairies and fairyland come to represent the workers and landscapes of industrial Britain resembles that of a dream, in which feelings are displaced from painful objects onto harmless ones metaphorically connected with them. Occasionally these dream-figures are condensed into one image which mirrors the range of Victorian anxieties about industrial modernity in a reversed form. Such is the case with Joseph Noel Paton's pair of paintings, *The Quarrel of Oberon and Titania* (1849; fig. 12) and *The Reconciliation of Oberon and Titania* (1847; fig. 13). These pictures show that fairyland is a place where lively elves play erotic games, and where nothing more is expected of them; it is a place where nature is harmonious, fruitful and beautiful, and where time and change have no dominion; where the body is free from the constraints of corporeality, and at the same time given over to sensual pleasure; where fairies and their world are completely in scale, not dwarfed by power looms or factories; and, of course, it is a place dreamed by humans.

The Quarrel of Oberon and Titania and *The Reconciliation of Oberon and Titania* were among the most popular fairy paintings of the period. Paton's first essay in a fairy subject, a small version of *The Quarrel*, was his diploma work at the Royal Scottish Academy. The next year, in 1847, he submitted *The Reconciliation* to the Westminster Hall Competition, winning a £300 prize and a favourable notice in *The Times*. Two years later he completed a larger version of *The Quarrel*: when this was exhibited at the Royal Scottish Academy in 1850 it was adjudged Picture of the Exhibition.[102] Paton's fairy paintings made his name and launched his career: he was courted by collectors wanting him to produce fairy paintings. He accordingly produced several smaller pictures based

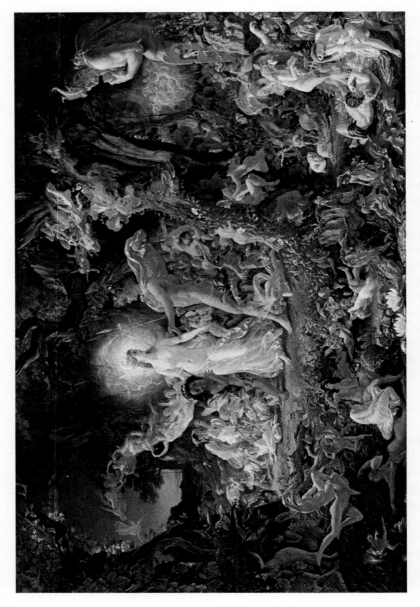

Figure 12. Joseph Noel Paton, *The Quarrel of Oberon and Titania.*

Figure 13. Joseph Noel Paton, *The Reconciliation of Oberon and Titania.*

on enlarged details of the two images, as well as replicas. Even later in his career, when he was increasingly occupied with religious subjects, he occasionally turned back to fairy painting, for example in *The Fairy Raid* (1867; Glasgow Art Gallery) and *Fact and Fancy* (1865; Private Collection). *The Quarrel* was bought by the Scottish Association for the Promotion of the Fine Arts, *The Reconciliation* by the Royal Scottish Academy; they were re-exhibited throughout Paton's lifetime, and are now permanently hung at the National Gallery of Scotland.

The two paintings, which are pendants, are thematically and compositionally very closely linked, using with only minor changes the same setting and background and many of the same figures, and showing a clear narrative development from one picture to the other.[103] The proliferation of detail makes it hard to know where to start looking at them, but perhaps the easiest point of entry is the centres of the paintings, through the figures of Oberon and Titania. What is remarkable about these figures (which are derived, as are many others in both paintings, from works by Renaissance painters, especially Raphael) is their vacuousness: the emptiness of their gestures (it is hard to discern signs of disputation in the one or amity in the other) and the stilted postures of their rather flaccid limbs. For a couple whose sexual desires are so potent, they are strangely unerotic; their genitals are carefully masked, for instance. Indeed, though they are highlighted, the eye tends to slip away from the bright centre of the image towards the light and shade of the surrounding areas where their attendant fairies disport themselves. It seems as if, though ostensibly the point of the pictures, Oberon and Titania function as the 'empty centre' around which the secondary and marginal figures and scenery take meaning.

The setting in both pictures is a woodland scene with trees on either side, a pool at the front and, at the left, a glimpse of sky and far background. Although the background is obviously meant to convey a sense of depth, because all the figures are concentrated on two parallel planes close to the picture plane – one right at the front, the other close behind it – the perspectival effect is negligible. In fact, the trees to the left and right, combined with the strong central highlight, work to give a strong theatrical sense to the setting, almost as if they were the wings of a stage set. Looked at in this way, the far distance appears like nothing so much as a backcloth or panorama of the type used in spectacular theatre. (Paton arrived in London in spring 1841, too late to see Madame Vestris's Production of *A Midsummer Night's Dream*. It is inconceivable that he did not hear about it, however, especially as one of his acquaintances in

London was S. C. Hall, who promoted 'theatrical' fairy painting in the
Art-Union.)

The theatricality of the scene is important, because it introduces two
further considerations: the question of scale, and that of dreaming. In
The Reconciliation, to the left and right of the central figures, are the sleeping bodies of Hermia and Bottom, with Lysander dimly visible at the far
right. These human bodies disrupt the scale relations of the picture in
a very obvious way, since trees, flowers, foliage and so on are clearly in
scale with Oberon and Titania. The scale relations are the same in *The
Quarrel*. Hermia and Bottom appear giant-size in relation to the fairies
around them, and nothing in the picture undermines this effect of scale.
The humans have fallen asleep in fairyland, a world scaled to accommodate fairies, a closed-off realm like the illusory world of a stage set, or
a dream, which one can never walk into the distance and out of. One
can only wake up and be in the human world once more, with no sense
of transition or journey. It is also a marvellously fruitful world, exemplified by the two ripe peaches nestling below Bottom's arm, and a bower
of various kinds of plants, flowers and animals. The paintings depict a
dream-like, sealed world, a fairyland in which nature bountifully creates
a miniature playground for fairies.

When one looks closely at the postures and actions of the fairies who
inhabit this playground, the vacuity of the paintings' centres is forgotten
in the wealth of narrative detail one finds there. The fairies are at their
revels: a group attacks a captured owl (*Reconciliation*); one caresses a pet
lizard (*Quarrel*); but mostly they are given up to the sport of love. The
task of enumerating the entwined bodies, kisses, languishing glances,
ménages à trois, rivalries, peeping toms, and embraces of all kinds would
be long and tedious, so many and varied are they. But in comparison
with the chasteness of the central couple, their fairy train is a riot of
abandoned sexual activity. There are several subsidiary details which
reinforce the eroticisation of the scene: the figure of Pan, for example,
who is associated with abandonment to the desires of the body; and the
exaggerated efflorescence of the plants and fungi (especially on the tree
trunk in *The Quarrel*), clearly a metaphor for sexual flowering. In fairyland, while the grown-ups behave with becoming modesty even in the
vicissitudes of jealousy and love, the children (that is, the smaller fairies)
manifest and act upon their desires pretty much as they please. Even the
humans are implicated in this sexual playground where erotic fantasy
appears to be given free rein, for in the narrative of which the paintings
illustrate a part, they too follow their desires as they like. In the pictures

themselves, it is the fact that the humans are asleep which implicates them, for they stand for the dreaming human spectator, arrested by the paintings' erotic spectacle. They metonymically connect the dream-world, the fairyland inside the pictures, with the real human world outside them.

In fairyland, where life is play, and where lively elves give themselves wholly over to erotic pleasures, the small drudges of the factories and the half-naked working men and women can be seen in a good form. The blighted landscape of the industrial towns is reimagined as a beautiful, unspoiled playground; the destructive force and power of industry is forgotten, for a moment, in dreaming of an enchanted world in which there are no cares, no responsibilities, no social divisions or conventions, and no bodily limitations. In *The Quarrel* and *The Reconciliation of Oberon and Titania* Paton represented for his audience the enchanted body and world of the fairy, a body and a world whose capabilities and attributes were the counterpart of anxieties about the effects of industrialisation on the human body and world. To look at these paintings is to see a 'dream-representation' of the oppressive fears which industrialisation brought with it; and it is also to see how middle-class Victorians escaped from those fears by looking directly at them in 'dream-representations'. Seen as in a dream, the fairy's body is the human body as it is shaped by mechanisation, destabilised by the hugeness of the steam engine and factory, and vitiated by the monotonous drudgery of mechanised labour. Fairyland is a vision as in a dream of the landscape that the factories, foundries and mines despoiled.

To many observers at this time, it seemed that man was the master of the world, transforming and controlling nature through ever more perfect and powerful industrial and technological processes: this is the characteristic note of Victorian optimism. But this optimism was countered by fears, doubts and anxieties that material gain would enfeeble the physical prowess, moral agency and spiritual nature of humanity. To escape their haunting doubts and fears, Victorians escaped into fantasy and daydream; they liked to look at pictures of fairies. But in picturing fairies they saw images of themselves: what they felt they had been, might be, were now. In escaping to fairyland, they dreamed themselves back home. The anxieties that led Ure to think of child workers as 'light-fingered elves' were the same ones that found relief in a dream of fairyland, where the landscape and inhabitants are mirror images of the industrialised world inhabited by the paintings' Victorian spectators.

Dickens's playful, dreamlike image of 'some half-way house where there are flowers on the carpets, and a little standing room for Queen Mab's chariot among the steam engines' is the key to understanding the appeal of Paton's paintings. They were popular because they picture fairyland as a kind of Arcadia where all is pleasure and ease. But the anxieties which shape this Arcadia are those of industrial modernity.

CHAPTER 3

A few fragments of fairyology, shewing its connection with natural history

> A pretty fairy-land our science has brought us to. It is like the 'behind-scenes' of a theatre. There are all the things we admired so innocently at a distant view; we can't deny that we have got them; 'but oh, how different!' The dazzle, the sparkle, the romantic glory, where are they? Are these realities of life, also, only meant to delude an imagination that makes itself a party to the charm? *Is* all the world a stage?[1]

This rhetorical question is posed by James Hinton in an article called 'The Fairy Land of Science' published in the *Cornhill Magazine* in 1862. Hinton, a sometime doctor with interests in physiology, physics and philosophy, had previously written a series on recent developments in physics for the journal, and in this article was pursuing a philosophical reconciliation of religion and science. In this passage, Hinton likens the explanatory power of science to the unmasking of a theatrical illusion. Science shows us the 'behind-scenes' of our world, revealing that what we thought was magical, ineffable or numinous is in fact worked by a stage machinery of levers and props, forces and physical laws. Is all the 'dazzle' and 'romantic glory' of the world nothing more than an illusion produced by stage mechanics? Science promises us a fairyland in which our dreams can come true, Hinton argues, but it then robs us of our native sense of wonder at the ineffable. Instead of the wishful dream of Aladdin's magical lamp we have the reality of the telegraph; amazing as the latter is, it is proof that nowadays there is no place for magic in the world: 'The history of man is written in the gleesome fairy tales of old, and the heavy burden of modern life: picture of hope, and hope fulfilled.' Scientific and technological progress bring undeniable benefits, but, says Hinton, they also have a cost: the 'heavy burden' of disenchantment. Fairy tales were the entertainments of man's childhood, the time before modernity. Giving up the 'wantonness of fancy' for 'dull and sober fact' and the 'chains' of scientific knowledge is necessary, because modernity brings with it the 'destiny sublime' of man's maturity.[2] Modern man must put away the child's things, and take up the duties and knowledge of manhood.

Yet the burden of Hinton's article is that the dominion of 'dull and sober fact' can never be absolute. The explanatory power of science opens up a new, higher mystery which is beyond either biblical or empirical explanation: 'The achievements of which Science boasts . . . are permitted to it only by the adoption of principles which compel it to bear witness to a truth beyond itself. By science man may control nature, and work marvels that outrival magic, but in the very act he concedes that the world is not what it seems.'[3] Nature cannot be regarded in entirely materialistic terms, but neither can it be seen as animated directly by the deity.[4] Instead, Hinton proposes a metaphysics in which the universe is held in balance by twin forces of attraction and repulsion acting against each other. On the physical plane, 'all processes in the material world arrange themselves under' a unity of force; 'all are instances of the shifting forms, and permanent balance of force'.[5]

Hinton's metaphysics is derived from Kant, whom he had read in the original German, and who was an important influence on scientists working on those areas in which Hinton was interested.[6] As a physiologist, Hinton had probably come into contact with *Naturphilosophie*, which had been the dominant influence on German physiology institutes in the 1830s and 1840s.[7] An important conduit into England for Kant's ideas was Hans Christian Oersted, the discoverer of electro-magnetism, whose *The Soul in Nature* had been published in an English translation in 1852. Oersted's Kantian conception of a unity of opposing forces directly underlay his discovery of the action of electricity on a magnetic needle and the formation of an electric current perpendicular to the magnetic needle.[8] In *The Soul in Nature* he gave an account of his metaphysics which closely resembles Hinton's ideas:

This accordance between nature and [human] mind can hardly be ascribed to chance. The farther we advance, the more perfect you will find it; and the more easily you will admit to me, that both natures are germs springing from one common root . . . But where something is to exist, to work, and to grow, the forces must have quitted their perfect equilibrium, and the struggle must have begun . . . While every thing in the great whole, down to the smallest part, varies between hate and love – while the inquirer himself must share in that vicissitude – while even his own human passions may be set in motion by external impressions of nature, he may yet preserve security and repose amidst this vortex; indeed, I may venture to say happiness, if he only steadily fixes his eye on the firm unity, which no power on earth can destroy.[9]

For Hinton, as for Kant, the order of the universe as we perceive it can also be found in the human mind, for such order as exists is imposed by us in understanding the universe, or, in Kant's terminology, the phenomenal world: that is, the 'world of facts' with which science deals. For Kant, the true nature of things, the noumenon, is absolutely unknowable by humans, though our knowledge of the phenomenal world necessitates the existence *a priori* of the noumenon. But Hinton suggests that the noumenal world, what he calls 'the actual', can be intuited, even if it cannot be known. For Hinton, it is this other realm, lying beyond and around the world of things, which gives science its transcendental meaning: 'For it is this recognition of the hidden essence in all things (appealing as it does to the highest portion of our nature, and giving the freest scope to the imagination) which surrounds science in our day, in spite of the stringent severity of its attitude towards facts, with an unquenchable halo of poetry.'[10] It is this intuition of the 'actual', the 'hidden essence', which brings scientific endeavour into the realm of the spiritual and allies it with poetry.

The article starts by describing the disenchanting effect of science as turning fairyland into a theatrical illusion worked by props and machinery. But that is superseded by a description of the world as known by science and intuition:

Dwelling on this idea of one unalterable power, we begin to feel ourselves in a new world of fascinating interest and mysterious awe. The solid globe seems almost to melt and become fluent before our eyes. All things put forth universal relations, and assume a weird and mystical character. The world becomes doubled to us: it is one world of things perceived; and one unperceivable. The objects which surround us lose their substantiality when we think of them as forms under which something which is not they, not essentially connected with them, is presented to us; something which has met us under forms the most unlike before, and may meet us under other forms again. In short, all nature grows like an enchanted garden; a fairy world in which unknown existences lurk under familiar shapes, and every object seems ready, at the shaking of a wand, to take on the strange transformations.[11]

As physiologist and physicist, Hinton was interested in some of the questions which were at the heart both of the latest scientific developments and of the controversies they generated: the relation between mind and body, the nature of the 'life force', galvanism, the laws of thermodynamics. The disenchantment to which he alludes in the metaphor of the stage set of fairyland is the sense of knowing too much, of denuding the world of its proper mystery and reducing it to a purely material plane.

And, of course, disenchantment removes the spiritual and sacred from the centre of the universe. Hinton's metaphysics, however, offer his audience a re-enchanted world, for which he uses the entirely appropriate metaphor of fairyland: 'Have we not well said, therefore, that science wins its triumph in a fairy land, and in fulfilling one vision, teaches us to recognize another?'[12]

'The Fairy Land of Science' is unusual in that it attempts to argue for a Kantian metaphysics of science at a time when idealism was in low esteem: it was written after the interest in German philosophy generated by Coleridge and Carlyle had waned, and before the dominance of idealism in British philosophy during the last two decades of the century. But in another sense it is representative of attitudes towards science in the mid-nineteenth century. George Levine has commented that in the Victorian period science occupied a central place in culture and came to carry an enormous weight of cultural authority. It was a time when

science was most forcefully extending its authority in the realm of knowledge and even beyond, into religion and morals, and when it really did seem for a while that apparently insoluble problems could be solved, that the limits imposed on human society by material conditions could be broken, and that knowledge was an aspect of morality, so that the highest Victorian virtue was 'Truth' . . . The ideas of science were helping to form the general view of the nature of 'reality' itself.[13]

Two factors which contributed to the growing authority of science in Victorian culture were its increasing professionalisation and its division into clearly defined scientific disciplines. The professional physicist, biologist or chemist – or, among the human sciences, anthropologist or sociologist – could claim a secular authority akin to that of the clergy to speak on the 'nature of "reality"'. But the formation of scientific disciplines and the growth of a class of professional scientists was enabled by the discoveries in the natural sciences of gentlemen amateurs like Lyell and Darwin, both of whom were anxious to keep the structures of established belief and authority in place, in spite of the implications of their work. The cultural weight of science was conferred, in great part, by ideas which undermined the foundations of religious belief; its authority was gained at the cost of a widespread anxiety about the encroachment of science on religion and morals.

Even Thomas Henry Huxley, one of the most trenchant of those arguing for the supremacy of scientific naturalism, conceded that the progress of science could be a destabilising force. In his controversial lecture 'On the Physical Basis of Life' (1868), he admitted:

The consciousness of this great truth weighs like a nightmare, I believe, upon many of the great minds of these days. They watch what they conceive to be the progress of materialism, in such fear and powerless anger as a savage feels, when, during an eclipse, the great shadow creeps over the face of the sun. The advancing tide of matter threatens to drown their souls; the tightening grasp of law impedes their freedom; they are alarmed lest man's moral nature be debased by the increase of his wisdom.[14]

Huxley goes on to state that matter and spirit are an indivisible, natural phenomenon. The 'extinction' of the spirit by materialism, over which 'a great lamentation is arising, like that which was heard at the death of Pan' is merely the extinction of a mistaken categorisation of matter and spirit as different in kind.[15] For Huxley, science must of necessity deal with such matters as the mystery of consciousness, the origin of life, and the relation of mind and body, for these 'spiritual' things are in fact material phenomena admitting of scientific investigation. But even in a lecture which puts the claims of science in their most militant form, Huxley is forced to acknowledge that these claims undermine the certainties which, for most people, keep their views of the world secure.

Hinton's article, then, is typical in that it encompasses both optimistic and anxious attitudes towards science. It is typical in another respect: its use of the fairy and fairyland as a metaphor to convey both attitudes. Like the famous phrase of Tennyson's from which it takes its title, Hinton's article testifies to the wonders of science at the same time as it manifests doubt and anxiety about the implications of scientific knowledge. A fairy tale, after all, is something wonderful and untrue: science, it implies, is both. The use of the figure of the fairy to connote the marvels and diffi- culties of science is very widespread, though not all examples are as neatly ambivalent as those of Tennyson or Hinton. There are many writings in which the figure of the fairy is explicitly contrasted with the ideas and institutions of science. In these examples the target is very often the disenchantment of the world threatened by scientific progress. One such instance is *A Few Fragments of Fairyology, Shewing its Connection with Natural History*, a pamphlet published in 1854 by Michael Aislabie Denham. In it he catalogued a number of instances of traditional associations between fairies and mysterious natural phenomena. Denham's list includes Fairy Stones (Encrinites and Entrochi), Fairy Butter (Tremella Mesenterica), Elf Kirks (caves), Elf Fire and Fairy Sparks (Ignis Fatuus). He gave it an explanatory epigraph from John Brand's *Popular Antiquities* (1777): 'The naturalists of the dark ages owed many obligations to our *Fairies*, for whatever they found wonderful and could not account for, they easily got rid of it by charging it to their account.'[16] Modern naturalists, it is implied, need no recourse to the fairies, for they are able to account for all wonderful objects and mysterious happenings. While the ignorant and superstitious still attribute natural phenomena they cannot understand to the fairies, naturalists, men of science, have no need of fairy tales. Something rather different from theology, 'Fairyology' certainly has no claims to being a science.

Andrew Lang's and May Kendall's satire *That Very Mab* (1888) also rehearses the incompatibility of belief in fairies and scientific knowledge. Forced back to England by missionaries from her post-Reformation exile in Samoa, Queen Mab assumes the position of the innocent outsider who observes the follies and absurdities of the English manners, politics and intellectual fashions of the 1880s, as explained to her by a wise old owl. Her first encounter is with a scientist who catches her with a butterfly net, thinking she is some rare species. He takes her back to his house, where she is decanted into a glass jar, and studied by the scientist and his two friends, a poet and a divine. When the poet, as a pose, identifies the 'butterfly' as a fairy, 'the professor replied that fairies were unscientific, and even unthinkable, and the divine declared that they were too heterodox even for the advanced state of modern theology'.[17] The episode comes to a close when the scientist accidentally lets Queen Mab out of the glass jar, allowing her to escape through the window.

For Denham, science has overtaken superstition as a way of explaining the world; his collections of fairy beliefs preserve a curious relic of a vanishing world. For Lang and Kendall writing thirty years later, however, the idea of fairies stands in opposition, or even resistance, to the progress of science: '"Tell me exactly who the scientific men are," said the fairy. "I have heard so much about them since I came." "They are the men," sighed the Owl, "who go about with microscopes, that is, instruments for looking into things as they are not meant to be looked at and seeing them as they were never intended to be seen."'[18] The feeling that scientists know too much, that they have 'put everything under their microscopes' is proved by their inability to recognise a fairy ('an anachronism, hundreds of years on the wrong side') when they see one.[19] Believers in fairies and men of science have mutually incompatible ways of understanding the world, and the beliefs of the former must yield to the knowledge of the latter, even if this involves the loss of everything that fairies represent.

The same idea is given an elegiac rendering in Edmund Gosse's memoir *Father and Son* (1907). One of the most moving passages evokes the specimen-collecting expeditions on the Devon coast he made with his father in 1858. He describes how the rock pools, which had seemed so inexhaustible, are now empty:

> There is nothing, now, where in our days there was so much. Then the rocks between tide and tide were submarine gardens of a beauty that seemed often to be fabulous, and was positively delusive, since, if we delicately lifted the weed-curtains of a windless pool, though we might for a moment see its sides and floor paved with living blossoms, ivory-white, rosy-red, and amethyst, yet all that panoply would melt away, furled into the hollow rock, if we so much as dropped a pebble in to disturb the magic dream.[20]

Gosse goes on to describe the quest for scientific knowledge as necessarily involving a desecration: regretful in the case of his father, unthinking in the case of his followers.

> The ring of living beauty drawn about our shores was a very thin and fragile one. It had existed all those centuries solely in consequence of the indifference, the blissful ignorance of man. These rock-basins, fringed by corallines, filled with still water almost as pellucid as the upper air itself, thronged with beautiful sensitive forms of life, – they exist no longer, they are profaned, and emptied, and vulgarized. An army of 'collectors' has passed over them, and ravaged every corner of them. The fairy paradise has been violated, the exquisite product of centuries of natural selection has been crushed under the rough paw of well-meaning, idle-minded curiosity.[21]

It is because too many pebbles have been dropped into pools, too much knowledge has been insisted upon, that the fairy paradise has been lost. The pools and their creatures, 'the infinite succession of soft and radiant forms', survive only through the innocence of the wondering look: at the touch of the scientist's probing finger, they give over their secrets and die.

For Gosse, the child of an eminent naturalist, his father's science entailed the destruction of what it sought to know. Yet his lament for the destruction of the paradisaical natural world of his childhood is framed in the language of science: 'the exquisite product of centuries of natural selection has been crushed'. If the popularity of his father's natural history books stimulated the 'well-meaning, idle-minded curiosity' which destroyed the rock pools, evolutionary theory ('centuries of natural selection') ended his father's career as a serious scientist. Edmund Gosse could not see the desecration of the natural world in anthropomorphic terms as an allegory of the Fall, for he rejected his father's literal biblical faith and became an agnostic. But he still conceives it in supernatural terms. The lost world whose beauty he elegises is a fairy paradise, an enchanted world whose precariousness and vulnerability make it seem like a magic dream.

The fairy and fairyland, then, were widely used as metaphors for anxieties about the progress and implications of science. But these metaphors were equally current in scientific writing which, far from banishing the supernatural, seems deliberately to invoke it. *The Old Red Sandstone* (1841) by Hugh Miller, the working-class Scottish geologist, was at the time the definitive geological account of the Devonian sandstone layers of the east of Scotland and the fossils they contain. In the middle of a description of the burn of Eathie, a point at which the stratifications and fault-lines of the rock layers are particularly interesting, Miller breaks off into a long footnote which begins:

There is a natural connection, it is said, between wild scenes and wild legends; and some of the traditions connected with this wild and solitary dell illustrate the remark. Till a comparatively late period it was known at many a winter fireside as a favourite haunt of the fairies – the most poetical of all our old tribe of spectres, and at one time one of the most popular.[22]

The 'natural connection' is, rather, one which Miller forges by breaking away from his text into a note at its margin, so that note and description run parallel on the page. The artificiality of the connection between 'wild scenes' and 'wild legends' is both concealed and described by the 'it is said': this device allows Miller to introduce the fairies in a tone of scientific objectivity ('the most poetical of all our old tribe of spectres'). Yet in the tale that follows, Miller's involvement in the narration seems to suggest that, insofar as they may once have inhabited the burn of Eathie, the fairies are important to him. The story concerns a man journeying home alone at night:

The moon, at full, had now risen; but there was a silvery mist sleeping on the lower grounds, that obscured her light; and the dell, in all its extent, was so overcharged with the vapour, that it seemed an immense overflooded river winding through the landscape. Donald had reached its further edge, and could hear the rush of the stream from the deep obscurity of the abyss below, when there rose from the opposite side a strain of the most delightful music he had ever heard. He staid and listened. The words of a song, of such simple beauty that they seemed without effort to stamp themselves on his memory, came wafted in the music: and the chorus, in which a thousand tiny voices seemed to join, was a familiar address to himself.[23]

Miller was associated with the so-called 'scriptural geologists' who tried to reconcile the findings of geology with the Book of Genesis and calculations of the earth's age based on the Bible. In *The Testimony of the Rocks* (1857) he explored the idea that each geological age was a 'day' of the creation.[24] That was a later stage in his career, however; in *The Old Red Sandstone* he eschews religious controversy, merely recommending geology as a more wholesome pursuit for the young and restless than religion or politics. Yet Miller seems reluctant in his painstaking descriptions and catalogue of fault lines and fossils to accede to a wholly material view of nature, for it lacks the enchantment which can be supplied only by the supernatural. In an account which tactfully remains silent on the direct involvement of God in geological processes, the rock formations themselves are inhabited and enchanted by fairies: small supernatural beings who, in this case, substitute for the deity. Nature is animated and made beautiful by a supernatural presence, but one which can safely ('it is said') be relegated to legend or glossed over as a tale, without the embarrassment of a profession of faith.

Charles Lyell, who was on the opposite side of nineteenth-century geological controversies from Miller, also used the figure of the fairy in his writing. The first part of *Principles of Geology* (1830–3) is devoted to the history of the subject, and to exposing the various errors to which earlier geologists had been subject. Introducing his discussion of 'Theoretical Errors which have Retarded the Progress of Geology', Lyell explains that the gradual enlightenment of ignorance in respect of the earth's formation parallels that in human moral life:

In an early stage of advancement, when a great number of natural appearances are unintelligible, an eclipse, an earthquake, a flood, or the approach of a comet, with many other occurrences afterwards found to belong to the regular course of events, are regarded as prodigies. The same delusion prevails as to moral phenomena, and many of these are ascribed to the intervention of demons, ghosts, witches, and other immaterial and supernatural phenomena. By degrees, many of the enigmas of the moral and physical world are explained, and, instead of being due to extrinsic and irregular causes, they are found to depend on fixed and invariable laws.[25]

This is clearly an optimistic account of the progress of knowledge and the subjection of the world to reason. Errors in our understanding of the natural world, like superstitions and supernatural phenomena, will gradually be cleared away by the advancement of human understanding. A few pages later, however, Lyell has recourse to the supernatural himself. Showing how theoretical systems which extrapolate universal theories from limited human observations, such as that of Leibniz, must be wrong, he describes an ideal observer of the earth's interior:

> But if we may be allowed so far to indulge the imagination, as to suppose a being, entirely confined to the nether world – some 'dusky melancholy sprite,' like Umbriel, who could 'flit on sooty pinions to the central earth,' but who was never permitted to 'sully the fair face of light,' and emerge into the regions of water and of air; and if this being should busy himself in investigating the structure of the globe, he might frame theories the exact converse of those usually adopted by human philosophers.[26]

Of course, Lyell is using the figure of the fairy satirically, in order to debunk the fallacious reasoning and bad science of his predecessors. But it is curious that he should use the supernatural, the thing which science supersedes and disdains, in order to prove the necessity of proper scientific method. Scientific method is unable to sustain its claim to truth without recourse to a supernatural figure, representative of a system of belief which is utterly incompatible with modern science.

The genre of scientific writing in which fairies appear most frequently is the popular science book for women and children (elementary science books were commonly aimed at both groups).[27] A common topos is that nature is a kind of fairyland, whose wonders are introduced to the readers by a fairy guide. An example of this genre is *Fairy Know-A-Bit, or a Nutshell of Knowledge* by A. L. O. E. [C. M. Tucker] (1866). Such works often have an explicit, conservative Christian message in which the magic of fairyland is inevitably a metaphor for the wonders of the creation. A much more sophisticated handling of this theme occurs in *The Fairy-Land of Science* by Arabella Buckley, a former secretary to Lyell and prolific writer of popular science (for example, she published a revised version of Mary Somerville's *On the Connexion of the Physical Sciences* in 1877). The book opens with a forthright statement of the enchantments of science:

> I have promised to introduce you today to the fairy-land of science, – a some-what bold promise, seeing that most of you probably look upon science as a bundle of dry facts, while fairy-land is all that is beautiful, and full of poetry and imagination. But I thoroughly believe myself, and hope to prove to you, that science is full of beautiful pictures, of real poetry, and of wonder-working fairies; and what is more, I promise you they shall be true fairies, whom you will love just as much when you are old and grey-headed as when you are young ... and though they themselves remain invisible, yet you will see their wonderful power at work everywhere around you.[28]

The fairy tale Buckley tells her audience is of the magic of physics; her rhetorical ploy is to personify forces such as gravity and magnetism as wonder-working fairies. In place of the metaphor of nature as a magical fairyland to be either wondered at or demystified, in this work scientific concepts are given an allegorical guise as fairies in order to show how much more magical science is than the supernatural: 'There are *forces* around us, and among us, which I shall ask you to allow me to call *fairies*, and these are ten thousand times more wonderful, more magical, and more beautiful in their work, than those of the old fairy tales.' The intention here is to impart, or perhaps to inculcate, a sense of the wonders of science. But, like Lyell's use of the metaphor, Buckley's comparison of physical forces with fairies has an unintended consequence, for it suggests that reason is insufficient to comprehend the world, and that scientific ideas are a form of magical thinking.

These representative examples show that the fairy was a recurrent figure in various kinds of writing about science, and that fairies could represent widely differing attitudes to and feelings about science. On the one hand, fairies are magical, and magic and science do not mix; on the other hand, science has a magic of its own which can readily be compared to the fairy. Fairyland, with all its enchantments, represents the idea of a mysterious, magical world which is destroyed by the encroachments of science; the fairy is a perfect metaphor for anxieties about encroaching materialism because fairies are themselves the denizens of a disappearing world. Yet scientific writings frequently have recourse to the figure of the fairy to convey the wonders of scientific knowledge, and the 'dazzle and sparkle' of fairyland (as Hinton put it) lends itself to an optimistic expression of the wonders of science.

However, it is too simple to leave the matter there, and to say that fairies represent both positive and negative attitudes to science, as it were turn and turn about. As we shall see in the rest of this chapter, when we look at visual images of fairies in the context of the scientific debates of the mid-nineteenth century, these images function mainly as consolations for the anxieties produced by scientific progress, but they do this partly by representing the objects of the scientific gaze turned into fairies and fairyland. In the next part of this chapter, I will discuss works by John Anster Fitzgerald. I will argue that Fitzgerald's fairy paintings can be seen as a response, unsettling but ultimately reassuring, to changing views of the natural world occasioned by the debates in natural history which culminated in the publication in 1859 of Darwin's *On the Origin of Species by Means of Natural Selection*. In the final section of the chapter, I discuss

Richard Dadd's *The Fairy Feller's Master-Stroke* in the light of Darwin's
theory, and argue that it represents a fearful and deranged response to the
threat of evolution. Visual images are not like literary and scientific texts,
and though they come from the same cultural contexts and frequently
embody the same attitudes and emotions, they rarely evoke them in the
same terms. Though paintings of fairies do not refer directly to science,
and scientific illustrations rarely include fairies, we shall see that images
of fairies have nonetheless a great deal to tell us about how scientific ideas
and controversies shaped the ways in which the Victorians perceived and
represented the visible world.

'A CASE OF SUCH FAMILIARS AT HOME'

In 1859 John Anster Fitzgerald showed a pair of paintings, *The Storm*
and *The Calm*, at the British Institution. These 'two subjects of elfdom'
were noticed by the *Art Journal*'s reviewer, who commented: 'Such a
rendering of these hideous realities is terribly suggestive that the artist
must have a case of such familiars at home.'[29] The following year the
same journal remarked that *The Fairies' Barque*, with its 'curious inditing
of the habits of fairy people, [could] only be the gathering of a long
residence in faydom'.[30] The tone of both reviews seems whimsical; the
reader is seriously expected to believe neither that the artist has had 'a
long residence in faydom', nor that he has a case of fairies for use as
life models. But Fitzgerald must have spent a great deal of time with the
fairies, in his imagination at least, for he produced fairy paintings for more
than thirty years. However, Fitzgerald's fairies look nothing like those in
previous fairy paintings. From where did he derive his ideas about how
fairies look, if not reality? The reviewer's observation that Fitzgerald's
pictures of fairies look so lifelike they might have been drawn from 'a
case of such familiars at home' may seem like a joke, but it should, in
fact, be taken seriously. For by following the clue of this seemingly playful
comment, we can begin to understand the contemporary significance of
Fitzgerald's fairy paintings, and to discover why this reviewer found them
so disturbing.

In the 1860s Fitzgerald produced a number of paintings of fairies
hunting, capturing and killing robins, and then colonising their nests.
Though not a formal sequence, images such as *Cock Robin Defending his
Nest, Who Killed Cock Robin?* and *Fairies Sleeping in a Bird's Nest* (Private
Collection; London: Maas Gallery; figs. 15–17) are certainly very closely
linked, and can be arranged to form a narrative.[31] Jeremy Maas and

Charlotte Gere have discussed at some length Fitzgerald's pictures of
dreaming sleepers surrounded by fairies, and have argued that these
images show the influence of Fitzgerald's employment as a theatrical
scene painter, as well as of an imputed laudanum addiction.[32] They pay
little attention, however, to the greater number of works by Fitzgerald
which show fairies not in relation to humans, but in an outdoor setting,
engaged in their own pursuits. The 'Cock Robin' paintings are typical
of works Fitzgerald was exhibiting in the 1860s and 1870s, and were
clearly saleable enough for him to execute numerous versions of similar
subjects. Yet Fitzgerald was not simply producing hackneyed copies of
the kind of fairy painting that had become popular in the 1840s, for his
fairies look strikingly different from any other images of fairies produced
at the same time or before.

Fairy painting originated as a sub-genre of history painting. By the
mid-1850s, when Fitzgerald began to produce his fairy pictures, however,
paintings of fairies had become more naturalistic in style. This was partly
due to the influence of early Pre-Raphaelitism, with its intense concen-
tration on the faithful representation of natural forms and on observation
from nature. The only example of a fairy painting by a Pre-Raphaelite
artist is Millais's *Ferdinand Lured by Ariel* (1849; fig. 14), in which nymph-
like fairies have been discarded in favour of green bat-fairies supporting
a green child-Ariel. In place of the theatrical settings which frame the
figures in works such as Joseph Noel Paton's *The Reconciliation of Oberon
and Titania*, in Millais's painting the botanical detail of the plants and
trees of the background and the grotesque detail of the fairies compete
for space in a crowded composition. The setting of Paton's picture is
garnished with plants and insects, but these are subsidiary to the masses
of intertwined bodies swirling around Oberon and Titania. In *Ferdinand
Lured by Ariel* the outdoor setting is the focus of the picture, as the *Art
Journal*'s reviewer commented:

The emphasis of the picture is in its botany, which is made out with a microscopic
elaboration, insomuch as to seem to have been painted from a collection of
grasses, since we recognize upwards of twenty varieties; there may be more; and
such is the minute description of even one leaf, that the ravages of an insect are
observable upon it.[33]

Perhaps it is because the commitment of the picture is to the faithful
description of the botanical detail of the setting that the fairies are oddly
sketchy, squeezed into the too-narrow space between Ferdinand and
the picture frame. The realism of the setting, its components evidently

Figure 14. John Everett Millais, *Ferdinand Lured by Ariel.*

drawn from life study, is incompatible with the depiction of the fairies; the 'eccentricity' of the picture, as the reviewer termed it, is due to the incoherence of natural and supernatural in the same pictorial space.[34]

Like Millais's painting, John Anster Fitzgerald's work is part of a trend towards the naturalistic representation of fairies, and the two have common features. Both are small (Fitzgerald's works are characteristically about 25 × 30 cm), in contrast to the large exhibition pieces associated with fairy subjects within the genre of history painting. Fitzgerald's style could be termed 'post-Pre-Raphaelite' because of his predilection

Figure 15. John Anster Fitzgerald, *Cock Robin Defending his Nest.*

Figure 16. John Anster Fitzgerald, *Who Killed Cock Robin.*

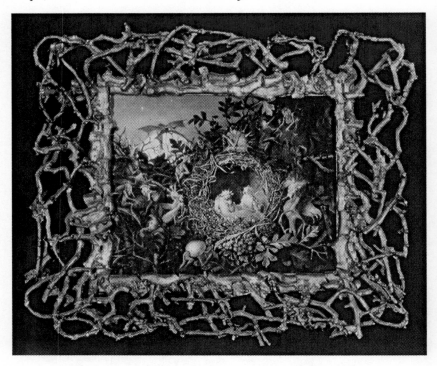

Figure 17. John Anster Fitzgerald, *Fairies Sleeping in a Bird's Nest.*

for detail and bright, pure colours; both painters reject the convention of nymph-like fairies derived from classical models, and depict the fairies as grotesque. On the other hand, Millais's painting illustrates a literary subject, whereas Fitzgerald avoids this. After the 1850s the subjects of fairy painting tend increasingly to be drawn from folk tales and legends, or from no literary source at all; Fitzgerald's fairy paintings, however, are the first and most emphatic rejection of literary subjects.[35] And although, like Millais, Fitzgerald places great emphasis on the natural setting of his fairy scenes, in his work there is none of the incompatibility of natural and supernatural worlds manifested by Millais's painting. Indeed, Fitzgerald's pictures are remarkable for the complete integration of the fairies and their natural setting.

Whether knowingly or not, Fitzgerald brought together in his fairy pictures motifs and styles from seemingly incompatible sources: religious art, natural history illustration, still life and taxidermy. The 'Cock Robin'

paintings bring together the natural and the supernatural in their depiction of fairies and fairyland; they put the material and the metaphysical
into the same picture. This in itself was not unusual in the mid-nineteenth
century, as testified by the numerous proselytising natural history books
published by Christian publishing houses, such as *Lessons Derived from the
Animal World* (1851). Such works continue the long tradition of natural
theology, which sees the natural world as 'God's work', complementary
to 'God's words', the scriptures. Nature is evidence of the designing hand
of the Creator, and studying the natural world leads both to knowledge
of the Creation and wonder at it. Fitzgerald's paintings, however, do not
simply reiterate some form of natural theology. Instead of implying a
supernatural world above and behind the natural one, they set natural
and supernatural together in the miniature, enclosed world of a fairyland
peopled with creatures a little like miniature humans and a little like
gigantic insects, and grant to the spectator the position of a giant who looks
in from outside. Though it draws on ways of representing nature which
can be seen as visual analogues of natural theology, Fitzgerald's work
in fact offers a much more disturbing picture of the natural world and
human beings' relation to it, and this is partly to do with its presentation
of that world in a miniature form.

Victorian perceptions of the relation between human, natural and
supernatural worlds found an especially vivid expression in the miniature,
because the miniature came to represent the problem of how that
relation could be conceived in an era of widespread religious doubt. The
miniature turns theological questions into perceptual ones, because it
makes visible an acute uncertainty about how large humans are. Before
the blows that Cuvier, Lamarck, Malthus, Lyell, Chambers and Darwin
cumulatively dealt to faith anchored in an immemorial conception of the
relation between God, man and other living creatures, the scale relations
through which man's size and place in the world were understood were,
generally, secure and stable. Man was to the animal kingdom as God
was to man: human superiority over animals was perfectly expressed in
the idea that man was the measure of all terrestrial things. As the dearest
of God's creatures, the one made in his image, man could be considered a scale model of the deity. This conception of human superiority
to the natural world was thrown into doubt by new scientific theories
and discoveries, which weakened and eventually demolished the anthropocentric belief that nature had been divinely created for man's use and
enjoyment, and that man was separate from animals. As Robert Young
has pointed out, the threat of Darwin's work lay in its implication that the

mind and soul were subject to the material laws of nature, that they had evolved in the same way as animal instinct. Instead of being a divine spark, man's moral and spiritual nature was inescapably animal.[36] The question 'How different are we from animals?' was translated into the question 'What size are we?'[37] It is in this context that Fitzgerald's miniature fairy worlds can be seen both to express and to allay an anxiety about how large the Victorians, metaphorically speaking, were.

Each of Fitzgerald's sources evokes such disturbances of scale; each in some way represents the relation between the human, the natural and the supernatural worlds. In the 'Cock Robin' paintings these are brought together to frame scenes which exclude the human viewer, and show a natural world apparently independent of human activity and observation. However, to take scenes of fairyland 'from life', as the re-viewer's apparently whimsical comment hints that Fitzgerald has done, is to suggest that these disturbances of scale and relation exist 'out there' in the world the viewer inhabits. But the paintings also place miniature beings, some of whom are a little like tiny versions of the viewer, inside the picture, and this implies that the world inside the painting is not as clearly separated from the world outside as one might like. Looking into a living miniature world, a doll's house come to life, say, is one of the most persistent and seductive fantasies provoked by the miniature, but, as anyone who has looked through a microscope will know, living miniatures are just as sinister as they are enchanting. Fitzgerald's fairy paintings offered their Victorian spectators just such an alluring and discomfiting opportunity.

Scientific writing is full of metaphor: this is one of the reasons why the interconnections of Victorian science and literature are so fascinating. The relationship between science writing and visual art is often less evident, because, as Marcia Pointon remarks in 'Geology and Landscape Painting in Nineteenth-Century England', 'the pictorial artist in the nineteenth century did not work with literary metaphor but through the articulation of the visible world'. She emphasises that in the geological landscapes depicted by William Dyce and John Brett, the 'eye and mind are activated through association in scenes that do not avoid the role played by the visual artist in observing and recording, rather than philosophising and discoursing'.[38] Such an 'articulation of the visible world', most famously theorised in Ruskin's injunction to optical truth and rigorous empiricism in landscape painting, has made the influence of the debates which shaped mid-nineteenth-century views of man's relation to the natural world hard to identify in visual art of the period.

The site of much of the conflict between natural theology and scientific naturalism, pro- and anti-Darwinian scientists and Christians was the relation of the material and metaphysical dimensions of the natural world, or as Ursula Seibold-Bultmann has put it, the 'flirt[ation] between the natural and supernatural'.[39] This relation demanded to be represented metaphorically; metaphor, however, was identified with the artist's failure or refusal to achieve optical truth. Fitzgerald's 'Cock Robin' paintings, however, should be seen as 'metaphorical landscapes', attempts to represent the natural world as both material and metaphysical, and to negotiate the problems caused to the anthropomorphic conception of nature by the scientific developments which culminated in Darwin's evolutionary theory.

I will first look at Fitzgerald's work in relation to that of Hieronymus Bosch, and show how visual features in Bosch's *The Garden of Earthly Delights*, which have close parallels in the 'Cock Robin' series, have theological meanings which are undermined by these scientific developments. Then I will compare Fitzgerald's paintings to still lifes by William Henry Hunt which visually embody the attitudes of natural theology, in order to show how anthropomorphisation is used to cover over the nastiness of the natural world, a process I call 'seeing with the loving eye'. Because of the way Darwin's work and the debates around it made anthropomorphisation problematic, the human figure became subject to a radical instability of scale. Both anthropomorphisation and instabilities of scale are especially problematic in natural history books on insects. The illustrations from such books have affinities with Fitzgerald's work. By comparing the 'Cock Robin' paintings with illustrations from books about insects published before and after 1859, I will show that his pictures are distinctively post-Darwinian. Finally, I will look at the practice of anthropomorphic taxidermy, and especially at the case which I suggest might have given Fitzgerald his subject, in order to demonstrate how the unsettling implications of Fitzgerald's representation of the supernatural and natural worlds are finally contained. I will argue, then, that in order properly to understand the meanings and contemporary resonances of these images, and to see how, though they cannot refer explicitly to the scientific and theological debates of the 1850s, they are in fact shaped by them, it is essential to take seriously the reviewer's conceit of 'horrid realities' drawn from 'a case of such familiars at home'.

Even the most casual glance at any of Fitzgerald's paintings of fairies will recall for the modern viewer the work of Hieronymus Bosch. Yet it is quite possible that the resemblance would have passed Fitzgerald's contemporaries by (neither of the reviews quoted earlier mentions it), as Bosch was obscure and unfashionable until the reawakening of interest in his work at the end of the nineteenth century.[40] He was, however, known to connoisseurs and collectors: the entry on Bosch in Pilkington's *General Dictionary of Painters* (both the 1829 and 1857 editions), gives a judgement on this artist which, though it emphasises the disturbing quality of the work, acknowledges its attractions:

He had a peculiar pleasure in painting spectres, devils, and enchantments; and though he possessed considerable powers as a painter, as well in the freedom of his touch as the strength of colouring, yet his pictures rather excite horror, mixed with surprise, than real delight. When he saw the Escurial [sic] in Spain, and considered the wonderful performances of the masters with which that palace was enriched, he despaired of producing anything comparable to them, and therefore fixed upon a style differing from them all, and which was full of fancy, whim, and wild imagination ... Though his subjects are disagreeable, his pictures have always been much esteemed, and yield considerable prices.[41]

Though he was not widely popular, and was certainly less well known than Pieter Brueghel, with whom his work was sometimes confused, re-productions of Bosch's work clearly circulated, for in the 1860s the South Kensington Museum bought a number of prints by Hieronymus Cock after Bosch. But whether Fitzgerald had seen Bosch's work in some form or not, the likeness between his figures and some of Bosch's is arresting, particularly between Bosch's demons and Fitzgerald's grotesque fairies.

There are other similarities: the fairy climbing into an eggshell in *Fairies Sleeping in a Bird's Nest*, for instance, appears in the central panel of *The Garden of Earthly Delights* (c. 1505–10, Madrid: Museo del Prado). In the latter work there are a number of birds, large in size in re-lation to the human figures; indeed, there are considerable disparities in scale between the sizes of humans, birds and animals. Such distortions of scale are consistent features of Fitzgerald's paintings. In *The Captive Robin* (1860s; Private Collection), for example, the (baby) robin is in scale with the plants surrounding the scene and much larger than the fairies. But sitting on a fairy's hand in the bottom left corner is another bird, in scale with the fairies, so that it is about as large in relation to them as a hawk would be in relation to a human. These parallels suggest that Fitzgerald may have looked at Bosch's work, perhaps even at a reproduction after *The Garden of Earthly Delights*.[42] In particular, Fitzgerald's division of fairies into 'human-esque' and grotesque varieties seems to mirror the distinction between the sinful mortals in the central panel of *The Garden of Earthly Delights* and the devils and damned in its right-hand panel. If the grotesque fairies resemble nothing so much as the therioanthropic monsters who inhabit Bosch's hell, the 'human-esque' fairies, with their thin bodies and child-like faces, are equally like his portrayal of humans.

The Garden of Earthly Delights is pervaded by a complex and idiosyncratic symbolism of the Fall, sin and judgement. Since there is no account of the picture from the mid-nineteenth century, one can only speculate about how it might then have been interpreted. But the visual qualities which seem most closely to parallel Fitzgerald's work – the disparities of scale, the miniaturisation of humans, the grotesqueness of the sinners and demons – all have obvious theological meanings. The perspective assumed by the picture is a panoramic, God's-eye view of the origins, present state and destiny of human life, and the human figures are tiny because, in comparison to God, this is their true size. The landscape in which animals, eggs, fruit and birds are much larger than the humans is symbolic of the immensity of the temptation offered by the sins of the flesh, and the meagreness of human virtue. The grotesqueness of the demons and damned makes physical the moral and spiritual perversions and deformities of sin.

In Bosch's work the disturbing qualities of the disparities of scale, miniaturisation and therioanthropic forms are tempered by the absolute fixity of forms and scale relations which, in fact, underlies the conception of human, natural and supernatural worlds presupposed by the images. The distortions of scale and form are intended to be interpreted allegorically rather than literally: humans can no more shrink to less than the size of birds than the forms of humans and animals can be fused together in one monstrous being. Such aberrations in nature would contradict a divine order in which relations and forms are fixed and immutable.[43] Indeed, such images as *The Garden of Earthly Delights* can function as allegories only because the scenes they depict are really impossible. The striking visual effects Fitzgerald echoed in his fairy paintings depend upon a theology which admits of no uncertainty as to the place of humans in the cosmos, nor to their size or form, nor their relation to the natural world.

The disparities of scale, miniaturisation and grotesque figures in Fitzgerald's paintings were no longer underpinned by the religious framework which lent them their original theological meanings in Bosch's work. The grotesque figures in the 'Cock Robin' paintings are not demons and damned souls but fairies, and instead of devising or enduring exquisite torments, they merely tease each other or the hapless robins. But this is not to say that in Fitzgerald's work the tropes of miniaturisation,

disparity of scale, and deformity are meaningless, or that these are reduced to purely visual effects, however striking. On the contrary, they are
given new, entirely different meanings by a new context: one in which
the perspective of the God's-eye view has been taken over by humans.
Science has attempted to usurp the point-of-view of the deity, for it has
adopted the perspective which sees and knows the world absolutely: now
scientists approximate the panoramic, transcendent vision formerly accorded only to God. But whereas God sees but is unseen, the God-like
perspective adopted by the scientist scrutinises humans' place in the cosmos. This in turn is a cause of further anxiety about scientific knowledge,
for it opens up the possibility that humans might know too much, might
learn more than they are morally fit for. These anxieties were widespread,
and were shared to some extent by scientists themselves; they shape some
of the most characteristic Victorian responses to the natural world. To see
why this is the case, and why they are evoked in *Cock Robin Defending his Nest*
and similar images, we have to turn to Fitzgerald's contemporary sources.

Since Edmund Gosse's well-known description of seeing Holman
Hunt's *The Finding of the Saviour in the Temple* (1860; Birmingham Museum
and Art Gallery) with his father, the naturalist Phillip Henry Gosse, it has
become commonplace to discern a similarity between Pre-Raphaelite
techniques and those of natural history illustration:

Some of the other visitors, as I recollect, expressed astonishment and dislike of
what they called the 'Preraphaelite' treatment, but we were not affected by that.
Indeed, if anything, the exact, minute and hard execution of Mr Hunt was in
sympathy with the methods we ourselves were in the habit of using when we
painted butterflies and seaweeds, placing perfectly pure bright pigments side by
side, without any nonsense about chiaroscuro. This large, bright, comprehensive
picture made a very deep impression upon me, not exactly as a work of art, but
as a brilliant natural specimen.[44]

Pre-Raphaelite painting, because of its commitment to the faithful description of natural specimens drawn from life, mimics the appearance of
the illustrations to the field guide or taxonomic reference book, which are
concerned to render the specimen with minute exactitude, to aid recognition in the field or the study. Natural history illustration, however, is
hardly free from stylistic conventions: it depends upon the understanding that the specimen illustrated is typical, that groups contain specimens of each sex and stage of development, and that the background,
where shown, is the creature's habitat, and may include its nest or food.
These conventions are disguised by the apparent complete realism of the

Figure 18. Plate IV, Phillip Henry Gosse, *Actinologia Britannica.*

illustrative style, so that we accept, for example, that caterpillar, pupa and butterfly are illustrated together on one plant, or that the stoat is shown in both summer and winter coats, or that the grasshopper is accompanied by a magnified section of the teeth on his wing with which he chirps. Of course, these features of natural history illustration are themselves products of the knowledge they seek to convey; the conventions of natural history illustration change according to the theories of animal behaviour and relation of species to habitat, knowledge of anatomy, and systems of taxonomy currently available.[45]

There are clear parallels between the style of illustration adopted by field guides, such as Phillip Henry Gosse's *Actinologia Britannica* (1858–60; fig. 18), and that of still lifes by William Henry Hunt.[46] Hunt specialised in still life, in the latter part of his career becoming particularly associated with fruit pictures, assemblages of plants and *nature morte*, and with birds' nests, these giving him his nickname, 'Bird's Nest' Hunt. *Primroses and Bird's Nest* (1840–50, London: Tate Gallery) is a typical example: a detailed, close-up view, in which the human agency which has brought the two elements of the picture together is disguised by the naturalism of the style. The popularity of Hunt's work was encouraged by Ruskin, who praised his 'keen eye for truth' and 'pure Naturalism'; it must have been influenced by Ruskin's repeated injunctions to study and draw from nature, and the taste he nurtured for painstakingly de-tailed sketches of plants and rocks.[47] But Hunt's popularity must also have been aided by the widespread interest in natural history which, according to David Allen, developed around the middle decades of the century into a 'craze'.[48] In these decades natural history publish-ing boomed, with an immense growth in the numbers of cheap field guides (these were often designed to accompany day trips by rail, and were sold at railway station booksellers), and instructional works aimed at children; both genres were lavishly illustrated. The bird's nest and plants (most of them identifiable species) which recur in Fitzgerald's 'Cock Robin' pictures are probably influenced by Hunt's still lifes.[49] They speak also of an informed public, who knew what animals, in-sects, birds' nests and wildflowers looked like, and expected to see them accurately portrayed in paintings, just as they were in natural history books.

Both field guides and Hunt's pictures grant to the viewer a transcen-dent position, looking down from above, with perfect knowledge and unimpeded vision. In other words, they grant to the human spectator the God's-eye perspective, in which seeing and knowing are identical. But for humans to take up this perspective is problematic, as Ruskin implies in a famous passage on the Pathetic Fallacy:

So, then, we have three ranks: the man who perceives rightly, because he does not feel, and to whom the primrose is very accurately the primrose, because he does not love it. Then, secondly, the man who perceives wrongly, because he feels, and to whom the primrose is anything else than a primrose: a star, or a sun, or a fairy's shield, or a forsaken maiden. And then, lastly, there is the man who perceives rightly in spite of his feelings, and to whom the primrose is for ever nothing else than itself – a little flower, apprehended in the plain and leafy fact of it, whatever and how many soever the associations and passions may be, that crowd around it.[50]

Ruskin introduces an important third term into the consideration of point-of-view: to seeing and knowing, he adds loving. The first of his observers sees and knows, the second sees and loves, the third observer sees, knows and loves; for Ruskin, this is the noblest perspective available to humans, because it is the closest to the all-seeing, all-knowing and all-loving perspective of God. Ruskin's trinity of perspectives suggests that by the mid-nineteenth century a quite new idea of point-of-view had arisen. It replaced the traditional conception of the perspectives available to God and man as heavenly, transcendent and perfect on the one hand, and terrestrial, limited and imperfect on the other, with a conception in which it is possible to see and know too much, to separate knowing and loving, and to take on a transcendent view akin to that of the deity.

Ruskin does not attribute the 'knowing' gaze to the scientist and the 'loving' gaze to the artist (indeed, he is concerned to argue that true art can only arise from a perspective that is both 'knowing and loving'), yet the terms in which he defines knowledge and love are already overdetermined by these categories. In Ruskin's schema, knowing is identified with exact description and enumeration of particulars, with an unflinching attention to structure, habitat, habits and appearance: these qualities were crucial to science's project to describe the external world truthfully and to understand it without the error of prejudice. Loving, on the other hand, is identified with imagination, metaphor, analogy, resemblance, and with a sense of other forms or realities behind or surrounding the physical: these attitudes are characteristic of the Romantic aesthetic which claims art as a conduit to a superior reality. Such a separation of science and art was already common by the time Ruskin was writing, as this instance from Hugh Miller's *The Old Red Sandstone* (1841), an important work of popular geology, shows: 'Will the reader spend a few minutes exploring this rocky trench, – it matters not as a scene hunter or a geologist?'[51] The 'or' here suggests the difficulty of taking up both positions at once, despite the contention that 'it matters not' which one adopts. A similar separation of 'knowing' and 'loving' perspectives is implied in T. H. Huxley's lecture 'On the Physical Basis of Life', in which he argues that all living things are constructed out of the same matter, protoplasm. Introducing his theme, Huxley asks:

What, truly, can seem to be more obviously different from one another, in faculty, in form, and in substance, than the various kinds of living beings? What community of faculty can there be between the brightly-coloured lichen, which so nearly resembles a mere mineral incrustation of the bare rock on which it grows, and the painter, to whom it is instinct with beauty, or the botanist, whom it feeds with knowledge?[52]

In the opening statement of his bold theme, the idea that the lichen, the painter and the botanist share the same fundamental physical nature, Huxley concedes that there are two clearly separable ways of regarding the natural world, the 'loving' gaze of the painter and the 'knowing' gaze of the scientist. Of course, this is the precipitate of a long historical process through which science became separated from other ways of knowing the world, and which led eventually to the professionalisation of science and the formation of scientific disciplines. Nevertheless, this seemingly casual separation of science and art, 'knowing' and 'loving' gazes, poses a problem for the representation of the natural world which Ruskin did not anticipate or account for.

The perspective which is both 'knowing and loving', which sees the primrose as 'itself – a little flower, apprehended in the plain and leafy fact of it, whatever and how many soever the associations and passions may be, that crowd around it', is the perceptual version of natural theology. The 'plain and leafy fact' of the primrose is made meaningful by the simultaneous perception of another reality which 'crowd[s] around it'; the observer is able to perceive both material and metaphysical realities at once. The problem this poses is the move from perception to representation, for while representing the object of the 'knowing' gaze is merely a matter of close observation and technical skill in realistic representation, the metaphysical, perceived with the 'loving' gaze, can only be represented symbolically. How could the 'associations and passions' which surround and give meaning to the natural world be literally and realistically represented? For Ruskin, the artist who was able to come closest to solving this problem was Turner, whose ability to suggest the numinous and the actual is celebrated at length in *Modern Painters I* (1843). But Turner's sublime landscapes can suggest only certain kinds of true and loving visions of the natural world. The problem is implicit in William Henry Hunt's still lifes, which certainly make no attempt to represent the primrose as anything other than a primrose. Despite Ruskin's contention that anyone might discern the 'simple love' which suffuses Hunt's work, the growing exploration in painting of the 1850s of symbolic elements in otherwise literal depictions of the natural world suggests the failure of still life and realistic landscapes to represent the attitudes of natural theology.[53] This tendency is especially marked in the work of the Pre-Raphaelites and those associated with them, as images like Charles Alston Collins's *Convent Thoughts* (1849; London: Tate Gallery) and William Holman Hunt's *The Hireling Shepherd* (1851–2; Manchester City Art Gallery) demonstrate.

The difficulty artists faced in attempting to represent visually a perception of the natural world which is both 'knowing' and 'loving' becomes most testing when the natural world is least amenable to an ideal, transcendent viewpoint. The contemplation of plants and *nature morte* presents little threat to the human observer, because, *pace* Huxley's claim that all living things are made from the same basic substance, they seem to be utterly unconnected with human beings, from another, almost inanimate, order of life. But this is not the case with animals, birds and insects. Even before Darwin, the contemplation of the animal kingdom was potentially disturbing, because what the observer saw there did not confirm that the natural world is necessarily beautiful, or benign. The insect world provoked particular difficulties in reconciling knowledge with love, for insects are the least homely (in the Freudian sense) of all life forms; their beauties, less evident to the casual viewer than those of birds or animals, are least apparent when they are closely observed.

The difficulty of representing insects is abundantly clear from popular natural history books. Most, like Jules Michelet's *L'Insecte* (1858, first English translation 1875), relentlessly anthropomorphise insects in an attempt to make them lovable as well as knowable. Michelet's work is divided into chapters with titles like 'World Builders', 'Love and Death' and 'The Home and Loves of the Spider'; this anthropomorphising tendency, however, cannot entirely efface the alien qualities of insects, seen for instance in the illustrations to the chapter 'Insects at Work' (fig. 19), which depicts insects scavenging on the dead body of a bird.[54] A surprisingly common strategy of popular entomology is to connect insects with fairies, as does *Fairy Frisket, Or Peeps at the Insect Folk* by 'A. L. O. E.' [C. M. Tucker], in which two fairies conduct a tour of the insect world, pointing out moral lessons to be learned by the child reader.[55] Fairies are connected with insects by a form of metonymy, through their wings. From the moment when fairies began to have wings, at the end of the eighteenth century, they were almost invariably given butterfly wings, because feathered wings belong to angels, and bats' wings to vampires.[56] Fairies and insects have the same wings, so it is natural to connect them; it is then a short step to turning insects into fairies and using this to cover over insects' alien qualities.

Episodes of Insect Life by 'Acheta Domestica' [L. M. Budgen] (1849–51) uses the device of identifying fairies with insects several times. The book intersperses descriptions of insects and their habits with 'episodes' which portray insects in human contexts (a despairing poet, for example, saved from suicide by a humble fly), or allegorise insect behaviour in human terms (the beehive is represented as the 'queendom' of 'Amazonia'). The author, himself taking on the persona of an insect, the hearth cricket, explains his aim as being to render the unpalatable appearance and reputation of insects both beautiful and friendly; in other words, to subject them to the 'loving' gaze. The opening chapter, in which this account is given, contains the following long apostrophe to Entomology:

Figure 19. 'Insects at Work', Jules Michelet, *The Insect*.

Dear Entomology! We have called thee a hobby, we have likened thee to a hack; but thou art more. Thou art a powerful Genie, a light-winged Fairy, not merely bearing us through earth, and sky, and water, but peopling every scene in every element with new and living forms, before invisible. For *us*, nature has now no desert place: touched by thy magic wand, every tree has become a peopled city, teeming with busy multitudes; every flower, a pavilion, hung with gorgeous tapestry, for the summer occupation of Insect nobles, clad in velvet, gauze, or coat of mail; nay, the very moss that grows upon the tree or clothes the stone has become to us a forest, where, as in forests of larger growth, roam the fierce and the gentle, preying or preyed upon by each other; and the stone, we have only to turn it, and we are certain to discover beneath, some hidden lurker, or some wondrous subterranean structure, perhaps a solitary dwelling, perhaps a nursery, perhaps a general home of refuge. Yes, our darling pursuit, of all the most lightsome and life-giving, with thee for our companion, the bare, the barren, the desolate, and the death-like become instinct with life. The arid heath, the decaying tree, the mouldering wall are converted at once into fertile fields of interest and inquiry, while the summer skies grow brighter yet with glancing wings and oar-like feet; and with the knowledge that both are plied by a multitude of happy creatures.[57]

The study of insects becomes a way of enchanting the natural world, of covering over 'the bare, the barren, and the death-like' and turning it into fairyland. The 'loving' gaze of Entomology imagines the natural world as a quasi-human, fairy-like domestic life taking place among the flowers or under the stone. In the miniature world of the forest in the moss, the law of eat or be eaten has become less fatal precisely because it is miniature; and, when juxtaposed with the home of the many under the rock and the medieval summer palace inside the flower, its threat disappears entirely. The 'darling pursuit' (the epithet could not suggest more plainly the 'loving' gaze), the 'light-winged Fairy', transforms nature by three separate devices: first, the insects are imagined as humans (anthropomorphised); second, they are invested with attributes of the past (made nostalgic); third, the world is seen at the insect's scale (miniaturised). Out of a nature ruled by death ('the arid heath, the decaying tree, the mouldering wall'), these devices produce a magical, enchanted nature: 'For *us*, nature has now no desert place: touched by thy magic wand, every tree has become a peopled city, teeming with busy multitudes.'

The 'multitude of happy creatures' who inhabit this enchanted natural world bear very little resemblance to insects, and perhaps that is the point. Insects as insects must always remind us of the alien strangeness of the processes of nature; what this apostrophe invokes is a kind of insect that is rather like a human, though much smaller and supernaturally magical:

an insect, in fact, that is rather like a fairy. In this sense, the 'light-winged Fairy' is the insect itself, rather than its study. Seen with the 'knowing' gaze, the insect world is filled with nastiness and death; with the 'loving' gaze, just as Ruskin's primrose was transformed into a fairy's shield, it is transformed into fairyland.

One of the most interesting of the book's narrative 'episodes' is a long poem called 'The Fresh Water Siren'. This is an allegory of the mutual preying of the Water Spider and Great Water Beetle, in which their battle to the death is transformed into the fatal love of a knight for a fairy – though it turns out fatal for her. An illustration of the interdependence of life forms in the food chain becomes a miniature 'La Belle Dame Sans Merci'. In this poem, the work that the 'loving' gaze performs to ameliorate the ubiquity of death in the insect world is made almost too plain. As the last lines show, the poem insists almost too hard that insects can be made wonderful, their battles chivalrous, and their habits magical, by making them into fairies:

> Ye lovers of marvel and fairy lore,
> Say not that the days of enchantment are o'er,
> That the well-springs of Fancy and Fable fail,
> For they water the streams whence we've drawn our tale.
> There are streamlets yet where the water sprite
> With his harlequin changes bewilders the sight;
> There are castles yet of ivory and gold,
> Hung with fabrics by sunshine unroll'd,
> Within whose luxurious recesses recline
> Fays of exquisite form, quaffing exquisite wine:
> Some in gossamer veiled of ethereal dyes,
> Which have only their match in the rainbow'd skies;
> Or in mail that does shame to the armourer's trade.
> These are haunting us ever for ill or for good,
> Through earth and through air, field, forest or flood:
> To transport our thoughts, as by magic spell,
> From the sordid objects whereon they dwell,
> To a land of the Marvellous dimly displayed,
> Where the light-winged Fancy by wonder stayed,
> Still delighteth to hover and joyously say: –
> 'Oh! my darling elves, ye're not chased away;
> 'There's a region still where you have a place, –
> 'The mysterious world of the Insect race.'[58]

The insect recalls the fairy, which in turn figures the insect; a 'Marvellous' vision of nature recalled as a consolation, in a metaphorical, miniature form, for nature's own 'sordid objects', struggle and death.

Episodes of Insect Life is profusely illustrated with vignettes related to each of the 'episodes'. These show the insects in closely observed detail, but in anthropomorphic settings, activities and attire. Insects are shown taking tea, playing musical instruments, writing, reading and so on. The illustration to 'The Fresh Water Siren' (fig. 20) shows a mail-clad knight attacking the fairy in the stream, and next to them, the Water Spider and Great Water Beetle. This illustration obviously refers to the conventions of natural history illustration, showing the habitat and food of species. It is unusual, however, in depicting the products of both the 'knowing' and 'loving' gazes. In a sense, the knight and the fairy really do illustrate the 'episode of insect life' suggested by the pictures of the insects themselves, for they do enact the way the two creatures prey upon one another. Yet they do so in a transformed fashion, as if such a natural and common occurrence can be safely represented only in a metaphorical form. The vignette is a perfect example of what might be called 'visual natural theology', an image which combines literal and symbolic, material and metaphysical, 'knowing' and 'loving'.

There is a clear parallel between the procedures of *Episodes of Insect Life* and Fitzgerald's 'Cock Robin' paintings. *Cock Robin Defending his Nest* is a typical instance. The scene depicted is the courtly pastime of hunting, connoted as historical rather than modern by the fact that the fairies hunt on foot, using swords and shields. Their attire – variously suggesting armour, helmets, and 'medieval-esque' robes and headgear – reinforces the suggestion of a historical setting for the scene. The relations between the fairies also contribute to this impression, with a division between 'knights' (those carrying thorn swords), 'ladies' (clinging together in the top right-hand corner), and 'serfs' (the smaller, grotesque fairies looking on or slain in the battle for the nest). This image presents a similar nostalgic scenario to 'The Fresh Water Siren' or the apostrophe to Entomology: a courtly, medieval past represented in miniature. A similar figuring of insects as fairies takes place here, but in a more complex form. The 'knights' and 'ladies' have human faces (and are derived from Bosch's human figures), but in other respects borrow from insects: they have iridescent wings; their headgear recalls antennae; the fairy immediately to the right of the nest has brown clothing which resembles the furry thorax of a hawk-moth. In the case of the 'serfs' the borrowing of an insect-like alien-ness is even more marked. It is not merely that the insect is made attractive by being represented as a fairy, but rather that the distinction between insect and fairy itself is made unclear. These figures are simultaneously both fairy and insect.

THE FRESH-WATER SIREN.

Part the First.

" My air-built bower come and see,
   " Stranger, come and dwell with me."
An armour-clad Rover is sauntering near ;
At the Siren's sweet accents he pricks up his ear :
" Gramercy ! " quoth he. " She bespeaketh me kind,
" And to pay her my devoirs I've almost a mind,
" If saint or if sinner would show me the road
" To this good-natured damsel's *al-fresco* abode. "

Figure 20. 'The Fresh Water Siren', 'Acheta Domestica', *Episodes of Insect Life*.

The scene depicted in this image is a disturbing one in which a robin, the epitome of avian domesticity, is attacked by beings who recall both insects and humans; it is a transformed version of the struggle for survival, in which nature's 'sordid objects', struggle and death, are explicitly represented. But the purpose of representing insects as fairies is to disguise the nastiness of the natural world and to make nature lovable. The nostalgic miniature world of *Who Killed Cock Robin?* should work a magic on nature: it should show the 'death-like become instinct with life'. As Susan Stewart remarks in her study *On Longing: Narratives of the Miniature, the Gigantic, the Souvenir, the Collection* (1984), the miniature is always nostalgic, because the reduced version of the world the miniature presents is metaphorical:

> The miniature does not attach itself to lived historical time. Unlike the metonymic world of realism, which attempts to erase the break between the time of everyday life and the time of narrative by mapping one perfectly upon the other, the metaphoric world of the miniature makes everyday life absolutely anterior and exterior to itself. The reduction in scale which the miniature presents skews the time and space of the everyday lifeworld, and as an object consumed, the miniature finds its 'use value' transformed into the infinite time of reverie.[59]

The miniature world of the insect is like fairyland, a world where time stops and is lost in dreaming: a place that is no-place and a time that is no-time. As 'Acheta Domestica' puts it, the miniature 'transport[s] our thoughts, as by magic spell' to a time before and outside the time we ourselves live in, an 'interior temporality' incommensurable with experience which continues over time.[60] The nostalgic world of the miniature represents a version of the world reduced for contemplation and separated from lived experience. This is indeed one aspect of Fitzgerald's 'Cock Robin' pictures, for the bright colours and tiny details do pull the spectator into a contemplative reverie. The experience of looking at these images is a little like looking through the windows of a dolls' house; like dolls' house food and furniture, the scenes represented grow more fascinating the further they are reduced in scale.

But *Who Killed Cock Robin?* is not entirely comforting. The nostalgic effect of miniaturisation does not entirely remove the threat posed by the depiction of struggle and death in the natural world. To put it another way, the 'loving' gaze cannot entirely efface what the 'knowing' eye sees. This is not the case for the illustration to 'The Fresh Water Siren', the whole purpose of which is to assure the reader that the 'knowing' and 'loving' gazes can be reconciled. Between the publication of *Episodes of Insect Life* and the inception of Fitzgerald's 'Cock Robin' series in the early 1860s a shift in attitudes to the natural world occurred, caused mainly, though not wholly, by the publication of Darwin's *On the Origin of Species by Means of Natural Selection* (1859). Though Darwin's work was at first known only to a small readership, it quickly caused an enormous controversy, the main point of which, despite Darwin's careful avoidance of an explicit statement to this effect, lighted on the implication that human beings were descended from primates, and thus from other members of the animal kingdom. Humans were no longer part of nature only insofar as they were equally part of God's creation, but of a superior kind, fashioned in the deity's image; rather, humans had their origins in the natural processes of the struggle for scarce resources, the survival of the fittest, and the evolution of new forms by chance mutation, just as all other life forms did. Looking at the natural world, one might see there, in miniature, the very same processes which had allowed the evolution of human beings.

To produce a comforting, nostalgic effect, the miniature must maintain a stable and transcendent viewpoint for the spectator; the observer's full size must be confirmed by the reduction in scale of the miniature. One symptom of the shift in attitudes to the natural world occasioned by evolutionary theory was that the relation between observer and observed became utterly unstable, because if the laws of material nature govern human beings as well as animals and plants, then to look at nature is also to look at human beings. The transcendent viewpoint of natural theology is made impossible, because now the scientist looks also at himself. An example of this can be seen in the text and illustrations of *The Population of an Old Pear Tree* (1870), a natural history book about insects written as a series of narratives. In the introduction, the narrator lies down in a meadow, underneath a pear tree, and falls into a dreamy haze. He awakes to find that he hears, sees and feels as an insect does: 'It seemed as if all the pores of my skin were being furnished with wondrously sharp and piercing eyes. All my senses at once became marvellously acute. The hum of a gnat seemed like the sound of a trumpet, and the perfume of lilies of the valley, wafted on the breeze, was strong enough to intoxicate my sense.'[61] The narrator has the senses of an insect, though it is unclear whether he has shrunk to the size of one. He sees the world of insects not as a miniature, but gigantically enlarged, and this enlargement lends it a frightful and demonic aspect:

I remembered that I had lain down at the foot of a pear-tree, just bursting into leaf with the warm breath of spring, though much injured by the winter's cold. I saw it again, but so wonderfully enlarged, that I really could not take it all in at once. Its bark had quite disappeared, giving place to a rich carpet of white, green, or yellow moss, in the most whimsical patterns. At times this verdant veil was raised by certain flat, bald heads, with great glaring round eyes, and bearing powerful hooks instead of jaws, which took a curious survey of me.[62]

The narrator sees the insects as huge monsters, which remind him of 'a picture of Brueghel's, of the infernal regions, in which the demons are drawn with cloven feet and large stomachs, grinning, leaping, and dancing, and with a human form struggling among them'.[63] This is a very similar conception to that of Fitzgerald's paintings: they both use the grotesque demons of Bosch and Brueghel to represent the monstrousness of the animal kingdom, and in both of them scale is unstable. In Fitzgerald's paintings the giant spectator looks in from outside only to see tiny 'human-esque' beings inside the picture. Here, the narrator sees the world as if he were a miniature human, and perceives the insects to be giants; in turn he is punished for being a giant by being made to see the natural world as if he were not.

The illustrations betray the same uncertainty about the relative sizes of human beings and insects. The two plates which illustrate the introduction each show the narrator in a different scale relation to the natural world. In the first, only the narrator's foot and ankle can be shown, crushing helpless insects, which cluster around his foot as if to beg for mercy. It is a characteristic of the gigantic that only a part can ever be represented; the presence of the insects as scale markers means that, if they are to be shown in any detail, the human figure cannot be shown whole. In the second plate, the scale relations between human and insect are completely reversed, for the narrator has shrunk dramatically, and is dwarfed by a vast spider hanging threateningly above him. The first plate emphasises the dominance of a human perspective by exaggerating the size of the human; the second shows that the human perspective is relative, one amongst many, and that humans may be seen as tiny as well as gigantic. The book's frontispiece (fig. 21) neatly encapsulates this reversal of scale in a visual joke: an artist is shown sketching under a tree, while the insects watch, waving merrily to him, from under another. The disproportionate size of the insects is the effect of the perspective: scale depends on where you are looking from. In one sense the joke is benign, reminding the reader that the 'book of nature' is superior to the book in hand. But

Figure 21. Frontispiece, Ernest Van Bruyssel, *The Population of an Old Pear Tree*.

in another sense, it suggests that human superiority over nature is merely a perspectival effect, one which is interchangeable with others in which humans are tiny or even insignificant. The radical destabilisation of scale between insect and human which these illustrations represent must also imply a similar uncertainty about the viewer. How large is the human body illustrated compared to that of the viewer? Does seeing things enlarged or in miniature imply a concomitant enlargement or reduction in the size of the observer? The human figure in the frontispiece stands for the viewer who, while he sees from one perspective, is himself seen from quite another: and who is to say which is the correct one?

The uncertainty which *The Population of an Old Pear Tree* betrays about the size and scale of the human body in relation to the natural world is a perceptual symptom of the uncertainty about humans' place in the natural world caused by the debates in the 1860s over evolution by natural selection. The immemorial conception of humans' place in nature which assumed that forms are fixed, and that humans are unrelated to other life forms, permitted to humans a transcendent viewpoint over the natural world, similar to God's. When Darwin's work suggested that forms were fluid and mutable, and that life forms were related because one evolved out of another, this transcendent viewpoint was made extremely problematic. To look at the natural world was no longer simply to see something separated from the human. After Darwin, to look at the natural world was also to see the human there. In this situation, the 'loving' gaze that transforms insects into fairies produces its own form of anxiety, because fairies are as much like humans as they are like insects. Covering over the law of eat or be eaten by turning beetles into fairies is not quite the same consoling move after Darwin as it had been for 'Acheta Domestica', for this move substitutes one form of anxiety for another. Instead of representing a natural world in which insects depend on each others' deaths, it represents a natural world in which humans do so.

This is the reason why Fitzgerald's 'Cock Robin' paintings are disturbing. They bring together references to a religious perspective on the place of humans in the world which was no longer tenable, and use them in a portrayal of nature which attempts to combine 'knowing' (the botanical detail of the plants) and 'loving' (the insect–fairies) gazes. Yet the fairies, even in their nostalgic miniature world, return the viewer's own regard. It is possible that the human spectator sees not insects but humans inside the picture frame, and thus is reminded of the ways in which human beings partake in the struggle for survival

common to the rest of the natural world. Instead of a magically transformed nature, an enchanted fairyland produced by the action of the
'loving' gaze on the external world, *Who Killed Cock Robin?* and the other
paintings throw back the image of the spectator as part of the world in
which 'roam the fierce and the gentle, preying and preyed upon by each
other'.[64]

This would explain why the *Art Journal*'s reviewer felt that Fitzgerald's
paintings depicted 'hideous realities', for, viewed in this manner, the
implications of the images are very disturbing. However, he also referred
to them as representations of a 'case of familiars', and this phrase gives a
clue to the means by which the distressing qualities of the 'Cock Robin'
paintings are ultimately made safe. Here is Susan Stewart on a further
aspect of the miniature:

As is the case with all miniatures, it is absolutely necessary that Lilliput be
an island. The miniature world remains perfect and uncontaminated by the
grotesque as long as its absolute boundaries are maintained. Consider, for example, the Victorian taste for art (usually transformed relics of nature) under
glass, or Joseph Cornell's glass bells. The glass eliminates the possibility of contagion, at the same time that it maximises the possibility of transcendent
vision . . . Yet, of course, the major function of the enclosed space is always to
create a tension or dialectic between inside and outside, between public and
private property, between the space of the subject and the space of the social.
Trespass, contamination, and the erasure of materiality are the threats presented
to the enclosed world. And because the interiority of the enclosed world tends
to reify the interiority of the viewer, repetition also presents a threat.[65]

The 'Victorian taste for art under glass' was a phenomenon of the
middle decades of the century. In 1845 the duty on glass was repealed,
making glass windows and ornaments affordable to a much wider public, and dramatically reducing the price of scientific equipment made
of glass, such as specimen jars and cases; the allure of glass as an orna-
ment was greatly magnified by Paxton's Crystal Palace of 1851. The
following decade marked the height of the craze for natural history
and for the collection of ferns, seaweeds, rock-pool creatures, butterflies,
moths and other insects. All of these could be kept alive under glass: in
aquaria, vivaria and Wardian sealed cases.[66] Even when the specimens
were dead, they were still kept under glass in the form of taxidermic
displays.

Although naturalists had attempted since the eighteenth century to
preserve animals, birds and fishes by stuffing them, it was only in the
1830s that techniques of preservation (using arsenic) and mounting were

developed that enabled reasonably robust and lifelike preservation of stuffed specimens.[67] The popularity of taxidermy as a decorative art, rather than a technical study aid for naturalists, was enormously increased, if not initiated, by the Great Exhibition, at which thirteen British taxidermists showed cases of birds and animals. The most celebrated taxidermic exhibits, however, were the cases submitted by Herrman Plouquet of the Stuttgart Royal Museum. Plouquet specialised in what came to be called 'artistic taxidermy'. In contrast to 'scientific taxidermy', which merely sought to present the specimen in a lifelike pose, 'artistic taxidermy' invested animals with human attributes and posed them in narrative scenes. Plouquet's work was so popular (Queen Victoria described his cases as 'really marvellous'[68]) that a collection of animal tales and fables, illustrated with engravings of the cases, was published the same year. The frontispiece to *The Comical Creatures from Wurtemberg* shows a case titled 'The wonderful Hare Hunt' (fig. 22), in which weasels hunt a pack of hares with guns, clubs and a dog.[69] This extremely disturbing scene, replete with incongruities of scale, explicitly replicates for the amusement of the spectator the anxieties about humans' place in the natural world which I have been discussing. Instead of depicting the way weasels might really hunt hares (or leverets, as they must be from their size), they hunt them as humans would. The spectator of the case simultaneously sees an 'amusing' or comforting representation of preying animals as civilised humans, and a representation of the ways in which humans behave like animals.

The vogue for anthropomorphic taxidermy started by Plouquet's cases was continued by the British taxidermist Walter Potter, who in 1861 exhibited a case entitled *The Death of Cock Robin* (fig. 23) at his parents' inn at Bramber, Sussex. *The Death of Cock Robin* illustrates the nursery rhyme, using ninety-eight birds and a cow made of skin stretched over a wooden frame. Potter took forward Plouquet's work by including props and a painted background in his case (these features were also becoming popular in 'scientific' taxidermy, where it was increasingly common to mimic the conventions of natural history illustration by including nests, plants from the creature's habitat, branches and rocks, and backgrounds painted to simulate sky or grass), and by manipulating the specimens to give them human expressions: one bird, for example, has a tear in its eye. *The Death of Cock Robin* was widely publicised, and attracted a great many visitors to Bramber; Potter made a career of anthropomorphic taxidermy, producing cases like *The Rabbits' Schoolroom*, *The Kittens' Tea Party*, and *The House that Jack Built*.[70]

Figure 22. Frontispiece, *The Comical Creatures from Wurtemberg.*

Figure 23. Walter Potter, *The Death of Cock Robin.*

It is impossible to know whether Fitzgerald saw *The Death of Cock Robin* (as it is to say whether he saw *Episodes of Insect Life*); the coincidence of subject, however, is striking. Whether he saw the case or merely heard about it, it seems very likely that he took the idea for his paintings from Potter's work. But the likeness does not end with the subject. Fitzgerald's 'Cock Robin' paintings look very like glass cases, both the living microcosm of the Wardian case and the lifelike arrangement of the taxidermic display. The resemblance is particularly strong in the case of *Cock Robin Defending his Nest* – the oval shape of which resembles the kind of newly inexpensive glass dome, containing wax fruit or a bird's nest, that was found in many middle-class Victorian homes – and *Fairies Sleeping in a Bird's Nest*, which has a frame made out of gilded twigs and branches, so that the picture itself is 'in the nest', framed as a lifelike arrangement.

It is significant that the theme of the 'Cock Robin' pictures is death, for this is also the preoccupation of taxidermic cases. Taxidermy presents death as a spectacle, in the form of bodies arranged to create the illusion of resurrection, and the allure of taxidermy lies in the tension it presents between the spectacle of dead bodies and their illusionistic presentation as lifelike. When the animals mimic humans, this tension is even stronger, because the implication that humans are animal-like is added to the representation of life-in-death. Anthropomorphic taxidermy does not explicitly represent the inclusion of humans in the law of eat or be eaten, kill or die; nevertheless, it suggests it, just as Fitzgerald's paintings do, through its identification of human and animal behaviour.

Susan Stewart describes how miniature worlds, like the taxidermic case or Fitzgerald's paintings, are always enclosed to prevent the contagion of the world outside, and to foil contamination by the grotesque. This, apart from the practical necessity of preventing damage and moth, is the function of the glass which surrounds the taxidermic specimen and, I believe, of the resemblance of Fitzgerald's pictures to enclosed glass cases. A picture like *Who Killed Cock Robin?* depicts a miniature natural world filled with death, and peoples it with beings who stand in for both insects and humans, but makes its revelation safe by mimicking the enclosure of the sealed glass case. Nothing can get out: the world of the spectator cannot be contaminated by the scenes of violence inside. Yet, as Stewart observes, there is a 'tension or dialectic' between the world inside and that outside the case. The nostalgic quality of these images produces a moment of reverie in the spectator, an imaginative return to fairyland, to an enchanted and magical natural place long since vanished from the world the spectator inhabits. On the other hand, what the spectator also sees, in this moment of reverie, is a representation of human life caught up in the terrible processes of mutual struggle and death: 'because the interiority of the enclosed world tends to reify the interiority of the viewer, repetition also presents a threat'. As much as the enclosure of the glass case or its mimetic equivalent holds off the threat that the spectator sees him or herself in the painting, it presents the same threat through the structure of the miniature. As the reviewer said, inside a 'case of familiars' one sees 'horrid realities'.

In painting fairies in the way he did, Fitzgerald drew on an anxiety about the relationship of human beings to the natural world which was widely diffused in mid-Victorian culture. The distinctive features of his painting – the forms of the fairies, the brightly coloured, highly detailed close-up views of the landscape settings, the discrepancies of scale, the size of the images, and the casual cruelty of the narratives – all draw their resonance from this anxiety. Whether he meant to or not, Fitzgerald represented in a particularly graphic form educated Victorians' fears about their implication in nature, and his work in the 1860s made fairy painting into a medium that could both express and allay those fears.

'ENTANGLED BANKS'

It is interesting to contemplate an entangled bank, clothed with many plants of various kinds, with birds singing on the bushes, with various insects flitting about, and with worms crawling through the damp earth, and to reflect that these elaborately constructed forms, so different from each other, and dependent on each other in so complex a manner, have all been produced by laws acting around us.

This is the opening of the final paragraph of Charles Darwin's *On the Origin of Species by Means of Natural Selection*. Summarising the thesis which the book as a whole has put forward, Darwin uses a hedge bank, something which might be seen by anyone on a country walk, to exemplify the workings of the natural world in general. In the contemplation of the entangled bank, with its seemingly random combination of life forms and activities, Darwin invites his reader to see the underlying order of the natural world, and to recognise that order as both inevitable and wondrous. He concludes:

Thus, from the war of nature, from famine and death, the most exalted object which we are capable of conceiving, the production of the higher animals, directly follows. There is a grandeur in this view of life, with its several powers, having been originally breathed into a few forms or one; and that, while this planet has gone cycling on according to the fixed law of gravity, from so simple a beginning endless forms most beautiful and wonderful have been, and are being, evolved.[71]

Looking at the entangled bank, scientist and reader see the interdependence of life forms, bound together in a war for scarce resources, in the chances of eat or be eaten, adapt or die, all subject to the expendability of the individual, and to the survival of the few at the cost of the many. Yet Darwin asks his reader to recognise this vision as wonderful. Though the entangled bank is not benign, the singing birds, flitting insects and crawling worms are grand; the war of nature, famine and death are exalted; evolution by natural selection, figured by the entangled bank, is beautiful.

In this final paragraph of *Origin of Species* Darwin's claims are both scientific and aesthetic: to look at, to really see the natural world, is both to know it and to wonder at it, to investigate it and to admire it. But the beauty Darwin asks his reader to see in nature is a strange, perhaps even a shocking one, founded not on harmony, proportion, agreement, symmetry or design, but on chance and change, mutation and struggle. The 'grandeur' of the vision of the entangled bank lies in the evolution, through the process of random mutation, and from the struggle for life in the face of the overwhelming chances of famine and death, of new, beautiful and wonderful forms of life. The entangled bank is a dialectical image, in which death leads to life in endlessly new and different forms. And instead of being a small instance of the grand design of nature in which God's patterns could be traced in miniature, as it might have been for earlier writers,[72] for Darwin the order of the entangled bank is entirely unplanned, existing fortuitously by virtue of the independent working of the laws leading to evolution by natural selection.[73]

Darwin's scientific and aesthetic claims were, needless to say, controversial. Even though Lyell's *Principles of Geology* and Robert Chambers's *Vestiges of the Natural History of Creation* (1844) had to some degree anticipated, and indeed helped Darwin formulate, evolutionary theory, it was the completeness of Darwin's account of the processes of natural selection and the imaginative power of his work that gave *Origin of Species* its particular importance. The effects of Darwin's work on contemporary representations of nature were profound. However, the ways in which writers and artists responded to his claims about the workings of the natural world were diverse, because the theory was so controversial. Looking at versions of the entangled bank by Robert Browning and Richard Dadd, I will argue that they each struggle, in very different ways, with the implications of evolutionary theory for the perception of order and meaning in the natural world. Gillian Beer has described Darwin's writing as partaking in an aesthetic sense of the 'wondrous strangeness' of the actual characteristic of Victorian culture in general: 'The grotesque, the beautiful and the wonderful in the everyday was a major Victorian imaginative theme. The study of "fact" was for Dickens and for Carlyle and for Hopkins an exploration of the fantastic. Darwin shared this pleasure in "making strange", in skimming off the familiar and restoring it, enriched and stabilised.'[74] Darwin's work made the natural world newly strange for his contemporaries, and posed the problem of how it might be represented 'enriched and stabilised' if the familiar were 'skimmed off'. Browning responded to the implications of Darwin's work by representing the natural world as grotesque: he developed a grotesque aesthetic which embodies a response to the idea of evolution. Dadd, on the other hand, produced a representation of the natural world whose grotesqueness is brought about by its inability to witness the processes which animate, and constitute the hidden order of, Darwin's entangled bank. Each of these responses deals in a different way with the loss of divine inspiration as the origin and centre of the natural world, and of a transcendent, spiritual significance to be found in nature, which evolution by natural selection entails. I will suggest that whereas the grotesque in Browning both encompasses the dialectical energy of the entangled bank and offers some consolation for the loss of a transcendent view of nature, Dadd's use of the grotesque is a reaction to the terrible costs of trying to contain the terror, the *horror vacui*, caused by the loss of the natural world as it is conceived by natural theology, ordered by the hidden hand of the divine designer and creator.

The first person to identify Robert Browning's poetry as grotesque was Walter Bagehot, in a review of Browning's *Dramatis Personae* and Tennyson's *Enoch Arden* (both published in 1864). Bagehot's review, titled 'Wordsworth, Tennyson and Browning: or Pure, Ornate and Grotesque Art in Poetry' (1864) used these terms to characterise and evaluate the qualities which, he argued, typified the poetry of these three writers. It has since become commonplace to call Browning's work grotesque, especially his representations of the natural world and its workings, though the word is generally used in a rather different sense to Bagehot's. Browning's grotesque is often thought of as made out of and representing a sense of the vital energy of the natural world.

'Sibrandus Schnafnaburgensis' (1842), an early example of Browning's grotesque manner, describes the decay of a dull, pedantic book abandoned in the garden to rot:

> How did he like it when the live creatures
>   Tickled and toused and browsed him all over,
> And worm, slug, eft, with serious features,
>   Came in, each one, for his right of trover?
> – When the water beetle with great blind deaf face
>   Made of her eggs the stately deposit,
> And the newt borrowed just so much of the preface
>   As tiled the top of his black wife's closet?
> All that life and fun and romping,
>   All that frisking and twisting and coupling,
> While slowly our friend's leaves were swamping
>   And clasps were cracking and covers suppling![75]

The insects invade the book, burrow into it, play in it, and make their homes out of its decay, so that instead of an inert leaching away of the book's substance, what is described is an active process of re-use and transformation. The verbs and participles, 'tickled and toused and browsed', 'frisking and twisting and coupling', draw attention to the natural processes at work, and to their energy. The deadly sterility of the book's contents gives way, via its decay, to the energetic otherness, the 'life and fun and romping' of the natural world. Commenting on this poem, Carol Christ remarks that 'Browning changes a lifeless, static object into a location of a crawling, vital conflux of life. Propelled by its peculiar energy, each creature tries to transform the book into its own environment. In the process, they change it from a closed, completed unit, to a continually evolving stage on which the natural elements act out their individual energies.'[76] She goes on to argue that in the 'vital conflux of life' which Browning's poems repeatedly represent, each particular element is engaged in struggle with the rest for its own place, both in the poem (hence the syntactical compression typical of Browning's work), and also in the environment. It is the struggle of these particulars for space in the poem and for existence in the world that constitutes the grotesque. 'In Browning ... the grotesque is a source of exuberance and vitality ... Browning attains his grotesque by his bizarre location of this energy.'[77]

Walter Bagehot defines the grotesque in relation to what he calls 'the type', which appears either 'pure', as in Wordsworth's poetry; ornamented, as in Tennyson; or distorted, as in Browning. The poetic grotesque

takes the type, so to say, *in difficulties*. It gives a representation of it in its minimum development, amid the circumstances least favourable to it, just while it is struggling with obstacles, just where it is encumbered with incongruities. It deals, to use the language of science, not with normal types but with abnormal specimens; to use the language of old philosophy, not with what nature is striving to be, but with what by some lapse she has become.[78]

Bagehot's 'type' is derived from the Aristotelian idea of the form, central to Aristotle's biology and influential in science at least until the seventeenth and early eighteenth centuries. The form for Aristotle is the *telos* of natural organisms, the thing which they become by maturing, and which they are becoming in every stage of development. Forms for Aristotle are ideas embodied in the material of each organism, so that they are compound of shape and substance, and are inherited directly and identically from father to son, thus constituting the eternal and intelligible nature of each species.[79] In the 'language of old philosophy', the type is the *telos*, 'what nature is striving to be', and what, under normal conditions, it will become. It is also, to use the 'language of science' (that is, of Linnaean classification), the normal specimen which runs true to the species, whose characteristics are clearly identifiable and identically inherited from generation to generation.[80] The grotesque, for Bagehot, is equally the organism in which 'by some lapse' the form has not been achieved, and an abnormal specimen which deviates from the true species, because in both cases a departure from the type constitutes a departure from the truth. As he goes on to say, the grotesque deviation 'shows you what ought to be by what ought not to be'; the grotesque is the individual which escapes definition, the imperfect 'not-species' which has departed from its true nature.[81]

Darwin's account of the evolution of species challenges the Linnaean conception which assumes that species are constant and distinct in number and form, fixed both in time and in relation to other species. Evolution undermines both kinds of fixity, because new forms appear and old ones vanish, and the new species appear as mutations from the old. Evolutionary theory, therefore, proposes a conception of the species in which life forms are fluid and can be described only for a particular moment, since chance mutation and the struggle for survival encourage not the stability of life forms but their continual change, increase and extinction. Whereas Linnaean classification envisages the species as a type which might 'get into difficulties', in Bagehot's words, *Origin of Species* replaces this with a conception of a natural world tending to diversity rather than homogeneity, in which life forms are fluid, mutable, unstable: as Bagehot puts it, 'struggling with obstacles, encumbered with incongruities'.

It is clear that in Bagehot's terms Darwin's evocation of the entangled bank would be an example of the grotesque. The entangled bank is a dialectical image, in which death, through change and chance, leads to life in endlessly new and different forms; it is the tangling together of the various plants and creatures in relations of mutual dependence and warfare that Darwin asks his reader to recognise as grand and wonderful, full of a strange beauty. But this is precisely the vision which appals Bagehot, for it envisages a world of types in struggle and contention, a world in which the type evolves, no longer delimited by fixed boundaries, but always in a process of change and adaptation. By implication, the horror of the grotesque lies for Bagehot in its tendency to imagine evolution, and the interconnectedness of struggle, death and life which it represents. The grotesque as formulated by Bagehot, then, is not simply a descriptive term. Because it relies on precisely those conceptions of the order and meaning of the natural world which Darwin's work exploded, it implies a response to Darwin's challenge to fundamental scientific and aesthetic conceptions of the natural world. And Bagehot's response, his desire for the purity, immutability and stillness of the type, is a reactionary one.

Bagehot's critique of Browning's work is that not only is it grotesque, but that it positively revels in a grotesque aesthetic. One of the poems from *Dramatis Personae* he singles out for greatest censure, 'Caliban Upon Setebos', is normally taken as a satire on the so-called 'primitive mind'.[82] Looked at in relation to Bagehot's criticism, however, it is clear that Browning's grotesque too implies a response to the Darwinian vision of nature; in this case, though, the representation of nature as a grotesque entangled bank is a much more positive response than Bagehot's, one which recognises the animating energy of Darwin's image.[83] At the same time, it imagines a way for the loss of the idea of a divinely ordered natural world, an idea which Darwin's work fatally undermined, to be made bearable. 'Caliban Upon Setebos' is a dramatic monologue in which Caliban (from *The Tempest*) speculates on the nature of his god, Setebos. Subtitled 'Natural Theology in the Island', it parodies William Paley's *Natural Theology* (1802), an immensely popular work whose appeal was dramatically diminished after the publication of *Origin of Species*. Paley argued that the wondrous adaptation of life forms to their habitats, and the marvellous workings of the natural world, were direct evidence of the designing hand of the creator. How else might the eye have come about, except through the infinite wisdom of God attending to the minutiae of retina, lens, iris, nerves and muscles to produce a perfect organ of vision? For Paley, the 'evident design and fitness' of the natural world is *prima facie* evidence of the existence and works of the deity, for 'it is only by the display of contrivance, that the existence, the agency, the wisdom of the Deity, *could* be testified to his rational creatures'.[84] This is the reasoning parodied in 'Caliban Upon Setebos'. But whereas Paley sees a harmonious and ordered natural world as the expression of the just and beneficent nature of God, Caliban sees a world of random cruelty and chance which, he reasons, mirrors the equally capricious nature of Setebos.

The opening of the poem, a description of Caliban, presents a reworking of the idea of the entangled bank:

> ['Will sprawl, now that the heat of the day is best,
> Flat on his belly in the pit's much mire,
> With elbows wide, fists clenched to prop his chin,
> And, while he kicks both feet in the cool slush,
> And feels about his spine small eft-things course,
> Run in and out each arm, and make him laugh,
> And while above his head a pompion-plant,
> Creeps down to tickle hair and beard,
> And now a flower drops with a bee inside,
> And now a fruit to snap and crunch.[85]

From inside the entanglement, as part of it even, Caliban speculates on the creation, attempting to deduce the nature of the creator from the natural world. However, as the opening lines suggest, and as at least one critic has argued, the natural world here is not susceptible to the kind of reasoning Paley employs precisely because it is conceived in Darwinian terms. 'Caliban, like Paley, engages in speculation about the characteristics of God based on appearances in nature. However, the nature which is the basis of these speculations is not Paley's world of rational design and order, but rather Darwin's world of random chance and the struggle for existence.'[86]

The reasoning of natural theology cannot hold in the Darwinian world, because it is ruled by chance and change, and because it is not underpinned by the idea of design. If applied, the reasoning of natural theology produces a capricious deity whose only order is chance, and whose actions and nature are merely a projection of Caliban's own. Yet Caliban's vision of natural processes from inside the entangled bank, 'eft-things' crawling over him and the 'pompion-plant' creeping down to tickle him, nevertheless does envision another kind of order in the natural world, despite his adherence to the fallacies of natural theology. Caliban, as it were in spite of his beliefs, perceives a dialectical order in nature. This is an order that foregrounds process and connection rather than distinction and fixity; an order in which random chances generate an energy which binds together life forms in a tangled relation. Instead of a static one-to-one correspondence between the world and God, what is represented here is a natural world which makes its own order out of the relations between life forms. Two passages from the poem will illustrate what I mean:

> Yon otter, sleek-wet, black, lithe as a leech;
> Yon auk, one fire-eye in a ball of foam,
> That floats and feeds; a certain badger brown
> He hath watched hunt with that slant white-wedge eye
> By moonlight; and the pie with the long tongue
> That pricks deep into oakworts for a worm,
> And says a plain word when she finds her prize,
> But will not eat the ants; the ants themselves
> That build a wall of seeds and settled stalks
> About their hole – He made all these and more,
> Made all we see, and us, in spite: how else?
> . . .
> Thinketh, such shows nor right nor wrong in Him.
> Nor kind nor cruel: he is strong and Lord.
> 'Am strong myself compared to yonder crabs

That march now from the mountain to the sea:
'Let twenty pass, and stone the twenty-first,
Loving not, hating not, just choosing so.
'Say, the first straggler that boasts purple spots
Shall join the file, one pincer twisted off;
'Say, this bruised fellow shall receive a worm,
And two worms he whose nippers end in red;
As it likes me each time, I do; so He'.[87]

The multiplicity of the natural world and its random chances are inextricably linked. The hunting, feeding and building of the first extract are inseparable from the chances of mutilation and reward in the second. To adapt Darwin's phrase, they are 'complexly dependent' upon each other. And there is no doubt that Caliban's vision from inside the bank is a grotesque one: the focus on detail in these passages, on distortion and incongruity (for example the otter 'lithe as a leech'), and on the otherness of the natural world, are all typical constituents of the grotesque.

In both these passages, while each description is made up of grotesque constituents, what links these elements together is a sense of an energetic process or relation. In the first passage, each example of a life form 'grows out' of the previous one, syntactically speaking, so that one clause, 'the pie with the long tongue' who 'will not eat the ants' forms the basis of the next clause, 'the ants themselves...' Activity and process, too, are continually forced to the attention of the reader, because the creatures described are characterised through their activities: the auk who 'floats and feeds', the badger hunting by moonlight, the pie that 'pricks deep into oakworts for a worm', the ants building their 'wall of seeds and settled stalks / About their hole'. In the second passage Caliban's sport with the crabs emphasises the relentlessness of the struggle for life. The 'straggler that boasts purple spots' must carry on with the 'march from the mountain to the sea', even with 'one pincer twisted off'; the 'bruised fellow' and 'he whose nippers end in red' with their worms receive their advantages only by chance, that is, by Caliban's capriciousness: there is no sense that the column of crabs will not march because Caliban stones or feeds them, merely that some will reach the sea sooner or later, more or less healthy, because of his random actions.

Bagehot's criticism of this poem implies a horror at the vision of a natural world animated by struggle and contingency which it represents, but the energy with which Browning invests this world suggests that it is not meant to provoke such an alarmed withdrawal on the part of the reader. The grotesque in Browning should be seen as a way of 'fulfilling, bodying forth, and replenishing what has seemed humdrum, inexplicable, or taken for granted': Gillian Beer's description of Darwin's writing in *Origin of Species* is equally applicable to 'Caliban Upon Setebos', for in it, through the grotesque aesthetic, Browning recasts in poetic form Darwin's vision of the natural world.[88] The entangled bank in this poem is the location not of fixed types, rational design and order, but of competing energies and evolving life forms, and, as such, Browning's grotesque might equally well be called a Darwinian grotesque: a grotesque which can embrace Darwin's claim that the entangled bank, rather than being a terrifying chaos, is instead full of wonder and meaning.

In the context of this idea of the natural world, the reasoning used by Caliban to deduce the nature of Setebos cannot hold. Jeff Karr argues that in this poem Browning does not envisage the impossibility of God, but rather the impossibility of an anthropomorphic conception of the world and of God in the wake of Darwin's work: it is simply impossible to imagine God through the contemplation of the world, because nature no longer has either man or reason at its centre.[89] But Browning also offers his readers a consolation for the loss of a beneficent deity and of a designed, harmonious natural world in which man is the dearest and most important of God's creations; these losses constituted the grievous blow which Darwin's work dealt the Victorians.[90] In the form of the dramatic monologue, in which Caliban speaks directly to the reader, while at the same time the reader 'speaks', or reads, in Caliban's voice, Browning offers a space for the loss of a divine designer and creator to be projected elsewhere. Significantly, this space is the 'primitive' and non-European; the reader can recognise as reassuringly familiar the reasoning which assumes a one-to-one correspondence between God and the world, and he can reject it as 'primitive'. If the world Darwin gave the Victorians was a random one, ruled by waste and chance, without progress and without design, 'Caliban Upon Setebos' assures its readers that, at the very least, though they might have to recognise the truth of that world, they did not have to conceive God in its image.

Browning's poem reimagines the natural world made wonderful by its energy and complex relations of dependency, and implicitly recognises that the conceptions of species and their relations formulated by 'old philosophy' and by 'science' cannot adequately explain them. In a sense, he turns round Bagehot's dictum that the grotesque 'enables you to see, makes you see, the perfect type by painting the opposite deviation. It shows you what ought to be by what ought not to be.'[91] 'Caliban Upon Setebos' makes the reader see that what is, is deviation, and that the perfect type is a consolatory fiction which supports an anthropocentric conception both of God and the natural world. Nevertheless, to imagine the natural world in such terms does indeed involve a grievous loss: of transcendent significance, of the sense of the supernatural animation of nature, and for many, mystery and enchantment. For some this loss created a terrifying vacuum in a nature from which all anthropocentric significance had been emptied out; a loss which was felt to be unbearable, and could be met only by putting the mystery and enchantment back into nature, but in another form. If one might no longer believe in the hand of the deity at work in the wondrous construction of every snail shell or convolvulus, it was still possible to imagine them the habitation of another, smaller kind of supernatural being. If man could no longer be thought of as an imperfect image of God, at the centre of a divinely ordered natural world, it might be a comfort to imagine the entangled bank, image of nature's new order, inhabited by supernatural beings a little like humans, a little unlike: fairies. Alternatively, one might take refuge in a cosmology which antedated the knowledge of nature which had caused such a loss, and thus refuse to recognise it. Both these responses shape the nature Richard Dadd imagined in *The Fairy Feller's Master-Stroke*, an attempt to picture a still-enchanted natural world which has not suffered the loss of an ordering supernatural presence, and which still manifests divine order and meaning. But because he represents the natural world as an entangled bank, Darwin's central image, what it comes to signify is the deathly sterility which is the cost of the disavowal of the entangled bank's dialectical, self-ordering, energetic relations. This is what constitutes the grotesque in Dadd's painting.

Dadd's interest in fairies was longstanding. He had exhibited several paintings of fairies, most notably *Titania Sleeping* and *Come Unto These Yellow Sands* (fig. 11), before his journey in 1843 to Egypt and the Near East, from which he returned mad, and following which he murdered his father, was found criminally insane, and confined first to Bethlem and then to Broadmoor hospitals.[92] It was an interest shared by many of his contemporaries, but Dadd's fairy paintings, and in particular *The Fairy Feller's Master-Stroke*, his most famous work, are among the best-known of the genre. *The Fairy Feller's Master-Stroke (quasi* 1855–64; fig. 24) is the second of only two paintings representing fairies made by Dadd after his committal to Bethlem, and it shares stylistic features with his *Contradiction: Oberon and Titania* (1854–8; Collection of Sir Andrew Lloyd-Webber).[93] However, though it is thought that Dadd worked on the two pictures simultaneously, the former occupied Dadd for much

Figure 24. Richard Dadd, *The Fairy Feller's Master-Stroke*.

Figure 25. Richard Dadd, *Songe de la Fantaisie*.

longer, despite remaining behind unfinished when he was transferred in
1864 from Bethlem to Broadmoor. Subsequently Dadd made a pencil
and watercolour version of the painting, *Songe de la Fantaisie* (1864; fig. 25),
and then wrote a poem called 'Elimination of a Picture and its Subject –
Called the Feller's Master-Stroke' (1865). The several versions of the

image suggest that he was in some way haunted by this subject, and that he returned to it until he could 'eliminate' it from his mind. Indeed, as it was his final picture of fairies, it is tempting to read the painting as Dadd's own 'master-stroke', particularly as he painted relatively little after his transfer to Broadmoor. The painting both represents and attempts to disavow this fascination; in the mad logic of the painting, the fairies come to figure a divine order in a natural world which resists relations of reproduction and inheritance at all cost.

Richard Dadd's case notes have been lost, and his madness is not now diagnosable as a specific mental disorder, but its two most important symptoms were beliefs that he was a descendant of the Ancient Egyptian god Osiris, and that he was persecuted by evil demons. Both of these are delusions typical of psychotic illness. In an account written for Dr Wood, the apothecary of Bethlem Hospital, he described his delusions and their consequences as follows:

On my return from travel, I was roused to a consideration of subjects which I had previously never dreamed of, or thought about, connected with self . . . My religious opinions varied and do vary from the vulgar; I was inclined to fall in with the views of the ancients, and to regard the substitution of modern ideas thereon as not for the better. These and the like, coupled with the idea of a descent from the Egyptian god Osiris, induced me to put a period to the existence of him whom I had always regarded as a parent, but whom the secret admonishings I had, counselled me was the author of the ruin of my race.[94]

Dadd conceived of his delusion as a conversion to the religion of Ancient Egypt and in particular to the cult of Osiris, to which he was introduced on his visits to the major Egyptian temples and through reading, on his return, Sir John Gardner Wilkinson's *Manners and Customs of the Ancient Egyptians* (1837). His reasoning was that the cult of Osiris was the original type of Judaic law and ceremonial: he wrote to David Roberts of his reading of Wilkinson, saying that 'Moses was a Priest at Heliopolis as also his brother Aaron and they were skilled in all the wisdom and learning of the Egyptians – and so they applied it to the Government of the People they led out of the Land of Egypt.' The religion of Osiris predated Judaism, and therefore had a claim to be its origin or type; moreover, the sophistication of the artefacts and buildings he had seen led him to question the veracity of the conventional dating of the Deluge. How could a people

so highly civilised and polished acquainted with Arts and Sciences to a degree that puts to shame our puerile notions of them and at so early a date in our

chronology as to make us laugh at the extreme youth which our modern antiquarians give to our Race – at any rate these Egyptians must have been a very
precocious and might[y] generation to have so soon after the general destruction
of the race, built such things as the Pyramids of Ghiza.[95]

In other words, Dadd appears to reject Christianity as the descendant
of an earlier and prior religion, a religion which was the faith of a
people whose works challenged the authority of the scriptural texts which
formed the founding account of the early history of the human race
and the creation of the world. As he comments, this revelation was 'so
terribly astounding ... that the call upon our Faith to believe in received
opinions is so great that I fear a great many will be found bankrupt in
that article'.[96] But this was not the only 'call upon our Faith' to which
Dadd was exposed. His father, Robert Dadd, was a sometime lecturer in
geology, and therefore must have been familiar with the controversy surrounding Lyell's *Principles of Geology*, which had argued that, instead of a
catastrophic deluge, the rock formations of the earth's crust were the result of infinitesimally slow processes over millions of years, thus implying
that the earth was much older than scriptural chronologies suggested.
Richard Dadd's marked interest in the forms and shapes of rocks, which
can be seen in many of his works, suggests the influence of his father's
geological interests. It is wholly possible that Dadd knew something, at
least at second hand, of Chambers's *Vestiges of the Natural History of Creation*
(1844), which managed to incorporate a developmental account of the
descent of species within a relatively orthodox theological framework
not incompatible with the anthropocentrism of natural theology:
'Man, then, considered zoologically, and without regard to the distinct
character assigned to him by theology, simply takes his place as the type
of all types of the animal kingdom, the true and unmistakable head of
the animated nature upon this earth.'[97] Central to Chambers's account
was the idea of the continuous variation in species through reproduction;
he argued, for example, that variation was frequently caused by foetal
monstrosities, and recognised the parallels between the stages of
development of the human embryo and the succession of categories
(fish, amphibian, reptile, bird, mammal) in the fossil record.

What links the content of Dadd's delusions with such 'calls upon our
faith' is the way in which all these ideas, whether originating in archaeology, geology or natural history, call into question notions of origins,
priority, inheritance and reproduction. Whether literally or symbolically,
each of these discourses substitute ideas of mutation, obscure or natural
origin, reversed priority and inheritance from lower to higher forms for

the 'received ideas' concerning these things. Dadd's madness, then, can be interpreted as at least partially culturally determined: his delusions assert a rejection of descendants and a claim for the priority of their origins. He rejected the religion of the son because it was the descendant of a religion of the sun-father, and he murdered his father in order to erase the traces of his own descent and inheritance. As the descendant of Osiris, Richard Dadd had not inherited the form, or soul, of the human being, which had been passed down through generations, but believed himself generated by a fresh act of supernatural creation. His psychosis, then, was intimately related to contemporary ideas about development, time and history which Darwin's formulation of evolution by natural selection drew upon. Dadd may not have read Darwin's work; nevertheless, *Origin of Species* and Dadd's psychotic delusions emerged from the same entangled cultural context.

This is significant for an understanding of *The Fairy Feller's Master-Stroke* because it enables the painting to be seen as engaging with contemporary anxieties about science, nature and the supernatural, rather than as merely the isolated if extraordinary work of a madman produced in entire seclusion.[98] Probably coincidentally, Dadd's representation of the natural world uses the entangled bank which is also Darwin's image; but in this entangled bank the relations of inheritance and reproduction which make up the dialectic of life and death are denied. What is represented here, in an attempt to assert a unique supernatural creation, is an entangled bank in which order has become alienation, generation sterility, and the processes of life have turned to death.

The Fairy Feller's Master-Stroke is an extreme example of the fragmentation of perspective characteristic of Pre-Raphaelite landscape painting. The surface of the painting is so densely packed with detail that it is almost impenetrable, and this impenetrability is intensified by the extremely compressed perspective, which appears both vertical and horizontal at once. On the one hand, the figures seem to be standing on a series of 'shelves' perpendicular to the picture plane, ending in the outcrop of rock in the top left-hand corner; on the other hand, there is no actual sign of such shelves, and the figures, when examined closely, appear to be on a parallel plane that recedes both backwards and upwards. This perspectival conundrum becomes even more puzzling when one realises that the buff-coloured ground at the bottom of the picture, which gives the impression of a 'floor' from which the composition 'rises', is in fact an unfinished area.[99] Were the painting finished, there would be no areas of differentiation in detail, tone, colour or size to signify near or far, up or down, here or there. The overall effect is of a paradoxical recession which appears to come nearer the spectator, as if the perspective has been turned round and the figures are going to topple out of the painting, except that they are 'held in' by the stalks of timothy-grass and hawkbit stretched like bars across the surface plane from left to right, so heavily painted that they stand out like an enamelled relief. These bars contain the scene: in fact, they do more, they imprison it.

In *Songe de la Fantaisie* the surface of the image is even more impenetrable, the figures are barely distinguishable from the background, and the bar-like stalks have become even more important, swirling and spiralling across the surface and virtually obscuring the figures. These swirls are also referred to in 'An Elimination of a Picture and its Subject ...'

> Turn to the Patriarch and behold
> Long pendants from his crown are rolled
> In winding figures circle round
> The grass and such upon the mound,
> They represent vagary wild
> And mental aberration styled.
> Now unto Nature clinging close
> Now wildly out again they toss,
> Like a cyclone uncontroll'd
> Sweeping round with chance-born fold
> Unto the picture bring a grace
> Which else were wanting from its face
> But tied at length unto a stem
> Shows or should do ad finitem rem —[100]

Such obscuring diagonals can be found elsewhere in Dadd's work produced during his years in Bethlem, for example in *Crazy Jane* (1855; Beckenham: Royal Bethlem and Maudesley Hospital), which illustrates a ballad in which a woman is deserted by her lover, and which is organised around a diagonal branch to which the figure clings; in *Sketch to Illustrate the Passions: Grief, or Sorrow* (1854; Beckenham: Royal Bethlem and Maudesley Hospital), which depicts an overgrown tomb crossed by diagonal branches; and in *Bacchanalian Scene* (1862; Private Collection), which has grasses crossing the painting downwards from right to left. Each of these pictures in different ways connotes loss of reason, whether through the depiction of madness, abandonment to the senses or mourning, and this correlates with Dadd's statement that the diagonals and spirals 'represent vagary wild / And mental aberration styled.' But in *The Fairy Feller's Master-Stroke* and *Songe de la Fantaisie* they are also 'tied at length unto a stem / [which] Shows or should do ad finitem rem'; that is, the tying together of the diagonals which represent Dadd's own madness is an attempt to contain it 'ad finitem rem', to the end of things. As my discussion of *The Fairy Feller's Master-Stroke* will show, such containment 'ad finitem rem' has deathly consequences.

The narrative of the picture, such as it is, is organised around the 'stroke' the Fairy Feller is poised to make, a blow that will cleave the nut in two. The nut is an obvious metaphor for fertility, one of a number with which the image is littered: the dandelion heads, plane-tree fruits and flowers are others. To cleave the nut would mean that it could never germinate, because the kernel would be shattered by the blow, but the moment of destruction is potential rather than actual. The deadly master-stroke is forever poised to fall. Around this arrested climactic moment, the fairies are gathered, seemingly attentive to the action, yet also uninvolved in it. And looking closely at the figures, one notices that only the few at the bottom of the picture are actually watching the Feller and the nut. The rest seem uninvolved either with this action or with each other. For example, the row of figures on the top 'shelf', the soldier, apothecary, farmer, tailor and so on, are, though grouped together, separate. They neither act, for there is no narrative to this part of the picture, nor interact, since they do not even look at each other. Similarly, the group of figures around the 'Patriarch' (the term comes from Dadd's poem) wearing the enormous hat in the centre of the painting seem to have little relation to one another. This lack of narrative is reinforced by 'An Elimination of a Picture and its Subject . . . ', which devotes most of its 600 lines to describing in detail each one of these figures without making any link, narrative or otherwise, between them. The image is crowded but static, and its stasis is due not only to the moment of arrest it depicts, but also to the fact that its crowd of figures, disposed around the picture seemingly at random, have no relation to each other.

Interspersed with the fairy figures are fragments of nature: the grasses, dandelion clocks, leaves, nuts and a grasshopper, almost hidden between the soldier and a fairy blowing a horn. Looking at these details, the variations of scale, already apparent in the fairies' sizes, become very marked. All these things are out of proportion to one another, so that it is impossible to tell which are enlarged or reduced. Which are the proper size: the daisies, grass and the Feller; or the nuts, grasshopper and Patriarch; or the leaves, dandelion clocks and apothecary; or all three? It is impossible to tell what should be the scale marker for the picture, since in the bewildering confusion of scales and sizes there is no perspective to give the spectator an idea of what the 'right size' should be. It appears, then, that the scene is one in which all kinds of relation, whether narrative, perspectival, of scale or of dimension, have ceased to hold, so that each separate object or figure, whether natural or supernatural, is entirely discrete. In addition, the fulcrum of the picture, the fairy feller's axe, is unfinished. This image, which seems composed of unrelated fragments distorted into an impossible perspective, has a literal blank space right at its centre.

The Fairy Feller's Master-Stroke is another version of the entangled bank of which Darwin wrote. But while Darwin's and Browning's entangled banks are full of life and of the various forms of life in relations of complex dependence upon one another, Dadd's entangled bank is marked by a lack of relation so extreme as to be alienation. It is as if, looking at the natural world, Dadd saw not process but stasis, not the dialectical relation of struggle, contingency, death and reproduction but a deathly stillness. The about-to-be-cloven nut, the unnaturally open daisies, the absurdly pointed breasts and huge calves of the female fairies, which should be signs of fertility, signify not reproduction but sterility. Even the narrative of the picture, its principle of binding and coherence, is, ultimately, reduced to a blank. And in the top row of figures, Dadd painted a portrait of his murdered father, the apothecary, half-hidden and looking over his shoulder, a reminder of his own disavowal of the processes of reproduction and inheritance. The grotesqueness of this picture, most apparent in the female figures, but equally present in the distortions of scale, the clarity of detail, and above all in the 'unnatural' juxtaposing of unrelated figures, plants and insects, is of a wholly different cast to the energetic 'Darwinian' grotesque of 'Caliban upon Setebos'. Dadd presents a sterile grotesque, the principle of which is stasis and alienation rather than a dialectic of life and death, struggle and reproduction. 'It shows or should do', in Dadd's words, 'ad finitem rem', the end rather than the beginning of things.

In some ways the confusion of perspective and scale, the frustration of the narrative, and the juxtaposing of natural and supernatural creatures recalls the image with which Paley begins *Natural Theology*: a heath on which a watch is found lying. Gillian Beer comments of this image that

The scene is, uneasily, both physical and provisional: its scale is unstable, moving rapidly between generality and articulated detail. It is at once authoritative and close to the absurd. Its project is to dramatise absurdity and misappropriated evidence, to rouse resistance, and then to satisfy our sense of congruity so that we accept as much – and more than – his analogy can imply. The process is like that of a riddle – the yoking of unlike objects, the unlocking of shared signification – and like a riddle it gratifies and disappoints . . . Both the bravura and the common sense are important in the learning process created by analogy: the abrupt shifts of scale and the fickle movements between concepts and objects set it always on the edge of fantasy, though claiming for itself a more than metaphorical status, a real presence in the natural order.[101]

The analogical purpose of Paley's image, to introduce the idea of design and purposiveness in the natural world, makes the image riddling and takes it to the 'edge of fantasy'. Beer's description of the process of analogy in Paley seems uncannily close to the 'shifts of scale and the fickle movements between concepts and objects' in Dadd's painting. However, in Paley the riddling, fantastic nature of analogy is transformative. As Beer points out, the analogy of the watch on the heath for the presence in nature of God the designer requires a transformation of 'the homely into the transcendent' like that of bread and wine into body and blood. Analogy is merely a way of figuring the real order and meaning in the natural world.

In *The Fairy Feller's Master-Stroke* the hierarchical figure of analogy is, as it were, compressed into one level. The designed order of the natural world, directly inherited from creation, is what Paley's analogy figures. His theology and his natural history and his figurative representation of them both depend upon clearly understood notions of inheritance, priority and equivalence – precisely the things which Dadd rejected as false or corrupted. Though Dadd's image looks as if it should be an analogy for the order of the natural world, it is in fact a psychotic, literal representation of it. Instead of the hidden hand of God lying behind the analogical riddle of the watch, as it does for Paley, in Dadd's painting the fairies represent the supernatural act of creation present in the scene. If Dadd rejected the distant origins of the natural and human worlds in geology, natural history and archaeology, he rejected equally the stories of a divine creation which those disciplines undermined. For Dadd, the natural and human worlds were created afresh in each generation, either by Osiris, or by the fairies. The fairies in this picture, then, represent the work of creation from nothing by supernatural power. The fairy feller does not need to split the nut, since the nut can have no meaning and purpose in this natural world which is entirely without sexual reproduction and generation, a natural world where the only creation is supernatural. The fairy feller is poised to split the nut because in the entangled bank inhabited by fairies, it is the fairies' supernatural power which supplies order and meaning. Dadd himself hints at this

in an extremely obscure passage from 'An Elimination of a Picture...'
which describes the feller's purpose in splitting the nut:

> The meaning thus, let's find –
> For idle pastime hither led
> Fays, gnomes, and elves and suchlike fled
> To fix some dubious point to fairies only
>   Known to exist, or to the lonely
> Thoughtful man recluse
>   Of power a potent spell to loose
> Which binds the better slave to worse
> Swindles soul, body, goods and purse
> T'unlock the secret cells of dark abyss
> The power which never doth its victims miss
> But may e[n]gorge when truth appears
> When fail or guns or swords or spears
> For some such end we may suppose
> They've met since day hath made its close
> Night's noon time haply extra bright
>   By fairie power made all so alight
> Doubtful if night or day might reign
>   To certain be in mind revolve again
> And say that common nature is not true.[102]

Like the whole of the poem, these lines are difficult to interpret, but the
implication here seems to be that 'fairie power' has something to do with
the reversal of the natural order, that it makes 'common nature ... not
true', and that this reversal has something to do with the way in which life
forms are bound together, 'Which binds the better slave to worse', and
in which their forms or natures are transmitted through the generations,
'T'unlock the secret cells of dark abyss / The power which never doth its
victims miss'. It seems from this passage that the idea of the fairy world,
filled with unnatural powers, in which common nature is untrue, and
in which the secrets of cells are unlocked, is horrible or frightening for
Dadd, and that the mystery of the fairies' purposes, which are known
to only themselves and him, 'the lonely / Thoughtful man recluse', is a
burden rather than an enlightenment. There is no doubt that Dadd's
psychosis, in part a response to a world from which stability, order and
meaning had been torn, gave him back the vision of a world in which
order and meaning were themselves terrifying.

Dadd concludes his poem, 'For nought as nothing it explains / And
nothing from nothing nothing gains.'[103] The reference to Shakespeare's
King Lear is unmistakable. Lear's words to Cordelia, 'Nothing will come

of nothing', are the thematic centre of a play concerned with inheritance, legitimacy and relationships between fathers and children.[104] It is possible that the bearded 'Patriarch' at the centre of the painting may be associated with Lear and the cross-eyed figure sitting at his knee with the Fool. Despite the play's tragic ending, in the last act Lear recognises his daughter, and Edgar is reinstated as Gloucester's legitimate son: the bonds of kinship and inheritance hold, finally. But in Richard Dadd's insane and terrifying vision, 'Lear' and his fool look impotently out at the viewer between the stems of grass which imprison the sterile world of the picture where, indeed, nothing will procreate and nothing will come of it.

Dadd's static grotesque is not 'Paleyite', since it refuses the hierarchies of meaning which suffuse Paley's natural world with beneficent divine purpose. It is, rather, 'Darwinian': not because it represents Darwin's entangled bank through a grotesque aesthetic, as Browning does, but because, like Darwin, Dadd rejects modes of representing the natural world which see its hidden order as metaphysical. For Darwin, the order of the entangled bank, though hidden, is material; it is the dialectical order of generation, struggle, death and life figured in the tangling together of life forms. For Dadd, since natural and supernatural exist in the same literal way, there can be no hidden order to the entangled bank; creation and creator, natural and supernatural are equally present within an enchanted world in which there is no distinction between them. But the cost of this vision, and the reason why it is grotesque, is that it is unable to admit the processes of life. It is stuck in a timeless and deathly moment of the arrested, continuous present in which, because there is no past, there can be no future.

Dadd's repeated return to the entangled bank in the various versions of *The Fairy Feller's Master-Stroke* bears witness to his horror at the image and his struggle to contain it. By imprisoning the bank within its swirls and bars, by pinning it down under its obsessively detailed surface, he attempted to control the force and vitality of the entangled bank. But the incongruities of form and scale, the incoherence of perspective, and the impotence of the narrative show how this attempt at control produces the distortion typical of the grotesque: the type, as it were, *in extremis*. *The Fairy Feller's Master-Stroke* is a deeply disturbing image because what it represents is the price of disavowal. It offers a deathly vision of the natural world in which the 'lifely' dialectical connection between life and death is arrested, in order to contain the terror of the randomness and contingency which are central to Darwin's account of evolution, and the tainted inheritance from father to son which is implied by evolution, by history, by archaeology and by geology. Whereas Browning's and Darwin's natural worlds teem with life and death, Dadd's is stuck in a moment of deathly stillness. In order to hold off the terror of the 'war of nature . . . famine and death' which produces the 'forms most beautiful and wonderful [which] have been, and are being, evolved', *The Fairy Feller's Master-Stroke* represents a natural world in which no evolution, no birth, no death, no future can take place, because relations of dependence and reproduction, struggle and chance, that is, the processes of life, are themselves disavowed.

Darwin asked his reader to recognise the entangled bank as wondrous and beautiful, but perhaps that was not possible for his contemporaries, in view of the shockingly new vision of the natural world it embodied. Browning's response, as Bagehot's criticism implies, was to frame the entangled bank as grotesque, and in this way to give expression to the wonderful, dialectical energy of the image. For Dadd, however, the grotesque became a way of taming and holding still the energies of nature, of insisting that nothing in nature has changed, and that nothing can change. It is because the dialectic of the entangled bank cannot be tolerated in this painting that its action is arrested and forms of relation are reduced in it to an alienated sterility and stasis. But the cost of this is a nothingness, from which nothing can come, as Dadd himself admits. If one refuses the lifely dialectic of the entangled bank, if one recoils in fear and horror, if one refuses to recognise loss, then nature, as in Richard Dadd's vision, stops dead.

CHAPTER 4

A broken heart and a pocket full of ashes

The fairies have been leaving since time immemorial. They had gone by the end of the fourteenth century, for Chaucer's Wife of Bath speaks of their departure; then Richard Corbet bade them farewell in the sixteenth century; they were again said to have disappeared in the late eighteenth century.[1] The departure of the fairies is a tradition in itself, a genre of lament for the passage of time and the loss of innocence. Fairies always belong to yesterday, because today's world is corrupt, sophisticated, urbane and disenchanted. The repeated elegy for their departure bespeaks a recurrent sense of the erosion of tradition by the demands of the present and the pressure of the future. The fairies leave at times of change and trouble when the stable order of society is pulled into a new shape, when new beliefs shake older faiths or when people leave the countryside and head for towns and cities: when the present pulls away from the past and people become conscious of the rapid pace of social change.

At the end of the nineteenth century and the beginning of the twentieth the refrain of the fairies' farewell was taken up again, but this time the tale of their departure was told differently. The burden of 'The Last Fairy' (1889) by Rosamund Marriott Watson is the melancholy emptiness of a world without fairies:

Under the yellow moon, when the young men and maidens pass in the lanes,
Outcast I flit, looking down through the leaves of the elm trees,
Peering out over the fields as their voices grow fainter;
Furtive and lone
Sometimes I steal through the green rushes down by the river,
Hearing the shrill laughter and song while the rosy-limbed bathers
Gleam in the dusk.
Seen, they would pass me disdainful, or stone me unwitting;
No room is left in their hearts for my kinsfolk or me.
Fain would I, too, fading out like a moth in the twilight,

Follow my kin,
Whither I know not, and ever I seek but find not –
Whither I know not, nor knoweth the wandering swallow;
'Where are they, where?'
Of-times I cry; but I hearken in vain for their footsteps,
Always in vain.
High in a last year's nest, in the boughs of a pine-tree,
Musing I sit, looking up to the deeps of the sky,
Clasping my knees as I watch there and wonder, forsaken;
Ever the hollow sky
Voiceless and vast, and the golden moon silently sailing,
Look on my pain and they care not
There is none that remembers . . .
O for the summons to sound! For the pipes plaining shrilly,
Calling me home![2]

In contrast to earlier versions of the departure of the fairies, where the tale is told by a witness, often at second or third hand, here the last fairy tells his own story, and the departure of the fairies is not even noticed by humans. Indeed, humans have utterly forgotten the fairies' existence. The last fairy is bereft in an uncaring universe because no-one remembers him; humans have become wholly engrossed in the present. Only the fairy remembers, for he is a remnant of a past to which he is the sole witness. The poem is infused with a melancholy sense that the past is about to slip away into oblivion without anyone noticing. Like the fairies, the past no longer exists for those who do not remember.

In her essay 'Origins and Oblivion in Victorian Narrative', Gillian Beer has drawn attention to some of the effects on the idea of memory of geology and evolutionary science. Their emphasis on the vast elongation of time, the incomplete and fragmentary record of the past, and the impossibility of recoverable origins marked Victorian culture with an anxiety about clues, decipherment, solutions and remembering. The past could no longer be encompassed, because its extent had become almost unimaginable, filled with deaths which are utterly forgotten. It is for this reason that the effort to remember and to recover at any cost what might be retrieved from the past found a cultural expression in literary forms such as detective fiction:

'The mind cannot grasp' what has been forgotten. The world is always full. Memory fills up the extent of life available to it and makes us forget what lies beyond . . . Through geology, prehistory, the extension of the past, the insistence in evolutionary ideas on change and loss of nameable origins, the forgetting and deforming of meaning in language, the debilitating of memory as an agent of transformation and control in Darwinian theory – through all these factors, together with a common insistence on growth, the Victorians were made to be aware of how much was irretrievably forgotten, and to set great store by those signs and traces, those acts of decipherment that relieved oblivion and reconstituted themselves as origins.[3]

The distant past overwhelmed the Victorians with the threat of oblivion (though their growing interest in pre-historic archaeology testifies to their anxiety about their distant origins in unremembered time).[4] The distant past was for the Victorians, conscious as they were of the length of time and the fallibility of memory, a source both of excitement and curiosity and intense sadness and regret. As Francis Palgrave put it so poignantly: '. . . we must give it up, the speechless past; whether fact or chronology, doctrine or mythology; whether in Europe, Asia, Africa or America; at Thebes or Palenque, on Lycian shore or Salisbury Plain; lost is lost; gone is gone forever'.[5] But the same was equally true of the recent past: it, too, was fading into forgetfulness, particularly those aspects of it which were threatened by modernity. The enchanted realm of the fairies faded before the advance of modernity, which overtook superstition with rational explanation and vanquished legend with news of the outside world. For the Victorians the fairy was an enchanting figure because it represented an escape from unbearable aspects of the present into a magical past almost, but not quite, beyond living memory. When the fairies bade farewell at the end of the century, they receded entirely into the past and became a metaphor for the evanescence of memory.

Folklore is an attempt to preserve the past as it is embodied in legend and tradition before it is extinguished by forgetfulness. In the second half of the nineteenth century anthropology, archaeology, geology and biology were all characterised by the attempt to reach back imaginatively into the distant past. The corollary of this endeavour was that of folklorists to record the more recent past lest it, too, be lost because legend and tradition are unwritten, embodied only in living memory. It is not surprising that towards the end of the nineteenth century folklore solidified into a discipline, with the foundation in 1878 of the Folk-Lore Society and its journal, the *Folk-Lore Record*. But, to the Victorians, understanding fairy legends could also unlock the distant past. As Carole Silver has shown, a heated and extensive debate was conducted by folklorists over theories of the origins of fairy belief.[6] The contending theories all reached back before written history: into the lost, unwritten past which might be partially reconstructed only through the fragmentary archaeological record or through studying its 'survivals' in legends and superstitions.[7]

For folklore theorists, the distant past and the origins of modern society could be recovered by reconstructing them from the distorted versions embodied in fairy legends. Theories of fairy origins postulated that fairies were the faint and fading memories of aboriginal conquered races, or invaders with metal-working skills, or the ancestors of the original inhabitants of Britain. For David MacCulloch, for instance, in *The Childhood of Fiction* (1905), 'the originals of the fairies were the ancient and modern "savages" and folktales were a direct reflection of their ideas, beliefs and customs', while for the anthropologist A. C. Haddon, fairy tales 'were stories told by men of the Iron Age of events which happened to men of the Bronze Age in their conflicts with men of the Neolithic Age'.[8]

The idea that legends of the fairies represented a story of origins or a version of history in disguised form connects the fairy with the desire to remember and decipher which Beer describes. The stories of the fairies and their exploits embodied a form of memory stretching back into the otherwise unremembered past, and the study of fairies became a way of recovering that distant time and of discovering in it the Victorians' own origins. That is why, as Silver shows, folklore theorists placed such great stress on the racial and national make-up of the fairies' originals.[9] It also helps to explain the attraction of fairy lore for Celtic nationalists and revivalists such as W. B. Yeats, Æ (George William Russell), James Stephens and Fiona Macleod (William Sharp). Most of these writers were especially interested in Irish legends of the Sidhe, part of the pagan mythology of ancient Ireland, which were also illustrated by the Scottish painter John Duncan in *Riders of the Sidhe* (1911; Dundee Art Gallery and Museum). But the myth of the fairy did not relate only to the prehistoric past. As folklorists repeatedly recorded, belief in the fairies had only lately died out, and they linked its extinction to the dissolution of the sense of locality and tradition preserved in rural communities: the world in which each village had its own fairies and each fairy had its own name and nature. This was the past from which modernity had so recently emerged, and the fairy symbolises this less remote past equally as much as, and perhaps more than, it does the Bronze or Neolithic Ages.

In contrast to modern, and particularly urban and metropolitan society, marked by anonymity, dislocation and alienation, the society in which fairies were a living tradition was one bound by community, stable and unchanging. It is this unchangingness that makes tradition possible. For modernity, the past is cut loose from the present, and not only does it stretch back further than memory, it is too vast and various to be embodied in the 'living memory' of legend. What folklore seeks to record is a past which was itself not subject to time, because it is constantly recreated in the stories and beliefs of legend. The time of myth and legend is not chronological; events do not happen in this year or that, but 'once upon a time'. It is this perhaps real and perhaps imaginary past that the fairy represents. And the fairy stands both for the past modernity has lost, and for what that loss means to modernity.

It is because the modern world in which they lived and which they had made was anonymous, uncertain and disenchanted that the Victorians dreamed of fairies, whose enchanted world gave back the things which they seemed to have lost. The idea of the fairies' farewell acquired such poignancy at the end of the century because it represented an anxiety that the condition of being modern was now so acute that no possibility of enchantment could offer consolation for it. If we forget the fairies, thought the Victorians, they will die, and then there will be no magic left in the world; representations of the last fairy and the fairies' farewell warn against such a forgetting, and remind of the necessity of looking backwards in order not to be swallowed up by the future.

This is the message of G. K. Chesterton's poem 'Modern Elfland' (1900), in which he uses the motif of the fairy to warn that modernity has extinguished the last gleams of magic in the world, and reduced human life to mere materiality. In his introduction to *The Magic Casement: An Anthology of Fairy Poetry* (1908), Alfred Noyes singles out this poem as making 'something like a definite "criticism of life". . . an attempt to draw magic from its natural source, the real world around us, and to shatter our materialism at one blow'. To evoke 'that golden time when the earth appeared "an insubstantial faery place" and a fit home for song' is inevitably to reject the modernity of the modern world and to recall the world of the past as a world of enchantment.[10]

> I cut a staff in a churchyard copse,
>   I clad my-self in ragged things,
> I set a feather in my cap
>   That fell out of an angel's wings.
>
> I filled my wallet with three white stones,
>   I took three foxgloves in my hand,
> I slung my shoes across my back,
>   And so I went to fairyland.

But lo, within that ancient place
    Science had reared her iron crown,
And the great cloud of steam went up
    That telleth where she takes a town.

But cowled with smoke and starred with lamps
    That strange land's light was still its own;
The word that witched the woods and hills
    Spoke in the iron and the stone.

Not Nature's hand had ever curved
    That mute unearthly porter's spine,
Like sleeping dragon's sullen eyes
    The signals leered along the line.

The chimneys thronging crooked or straight
    Were fingers signalling the sky;
The dog that strayed across the street
    Seemed four-legged by monstrosity.

'In vain,' I cried, 'though you too touch
    The new time's desecrating hand,
Through all the noises of a town
    I hear the heart of fairyland.'

I read the name above a door,
    Then through my spirit pealed and passed:
This is the town of thy own home
    And thou hast looked on it at last.[11]

The impulse to discover a fairyland underneath the deformity of modern life is a form of the wish to return to a past that seems utterly to have vanished. By depicting fairyland as the true and beautiful reality covered over and despoiled by modernity, the poem voices a desire that the past be somehow immanent in the present and that the enchanted world be not utterly forgotten by modernity. The angel's feather, three white stones and three foxgloves the speaker picks up are both natural and magic tokens, and are counterposed to the powers of science which lend a demonic aspect to the productions of industrialisation: 'Like sleeping dragon's sullen eyes / The signals leered along the line.' Yet even amidst the monstrous modern town, the speaker hears 'the heart of fairyland', because the enchanted world is our native country, 'thy own home', from which we are separated by modernity.

Fairies reappear in 'The Ethics of Elfland' from Chesterton's *Orthodoxy* (1909). In this essay Chesterton attacks the idealist metaphysics which then dominated English philosophy, especially philosophy of science. He uses the magic powers which operate in fairy tales as a counter-argument to expose the flaws of inductive reasoning, central to the conception of scientific laws such as evolution or thermodynamics. Chesterton sees as deadly and mechanistic the conception of a universe in which there is no agency, no order or existence except in the minds of humans; he argues for a realist, Christian metaphysics in which the universe is directly animated by God: 'The only words that ever satisfied me as describing Nature are the terms used in fairy books, "charm," "spell," "enchantment." They express the arbitrariness of the fact and its mystery. A tree grows fruit because it is a *magic* tree. Water runs downhill because it is bewitched.'[12] This is part of the book's polemical argument that the effects of modernity can be reversed, but only by a return to a wonder at the world which Enlightenment rationality and modern life have stripped away: 'We need so to view the world as to combine an idea of wonder and an idea of welcome. We need to be happy in this wonderland without being once merely comfortable.'[13] Chesterton looks forward by looking backwards; his call for a re-enchanted world is part of his wider conviction that the crisis of modernity might be healed only through a return to tradition.[14]

Chesterton, however, was unusual in the polemical, forward-looking uses to which he put the figure of the fairy. For most writers of the period, fairyland is a nostalgic idea, and their use of fairies and fairyland in their writings is as an imaginative escape from an intolerable present into the past. The recurring motifs of the last fairy and the fairies' farewell in poetry of this period are, for the most part, saturated with this nostalgia. Alfred Noyes turns the idea into an attack on Modernism in 'The Elfin Artist', the title poem of a collection published in 1920. The speaker comes across a fairy painting a picture deep in the forest away from human affairs, and watches as he depicts nature heightened into magic:

> For he painted the things that matter,
>   The tints that we all pass by,
> Like the little blue wreaths of incense
>   That the wild thyme breathes to the sky;
> Or the first white bud of the hawthorn,
>   And the light in a blackbird's eye.[15]

The implication here is that most of us do pass by the 'things that matter', that we are unable to see the transfigured world the fairy depicts on his magical canvas. The 'elfin artist' paints what most of us no longer have the ability or desire to see, and only the speaker of the poem (clearly Noyes himself) can bear witness to the remaining magic in the world by describing the process in the poem. As his praise for Chesterton suggests, Noyes was a social and aesthetic conservative: later in his life he too became a Catholic. In his essays on poetry Noyes largely ignores Modern poetry in favour of work, like his own, which espouses traditional forms and a late romantic aesthetic inherited directly from Tennyson and Swinburne. Yet he clearly realises such poetry is embattled; he admits as much in recounting an anecdote in which 'a very beautiful book of poems was once dismissed by the contemptuous ejaculation of a single word, "fairies!"'[16] In this context, it seems clear that 'The Elfin Artist' is an aesthetic manifesto, a call for the rejection of Modernism and a return to the poetic values of the past.

More often, however, the past which writers wish to return to is a more personal one, and the leaving of the fairies symbolises ageing and the gradual drawing away of childhood. One of many variations on this theme is 'The Fairies' Valediction' by Rosamund Marriott Watson (1889):

> Hear them cry 'Goodnight! Goodbye!'
> Piping voices sweet and shrill
> Pierce the dusk from hill to hill.
> 'We are weary of you all,
> High and humble, great and small.
> Mortal anguish, mortal rage,
> We will never more assuage;
> Mortal pleasures, mortal pain,
> Never will behold again.'[17]

Human mortality has caused the fairies' passing, for they regret the 'withered lips and faded eyes' dulled by time, which will 'never more behold / Moonlight magic, elfin gold'. The fairies still exist, but humans can no longer see them, our eyes clouded by age and the approach of death. To rue the disappearance of the fairies is the same thing as to regret the inevitable process of ageing, for we can no sooner hear the fairies' song than we can recapture our youth. Nostalgia for the time of the fairies is the longing for the time of our own pasts.

This is also the theme of 'Martha' from Walter de la Mare's collection *The Listeners* (1912), in which the speaker remembers a storyteller from his childhood:

'Once . . . once upon a time . . . '
  Like a dream you dream in the night,
Fairies and gnomes stole out
  In the leaf-green light.

  . . .

All fordone and forgot;
  And like clouds in the height of the sky,
Our hearts stood still in the hush
  Of an age gone by.[18]

The phrase 'once upon a time' evokes both the storyteller and the magic spell of the tale which conjured up the fairies. Martha belongs to the 'age gone by' when such enchantments were possible, the 'fordone and forgot' years of childhood which, like dreams and fairies, are full of sadness because they are only memories.

The idea that in growing old people lose the ability to see the fairies acquired enormous power in this period. At the turn of the century fairies made a return to the stage in a new genre: the 'fairy play'. Though some, like *The Fairy Maiden, or Thomas the Rhymer* (1907) and Maurice Maeterlinck's *The Blue Bird* (1909), were adult plays, many others were aimed at children, and often included music, dance and the effects typical of the spectacular theatre. One of the more successful was *Pinkie and the Fairies* by Walford Graham Robertson, first produced in 1909. Robertson's aim was to turn the imaginative life of the child into a dramatic spectacle, and to present, for children, a child's view of the world. Yet, as he records in his memoirs, throughout the play's highly successful run the theatre was full of soldiers, who came to the theatre to cry:

Apparently, what they found most devastating was the close of the second Act, when the children's dream ends the vision of Fairyland slowly fades, the lights twinkling out, the music dying away, until all is darkness and silence save for the murmur of the stream among the shadows. And, in the darkness Aldershot sat weeping for its lost Fairyland, and the lights went up upon rows of bedewed shirt-fronts.[19]

The fairyland that the soldiers have lost is childhood: they come to the theatre to have childhood restored to them and then to see it vanish again. Robertson claimed the play was the elaboration of an illusion staged for a child's birthday treat in which fairies 'appeared' at dusk in a nearby wood and 'vanished' as night fell. But it was adults who wished to be reassured that the 'gate to fairyland' was still open, as he

himself realised, for the words which moved 'Aldershot' so were 'Once
to Fairyland you found your way, dears; / Once upon a time.'[20] 'Once
upon a time' the soldiers were children; in that lost golden age they
might have found their way to fairyland. Such nostalgic visions of the
lost fairyland of childhood are intended to be pleasurable. The soldiers,
Robertson implies, wallow in their tears; they visit the theatre in order to
see the loss of their fairyland, their childhood, enacted in front of them.
Despite his claim that the play was intended for children, it is clear that
he knew who his real audience was, for he also produced a skit in which
a hapless 'Fairy Visitant', spurned by a family of sceptical children, finds
that only the parents are romantic enough to be interested in it.[21]

The same impulse lies at the centre of the most famous of all fairy
plays: J. M. Barrie's *Peter Pan* (1904).[22] Like most fairy tales, *Peter Pan* is
not actually about fairies: it is about children, and whether or not they
can or will grow up. Yet the play's best remembered moment, its dramatic
climax, does involve a fairy. In order to save Peter's life, Tinkerbell has
drunk the poison dissolved by Hook in Peter's medicine. As Tinkerbell
dies, Peter turns to the audience:

Why, Tink, you have drunk my medicine! It was poisoned and you drank it to
save my life! Tink, dear Tink, are you dying? . . . Her light is growing faint, and
if it goes out, that means she is dead! Her voice is so low I can scarcely tell what
she is saying. She says – she says she thinks she could get well again if children
believed in fairies! *(He rises and throws out his arms he knows not to whom, perhaps to
the boys and girls of whom he is not one.)* Do you believe in fairies? Say quick that you
believe! If you believe, clap your hands![23]

This is an extraordinarily powerful moment in the theatre, rarely forgotten by anyone who has experienced it. Many spectators feel compelled
to respond to Peter's appeal. A. J. Ayer was one such, recalling, 'In the
Christmas holidays I went at least twice to see *Peter Pan*, resolving not to
say yes when the audience is asked to bring Tinkerbell back to life by
saying that it believes in fairies, and almost certainly failing to keep my
resolve.'[24] For others, though, it is the moment when the dramatic illusion
founders, and they are disenchanted. Suzanne Langer (another philosopher) remembered the moment very differently from Ayer: 'Instantly
the illusion was gone; there were hundreds of children, sitting in rows,
clapping and even calling, while Miss Adams, dressed up as Peter Pan,
spoke to us like a teacher coaching us in a play in which she herself was
taking the title role.'[25] Barrie himself must have anticipated that Peter's

injunction 'Say quick that you believe!' would not work for every child, for it is followed by this stage direction. '*(Many clap, some don't, a few hiss. Then perhaps there is a rush of Nanas to the nurseries to see what on earth is happening. But TINK is rescued.)*'[26] The idea that children's disbelief in fairies would bring their concerned guardians to their sides is comical, but it implies that there is something wrong with a child who does not respond to Peter's appeal. What on earth is happening when children do not believe in fairies?

Jacqueline Rose has explored the role of *Peter Pan* in the 'ongoing sexual and political mystification of the child'.[27] She warns against mistakenly believing that *Peter Pan* is 'for children', and argues rather that it constructs the child as a consolatory myth for adults. Peter's appeal to the audience ('the girls and boys of whom he is not one') is central to the construction of this myth, for it suggests that only children can save Tinkerbell; only they can do so because to be a child is to believe in fairies. Children who do not believe in fairies are not proper children, and ceasing to believe in fairies is part of leaving childhood. Those who clap their hands signify that they have not yet learned that fairies do not exist, and so that they have not yet entered the disenchanted state of adulthood or even adolescence. Peter asks the children in the audience to show that they are children; but they do not clap for themselves. Whether the children believe in fairies or not, it is the adults who take them to the theatre who want them to clap their hands, in order to evoke for them a nostalgic remembrance of the childhood they have left behind for ever.

Such nostalgia was widespread. The desire to return imaginatively to the lost world of childhood infuses such popular works as Robert Louis Stevenson's *A Child's Garden of Verses* (1885) and Kenneth Grahame's *The Golden Age* (1895). The last lines of the latter's first chapter, 'The Olympians', might stand as a summation of all expressions of nostalgia for childhood:

Well! The Olympians are all past and gone. Somehow the sun does not seem to shine as brightly as it used; the trackless meadows of old time have shrunk and dwindled away to a few poor acres. A saddening doubt, a dull suspicion, creeps over me. Et in Arcadia Ego – I certainly did once inhabit Arcady. Can it be that I also have become an Olympian?[28]

In one sense, Grahame's regret is indeed at having irrevocably crossed the boundary between childhood and adulthood. But the longing which suffuses this passage seems to be for the past as such, be it Grahame's own, the recent or the very ancient past.

'The Olympians' was first published as an essay in the *National Observer* in 1891, then edited by the poet T. E. Henley, who was also associated with Rosamund Marriott Watson. Most of the chapters of *The Golden Age* were published first as periodical articles, some in the *Yellow Book*. The yearning for past times and the sense of loss which infuses Grahame's reminiscences and Watson's poems was not particular to them: it struck a sympathetic chord with the wider reading public.[29] But why should this kind of nostalgia have become popular at the turn of the century and the years following it? Malcolm Chase and Christopher Shaw have identified three conditions for the existence of a popular mood of nostalgia: 'a secular and linear sense of time, an apprehension of the failings of the present, and the availability of evidences of the past'.[30] Among the educated middle class, consciousness of each of these was particularly acute during this period. As Gillian Beer suggests, the Victorians' sense of the expansion of the past and their emphasis on memory and origins imply an acute sense of the linearity of time. The idea that time moves forward and that the past and present draw away from each other is opposed to a conception of time as circular, punctuated with moments when the past repeats itself, or destined to turn full circle. As Shaw and Chase point out, the circular conception of time is associated with the belief in an apocalypse and the literal resurrection of the body, with notions of pre-destination and final judgement. The increasing secularisation of society and the waning of belief amongst educated people, combined with a new awareness occasioned by evolutionary theory, geology and archaeology, of the multitudinous, incalculable numbers of deaths upon which human life in the present depended, caused the Victorians increasingly to dwell upon time's arrow. On the one hand, they saw themselves marching steadily and progressively into the future; on the other they pondered nostalgically the loss of the past.

This sense of the march of time, of days and years steadily ticking away, is counterposed by the quite different sense one has internally, in which time expands and contracts according to how bored or occupied we are. Shaw and Chase argue that adults and children have quite different relationships to these kinds of time: whereas adults experience both, and are particularly susceptible to the tyranny of time's march, in childhood we only experience the elastic time of the emotions.[31] The nostalgia associated with the consciousness of linear time is expressed as a yearning for time as experienced in childhood: 'once upon a time' that stretches out endlessly or is gone in a moment. The Victorians' nostalgia for childhood was at least partly a longing for this kind of time, but it could be otherwise expressed. The time of fairyland is very like that of childhood, for in contrast to the speeding up of time adults experience, in memory childhood seems both brief and endless. The passage of time in fairyland is similarly elastic, and in fairyland time's arrow has no effects, for no-one grows old. In fairy legends, human visitors to fairyland stay young as long as they linger there, and believe that they have spent only half an hour listening to fairy music, or a night and a day dancing and feasting; as soon as they return to the human world they find themselves grey and aged. And whereas in human affairs change is continual, in fairyland nothing ever changes: the fairy queen is always young and beautiful; Oberon and Titania are always quarrelling and always being reconciled; their attendants pursue their pleasures for ever. But if the country of the fairies is one which has no history, and in which time holds still, the figure of the fairy itself bears witness to the passing of time and the changes which history records in the human world. Fairyland, a place that is no-place with a time that is no-time, is the counterpoint to our own world, but the time when the fairies were is the time and place of our own past.

The elastic time of childhood and the supernatural time of fairyland are both connected to the changeless and eternal time of myth, yet another factor in the Victorians' nostalgia for the distant past. Grahame's metaphor of the Olympians is a telling one, for it connects up the child's sense of adults as all-powerful, capricious beings with the understanding of mythology developed by late Victorian folklorists and anthropologists, who came to see myths as exploring elemental truths about the human condition, and providing historical information about the way ancient peoples saw themselves in relation to nature. These theories also informed their interest in fairies, because fairies were the representatives in the recent past of those gods whose presence had animated the world of the ancients. For example, Alfred Nutt saw the origins of fairy legends in the myth of Dionysius:

The object of the sacrifice is to reinforce the life alike of nature and of the worshipper; but this inspires a conception, however crude, of unending and ever-changing vital essence persisting under the most diverse manifestations: hence the powers worshipped and appealed to, as they slowly crystallise into definite individualities, are necessarily immortal and as necessarily masters of all shapes – the fairy and his realm are unchanging and unfading, the fairy can assume all forms at will.[32]

The enchanted world of the fairies is a metonymy for the one where the Olympian gods walked the earth and animated the heavens. But the Victorians had come to occupy the roles of those formerly powerful deities, for to an increasing extent they could control nature and harness natural powers for human use and enjoyment. Grahame's realisation that 'I too have become an Olympian' is one that resonates more widely in late Victorian culture. By the end of the nineteenth century people had indeed gained Olympian powers, and they had irrevocably left behind the 'childhood' of society before modernity. Becoming an Olympian gives one great powers, of course; but it involves terrible responsibilities, and a daunting sense of the burdens of both present and future. It is no surprise, then, that grown-ups looked back to childhood, and that they wept for their vanished fairyland in the warm darkness of the theatre.

Yet the flaw in nostalgia is that it cannot evoke the past as one experienced it. Rather, the nostalgic impulse needs a representative fragment of the past as a figure for the past's richness: the sun that does not shine as brightly, the no-longer-trackless meadows. Images of fairies are one such representative fragment. These metonymies reduce the complexity of the past to a single note, and this is one reason that nostalgia is so often regarded as an inauthentic and oversimplified substitute for history. It is also partly why late nineteenth- and early twentieth-century representations of fairies seem so unsympathetic now. It was because the Victorians' ideas about fairies overlapped with those about the past in so many respects that the figure of the fairy was an enchanting one: the figure of the fairy conjured up in several ways the world the Victorians had lost, but its power to do so was specific to the period. Paradoxically, the fairy's evocative quality would have been most apparent to contemporary viewers in those representations which now seem utterly to have lost their meaning. Whilst the yearning for the past that suffuses turn-of-the-century fairy poetry is still palpable, the affective qualities of pictures of fairies from this period are harder to discern.

Nostalgic images suffer from a disadvantage which does not dog nostalgic writings, which can express their longing for what has been lost as well as representing its absence. The idea of a world empty of magic can be mourned and the departed fairies simultaneously invoked. But this is impossible in the visual arts, because one cannot visually represent something that is absent and it is harder visually to call up the longing for what is absent than to describe the feeling in words. Ann Colley suggests that this is a problem all artists caught up in the 'nostalgic moment' have to deal with: 'how it is possible adequately to represent the longing that invariably accompanies the experience – more specifically, what kinds of images satisfactorily signify a yearning for something that is absent'.[33] Late nineteenth and early twentieth century paintings of fairies exemplify this problem acutely. They seem stilted and shallow, lacking in the detail and incident which captivate the viewer of earlier fairy paintings. However, they are in fact suffused with nostalgia; they speak as poignantly as contemporary fairy poetry of the loss of and longing for the past.

Nearly all nineteenth-century fairy paintings depict fairies in groups – sometimes, as in Joseph Noel Paton's *The Fairy Raid* (1867; Glasgow Art Gallery), great troops of fairies of all shapes and sizes, which fill the picture with a mass of detail and incident. But at the end of the century a new trend emerged for paintings of a single female fairy, often by water, and always alone. An early example of this type of picture is John Atkinson Grimshaw's *Iris* (1886; Leeds: City Art Gallery). Here, a winged female figure (actually a Greek nymph, but possessing the insect-wings which characterise fairies) hovers just above a murky pool in deep woodland. The entire picture is dark, in shades of brown, so that it is difficult to distinguish the trees and the surface of the water; the only light source is Iris's halo, which glimmers off her iridescent wings and outlines the contours of her body. Though not actually a fairy painting, this image in its several versions set a precedent for a new image of fairies: female, solitary and evanescent.

Among such images are Herbert Draper's *The Kelpie* (1913; fig. 26), Elizabeth Stanhope Forbes's *Will o' the Wisp* (1900; whereabouts unknown), and *The Kelpie* by Thomas Millie Dow (1895; whereabouts unknown); in addition the theme was explored in a series of watercolours and etchings of marsh and water spirits made during the 1890s by Charles Prosper Stainton.[34] In such images the fairy is typically a beautiful and melancholy young woman alone in a landscape or, in the case of the Kelpie, sitting on a rock in the middle of a river. As an Academy painting *The Kelpie* seems wholly conventional, for it employs the approach to figure painting and painstaking technique which Frederic Leighton had developed in the 1870s and which was very dated, even in the conservative context of the Royal Academy. However, the conservatism of the image, which seems to proffer itself initially as a rather weary repetition of the clichéd figure of the water-nymph, is important in understanding its use of the fairy. In both its form and its theme, this is a painting about the loss of the past and the weakening of tradition. It is not easy to see at first why, for it is not unless one thinks about what the Kelpie is that the point of the picture can be grasped. According to Katherine Briggs's definitive *An Encyclopaedia of Fairies*, the Kelpie is, or was

the best-known of the Scottish water-horses [who] haunted rivers rather than lochs or the sea. He could assume human form in which he appeared like a

rough, shaggy man. In this shape he used sometimes to leap up behind a solitary rider, gripping and crushing him, and frightening him almost to death. Before storms, he would be heard howling and wailing. His most usual shape was that of a young horse . . . He was suspected sometimes of tearing people to pieces and devouring them.[35]

Draper's Kelpie has metamorphosed from a rough and shaggy man–horse to a lithe young woman, and though perhaps she is rather sharp-faced, there is little reason to suspect she would tear anyone limb from limb. Indeed, she seems little like a fairy at all: she has no wings and seems to be roughly human-size in relation to her surroundings. In what, then, does her fairy nature consist, and why has Draper portrayed her as the opposite of her traditional counterpart?

It seems superficially as if Draper has made the Kelpie safe, divesting her of the terrors associated with the traditional fairy. But this Kelpie is dangerous, though the hazard is perceptible only to the careful viewer. The Kelpie sits, disrobed for bathing, glancing shyly downstream, as if she has pulled herself out of the water to catch the sun. She evidently fears to be seen, yet her glance fails to discover the hidden spectator who does in fact watch her every move, for the viewer of the painting is positioned as if he or she were concealed by the frame like a watcher in a hide. The Kelpie appears to be at her ease, but in fact she is not. Her pose is not one of rest, but an arrested position: she is ready, at any moment, to slide back into the water. Just by uncrossing her legs, she will be ready to push herself off the rock. Her nervous glance indicates that she suspects that at any moment she might be seen, and have to disappear. The large size of the picture (the figure is almost life-size) and the high finish of the painted surface provoke the fantasy that the viewer might be able to get into the picture: but if one were to try to approach the Kelpie, she would instantly be gone with a splash into the stream.

The idea that the Kelpie might vanish is represented by this implied narrative in which the picture involves the viewer. But it also works at other levels. The 'real' fairy of legend, the murderous man-horse, has already disappeared, to be replaced by a creature not so different from the human spectator. In this sense the painting embodies the erosion of tradition, and the nostalgic substitution of a sentimental figure for a more complicated and difficult sense of the past. On the other hand, in its formal aspects the painting looks backward to an aesthetic tradition itself under threat from the emergence of modernism. In this sense, *The Kelpie* has much in common with 'The Elfin Artist'. Like that poem, this picture makes a deliberate connection between aesthetic conservatism and the importance of tradition, even though the tradition it depicts has already been consigned to oblivion.[36] The 'real' Kelpie was a perilous creature, but although Draper's Kelpie seems to have been divested of his terrors, she has her own dangers. In legend, these fairies led strayed travellers into bogs or leapt up behind them and dragged them into the river; in the painting, the danger is that she might disappear from sight, perhaps for ever. It is this threat of disappearance that makes Draper's *The Kelpie* and images like it nostalgic, and connects them to ideas of the last fairy and the fairies' valediction. The last fairy, like the fairies in these paintings, is a creature little different from ourselves, a being who speaks in a language humans can understand of the pain of loss and the ache of oblivion. The last fairy is almost indistinguishable from the human except for its evanescence, its quality of being-about-to-vanish or to disappear from the world for good. It is this evanescence which connects the fairy to memory, that most immaterial of all records of the past, the one which is most easily lost and yet carries an extraordinary affective weight. These last, about-to-vanish fairies represent an anxiety about the late Victorians' own ability to hold on to their own past in the face of modernity, to maintain through memory the few gleams of enchantment that were yet left to them.

A sense of the failings of the present is the second of the conditions Shaw and Chase identify for a widespread mood of nostalgia: the sense that whatever the benefits of progress it also exacts its costs, and that modern life, for all its possibilities and conveniences, is meaningless and hollow compared with life in the past. A meadow crossed with paths has lost an indefinable mystery compared with one that is trackless. This is the refrain of nostalgic writings about and images of fairies. Such feelings also underlie the efforts of folklorists to preserve the fragile traces of tradition, because in doing so they were trying to remember, and so keep hold of, whatever it was modernity had lost. This sense of modernity's failings also animates the work of theorists of modernity like the sociologist Max Weber, who sought to understand how social, cultural, intellectual and affective changes had combined to allow the development of modern society. Weber argued that modernity was different from what had gone before it, that it had emerged quite recently with the development of capitalism and industrialisation, and that it was a social, cultural and intellectual phenomenon. Most importantly, he thought that the tremendous material benefits of modern society were in tension with the deadening, stultifying effects of modern social organisation. In other words, his analysis of modernity weighed human progress against a pessimistic sense of human loss, and was shadowed by a nostalgic sense of the world of the past the present had lost.

Weber's ideas were not unique, for he was part of a school of German sociological thought, running from Herder and German Romanticism through to Walter Benjamin and beyond, whose 'characteristic response . . . to the onset of capitalist industrialisation was', to quote Paul Connerton, 'a mood of tragic pessimism'.[37] Perhaps the most poignant expression of this tragic pessimism, however, is in Weber's lecture 'Science as a Vocation', given in the year of his death, 1919. In this lecture Weber considers what the meaning of science is in the modern world, and what might constitute a vocation for science. Both the meaning of and the vocation for science are rendered pessimistically because of what Weber calls the 'disenchantment of the world'. 'Scientific progress', he wrote, 'is a fraction, indeed the most important fraction of that process of intellectualization which we have been undergoing for millennia and which is generally judged in such an extraordinary negative fashion nowadays.'[38] Intellectualisation does not mean that we know more about the world, for in practical terms modern humanity knows less about the workings of the world than 'primitive man'. In contrast to primitive man, who knew exactly how all the technologies he used and institutions he encountered worked, the advances in knowledge mean that modern man is surrounded by systems (like money), structures (like the economy) and technologies whose workings he cannot understand. Rather, intellectualisation means the

knowledge or the belief that, *if one only wanted to*, one *could* find out at any time; that there are in principle no *mysterious, incalculable powers at work,* but rather that one could in principle master everything through *calculation*. But that means the disenchantment of the world. One need no longer have recourse to magic in order to control or implore the spirits, as the savage did for whom such powers existed. Technology and calculation achieve that, and this more than anything means intellectualization as such.[39]

Weber's tone here should not be mistaken for neutral. Nor should it be thought, just because disenchantment has been going on for millennia, that its effects are not at their most intense, catastrophic even, in the modern period, the Enlightenment and after. The essay ends on a note of terrible pessimism:

The fate of our age, with its characteristic rationalization and intellectualization and above all the disenchantment of the world, is that the ultimate, the most sublime values have withdrawn from public life, either into the transcendent

realm of spiritual life, or into the brotherhood of immediate personal relationships between individuals. It is no accident that our greatest art is intimate rather
than monumental, nor is it fortuitous that today only in the smallest groups,
between individuals, something pulsates *in pianissimo* which corresponds to the
prophetic *pneuma* which formerly swept through great communities like fire and
welded them together.[40]

The alienated condition of modernity is the condition of disenchantment. Modernity transforms the world into a commodity to be used; the
world is, as Zygmunt Bauman points out, '*de-animated, de-spiritualized*, denied the capacity of the subject'.[41] And just as forests and rivers are transformed into timber and waterways, so human beings are also turned into
a commodity. 'As nature became progressively "de-animated", humans
grew progressively more "naturalized" so that their subjectivity, the
primeval "givenness" of their existence, could be denied and they themselves could be made hospitable for instrumental meanings.'[42] Modernity's 'war on enchantment' (the phrase is Bauman's) disenchanted
the world by transforming it into the object of instrumental reason; it
mastered the world through scientific knowledge, transforming the world
into the object of that knowledge, which sought to be comprehensive;
and it reshaped humans in the image of the world it knew and had made.
    Fairies are part of the lost enchantment of the world. The enchanted
world, in its purest sense, was inhabited by the gods of animistic religions:
supernatural beings with whom, in the course of daily living, primitive
man had to interact, and through whom the unknowable chanciness of
the world was mediated and made meaningful. In the enchanted world of
the primitive, the universe is ruled by capricious and therefore completely
unpredictable beings. The realm of the gods is another, incalculable
world whose operation is the cause of awe and wonder, and the source of
myth. To save the fairies from oblivion is to save some gleam of enchantment from modernity's armoury of intellectualisation. But representations of fairies are always tainted by the loss of enchantment: by sadness,
nostalgia and a sense of the tragic dimension of modernity. To dream of
fairies is to dream of the world modernity has lost; to imagine the fairies'
farewell is to say goodbye to it forever. Awareness of the inexorable
passage of time and of the failings of the present were the two impulses
which made the figure of the fairy such a powerful expression of nostalgia
in the late nineteenth and early twentieth centuries, and they combined
to produce the topoi of the last fairy, the fairies' farewell, and the special
ability of children to believe in fairies. The widespread sense of disillusionment with the present, foreboding about the future and longing for

the past which characterised the decades surrounding the turn of the century found a perfect expression in melancholy, nostalgic images of fairies.

The most startling examples of this emotional response to the modern world are those representations of fairies produced during World War One. The same feelings which caused 'Aldershot' to weep so copiously at performances of *Pinkie and the Fairies* in 1909 caused soldiers to dream of fairies amidst the horrors of the trenches. World War One has been widely understood as the defining moment of modernity: it marked the inception of industrialised warfare and the absolute loss of that innocence which retrospectively came to be associated with the 'golden' years of the pre-war period. With hindsight it has come to seem that the most heroic response to the war was to depict its horrors unflinchingly, to attempt some form of realistic representation of the monstrosities of modern warfare. However, first-hand observers were as likely to idealise soldiers and soldiering, or to give rein to escapist fantasy, and these responses have come to seem embarrassing evasions of reality and expressions of disturbing, conservative impulses. The occurrence of fairies in writings about the war is an example. In his discussion of a passage from Vera Brittain's *Testament of Youth* (1933) in which she recalls her period of service in Malta and tries to understand her own excitement about the war, Adrian Caesar argues that Brittain was excited by, enjoyed even, the contemplation of her own and others' suffering and anguish. But equally striking is her use of metaphors connected with fairies. She writes:

It is, I think, this glamour, this magic, this incomparable keying up of the spirit in a time of mortal conflict, which constitutes the pacifist's real problem . . . The glamour may be the mere delirium of fever, which as soon as the war is over dies out and shows itself for the will o' the wisp that it is, but while it lasts no emotion known to man seems as yet to have quite the compelling power of this enlarged vitality.[43]

The idea is that war is like a fairyland in which the combatant experiences a kind of magic, a glamour the enchantment of which he is powerless to resist, like a man who cannot help but follow a will-o'-the-wisp. This seems perverse, but when compared with other uses of the metaphor of the fairy can be understood as a more typical response to the horrors of war than first seems likely. In their glossary of soldier's slang from the Great War, John Brophy and Eric Partridge gloss 'Blighty' as 'England, in the sense of home. In this one word was gathered all the soldier's homesickness and affection and war-weariness . . . *Blighty* to the soldier was a sort of faerie, a paradise which he could faintly remember, a never-never land.'[44] The obscene horrors of the battlefield and the idealised comforts of home are connected through the metaphor of the fairy. Though they are polar opposites, they are brought together in the idea of fairyland in just the same way that in the mid-nineteenth century fairyland was both an imaginative escape from and a representation of the landscape of industrial Britain.

The Piper of Dreams (1914; fig. 27) by Estella Canziani was exhibited at the Royal Academy in 1915, where it was an enormous success. The reproduction rights were quickly acquired by the Medici Society, who produced it as a colour print. It instantly became a best-seller, and in the first year 250,000 copies were sold: many of these were sent to soldiers in the trenches.[45] The Piper, a young boy, sits with his legs crossed and his back against a tree in the middle of a gloomy wood. The bare ground is dotted with primroses, indicating that it is early spring, and also suggesting that this is a particularly British scene. Like Dickon in Frances Hodgson Burnett's *The Secret Garden* (1911), the Piper clearly has the power to tame animals, for a red squirrel approaches, and a robin is perching on his outstretched foot. He looks down, intent on his piping; he cannot see therefore the 'dreams' his playing has conjured up. Around him, faintly visible like wisps of smoke, almost transparent fairies float and hover. The picture plainly represents a vision of 'Blighty/faerie', an image of home as fairyland. It is also full of nostalgia. Not only are the fairies barely visible, their evanescence a sign that their existence is threatened; to become visible at all they require an intermediary between them and the viewer. A child must be the piper of adult dreams. To the soldiers who owned copies of *The Piper of Dreams* 'Blighty' was not only home, it was their 'lost fairyland', their childhood – which many of them had only very recently left behind. The print was popular because it was an idealised vision of home, and a representation of the gulf between past and present, the child's fairyland and the grim world of adulthood. It was pleasurable because it represented everything the soldier in the trenches had lost.

The same mixture of pleasure and pain – which is what gives nostalgia its particular poignancy – motivates Robert Graves's collection *Fairies and Fusiliers*, published in 1917. As the title suggests, the collection brings together poems describing and reflecting upon Graves's experience of the war, such as 'A Dead Boche', 'The Two Fusiliers', 'The Next War' and 'Dead Cow Farm'. These are interspersed with poems looking

Figure 27. Estella Canziani, *The Piper of Dreams*.

back to a pastoral vision of England, to childhood and to fairyland, such as 'Cherry Time':

> When I sound the fairy call,
>   Gather here in silent meeting,
> Chin to knee on the orchard wall,
>   Cooled in dew and cherries eating.
> . . .
> And you'll be fairies all.[46]

There is a deliberate confusion here about whether the speaker is a child or a fairy, and whether the enchantment evoked by the poem is the magic of fairyland or the magic of childhood. Perhaps, Graves implies, they come to the same thing. In 'Cherry Time' the pleasure of looking back is unalloyed, but in other poems it is mixed with sadness and regret. 'Babylon', for example, begins by making a connection between looking back and writing poetry, suggesting that it is only by recollecting childhood that the speaker can return to the state in which poetry can be written:

> The child alone a poet is:
> Spring and Fairyland are his,
> Truth and Reason show but dim,
> And all's poetry with him.

By the end of the poem, however, the speaker has bade farewell to poetry and to fairyland, and views this 'lost Babylon' with the melancholy but pleasurable tears which accompany nostalgia:

> None of all the magic hosts,
> None remain but a few ghosts
> Of timorous heart, to linger on
> Weeping for lost Babylon.[47]

Next to the realism of 'The Dead Boche' or the disillusionment of 'The Next War', Graves's apparently playful assertion 'I'd love to be a Fairy's Child' at first strikes a false note.[48] Nevertheless, the seemingly trivial fairy poems are integral to the conception of the book, because the complex emotional attitude to the war which seeks both to look directly at it and to escape from it, and which is both clear-eyed and nostalgic, is conveyed by the conjunction of the 'fairy' and the 'fusilier' poems. To write poems about fairies was for Graves not a 'wilful evasion of his war experience', but a means of expressing the nostalgia that was an inextricable part of his experience of war.[49] In this sense, Graves proves himself a typical soldier, not very different from those who wept in the theatre or owned prints of *The Piper of Dreams,* and this ordinariness is what Graves strives to project in the collection. It is in his declaration that 'I shall scrawl / Just what I fancy as I strike it, / Fairies and Fusiliers and all' that he asserts his common bond with his fellow soldiers.[50] Being a grown-up man in war-time means renouncing childhood for ever; those who returned bore witness to the gulf the experience of war opened up between them and their past. It is not surprising, then, that marooned in the present, they took to dreaming of, and weeping for, the lost world of the fairies.

It was not only soldiers who mused on fairies during the war years. Those at home also felt the attraction of fairies. During the summer and autumn of 1917 *Punch* published a series of poems by Rose Fyleman about fairies. 'Fairies', published on 23 May 1917, was her first published poem, and it was so popular that she then contributed at least one fairy poem a month for the rest of the year. These were followed by her collection, *Fairies and Chimneys* in 1918. The close connection between the popularity of her fairy poems and the war can be seen in 'There Used to Be – ', another version of the fairies' farewell:

> There used to be fairies in Germany –
>   The children will look for them still;
> They will search all about till the sunlight slips out
>   And the trees stand frowning and chill.
> 'The flowers,' will they say, 'have all vanished,
>   And where can the fairies be fled
> That played in the fern?' – The flowers will return,
>   But I fear that the fairies are dead.[51]

Fyleman's poems appear from their address to the reader to be aimed at children ('Have you watched the fairies when the rain is done . . . I have, I have! Isn't it fun?'), yet although *Punch* was certainly read by children, its primary readership was adult.[52] The address to the child reader is an alibi which masks the real intention at work. The idea that the war has killed off all the German fairies is an appeal to the same nostalgic impulses that mourned the 'trackless meadows' of childhood and the enchanted world of the time before modernity, the same feelings that made *The Piper of Dreams* such a best-seller and prompted Robert Graves to write about fairies in the trenches.

The publication of 'Fairies' had an unintended consequence. In the summer of 1917 Elsie Wright took a photograph of her cousin Frances Griffiths – and fairies. 'Frances and the Fairies' (fig. 28) was the first

Figure 28. Elsie Wright, *Frances and the Fairies*.

photograph Elsie Wright ever took, on a single plate loaded into a box camera for her by her father. The girls staged the photograph to show their family that Frances, the younger of the two, had got her dress wet playing with the fairies in Cottingley Beck, the stream at the bottom of the Wright family's garden. Later in the summer they took another photograph, this time of Elsie ('Elsie and the Gnome'), but this was not so successful. The photographs did not become public until 1920, when a family friend showed them to Edward Gardner (a leading theosophist), who had them 'improved' and made into slides. A correspondent of Gardner's mentioned them to Arthur Conan Doyle, who was then writing an article on fairies for the 1920 Christmas number of the *Strand*. Gardner and Doyle arranged for the publication of the two photographs in this article, and to this end had them attested by photographic experts. In the summer of 1920 (that is, before publication), Gardner sent Elsie Wright a new camera and plates, so that she and Frances could (or should) take some more photographs of fairies. They complied, producing three more: 'Frances and the Leaping Fairy' (fig. 29), 'Fairy Offering a Posy to Elsie' (fig. 30) and 'The Fairy Sunbath'.[53] He also visited Cottingley to meet Elsie and her family. When the photographs were published, using pseudonyms, there was a storm of publicity, and within a few weeks the family's identity was revealed and Elsie lost her job. The publicity

Figure 29. Elsie Wright, *Frances and the Leaping Fairy*.

Figure 30. Frances Griffiths, *Fairy Offering a Posy to Elsie.*

was furthered by the publication of the second lot of photographs in the *Strand* of March 1921.

Each of the first four photographs was a single exposure taken outdoors in Cottingley Glen, using fairies modelled from cardboard and supported with hatpins. Grey artist's chalk was used to disguise the edges of the models and to achieve a translucent effect. The final photograph was, apparently, an accidental double exposure. Elsie Wright made the fairies and arranged the composition of the photographs. Though the first two photographs were 'cleaned up' (re-photographed and retouched to eliminate blurring and the effects of under-exposure), the remaining three look exactly as they did when Elsie and Frances took them.[54] Between them Gardner and Doyle turned the photographs from images the girls made for themselves into documents in the public domain. Their interest in publishing the photographs was to show conclusively that fairies, the lowest rank in a hierarchy of spiritual forms, could be materialised and captured in such a way as to deny disbelief.[55] Their problem was that they believed that only children could do this. From the beginning of Gardner's involvement in the affair he was terribly concerned that the girls be and remain children. His fears about the ending of their childhood are made explicit in his very first letter to Conan Doyle: 'But children such as these are rare, and I fear that we are late because almost certainly the inevitable will happen, one of them will "fall in love" and then – hey presto!!'[56] When this letter was written, Elsie and Frances were 19 and 13 respectively. The appalling possibility that one of the girls will fall in love and so lose the ability to see fairies is produced with rhetorical flourish; in the correspondence that followed, both Gardner and Doyle anxiously watched for and speculated about the moment when the girls might cross the boundary between adult and child by falling in love.[57] The motivation of the two men who published the photographs was similar to that of adults who take children to clap their hands at *Peter Pan*. They wanted children to believe in fairies for them, and they wanted them to prove that they really believed.

The photographs were immediately controversial, and although it was not until 1983 that they were conclusively proved to have been 'faked', both believers and sceptics conducted vociferous debate in the press, much of which centred around the question of whether the fairies were real or imaginary. Major Hall-Edwards wrote in the *Birmingham Weekly Post*:

As a medical man, I believe that the inculcation of such absurd ideas into the minds of children will result in later life in manifestations of nervous disorder and mental disturbances. Surely young children can be brought up to appreciate the beauties of nature without their imagination being filled with exaggerated, if picturesque, nonsense and misplaced sentiment.[58]

For commentators such as Hall-Edwards, purely imaginary fairies were as disturbing as the real thing, precisely because they were imaginary. In later life, Elsie repeatedly called the photographs 'pictures of figments of our imagination', and while this statement has been taken as a wily evasion of responsibility for a famous fraud, it also signifies the alternative meanings the pictures might have had for Elsie and Frances, which have less to do with proof and authenticity and more to do with fantasy and representation.[59]

The photographs have normally been understood as snapshots which are intended to record or to simulate a moment's happening. This was how Gardner and Doyle interpreted the photographs, and it was what enabled them to appropriate the images as evidence. The girls' own explanations of how they took the photographs and the fact that the snapshot is the typical form of domestic photography also supported this interpretation. Looked at closely, however, the photographs begin to look very much less like snapshots, and not at all like pieces of documentary evidence. Frances and Elsie did not intend to produce fakes or to stage a fraudulent proof of the existence of fairies, because, for the two girls, their photographs were works of the imagination.

It is not certain that Elsie and Frances saw 'Fairies' when it was first published in 1917, although Elsie's parents took *Punch*.[60] Nevertheless, there are several correspondences between the poem and the pictures, and they have become welded together in the phrase 'fairies at the bottom of our garden', the first line of the poem which is so often used to describe the photographs. These are the first and final verses:

> There are fairies at the bottom of our garden!
>   It's not so very, very far away;
> You pass the gardener's shed and you just keep straight ahead –
>   I do so hope they've really come to stay.
> There's a little wood with moss in it and beetles,
>   And a little stream, that quietly runs through;
> You wouldn't think they'd dare to come merry-making there –
>   Well, they do.
>
> There are fairies at the bottom of our garden!
>   You cannot think how beautiful they are;
> They all stand up and sing when the Fairy Queen and King
>   Come gently floating down upon their car.

The King is very proud and very handsome;
   The Queen – now can you guess who that could be
(She's a little girl all day, but at night she steals away)
         Well – it's me![61]

Cottingley Glen, with its wood and stream, was at the bottom of Elsie Wright's garden, and her parents didn't think the fairies were 'merry-making there': in a sense, the photographs are a visual 'Well, they do', with all its childish petulance.

Like the photographs, however, the childish voice of the poem is more complicated than it initially seems. The ambiguity lies in the last two lines of the final verse. The naive tone belies the contradictions between the two propositions that the poem puts forward: first, that the speaker has seen the fairies; second, that she is one of them. The credibility of the claim to have seen the fairies is undermined by the possibility that they are merely imaginary. If the speaker is the Fairy Queen, then the fairies are nothing more than a 'pretending game'. The shift from 'I' to 'she' also makes it apparent that the speaker stands outside as well as inside the poem, even though there seems only to be one voice. The fact that this shift from inside to outside is marked by a parenthesis gives the impression that this is an adult interjection, so that there is a shift from narration by a child ('There are fairies at the bottom of our garden!') to narration as if by a child ('She's a little girl all day'). Instead of a proper distinction between truth and falsehood, real and imaginary, this shift produces two irreconcilable truths: the fairies exist and they are also imaginary. The closing line, 'Well – it's me!' attempts to unite these two possibilities, yet this, the most embarrassing line in the poem, serves only to echo what the poem as a whole asks: are imaginary things true or false, and who is to say so, adults or children? This poem invokes the adult's voice as a way of distinguishing between truth and falsehood, only to insist that the products of the imagination are as real as the 'really true'. And it does so by making the child voice her belief in fairies.

In the context of 'Fairies', Elsie's statement that the photographs are 'pictures of figments of our imagination' looks less like a sly evasion of forgery and more like an honest account of what she and Frances were really up to. Critics of the photographs complained that the fairies were too conventional to be real: that their diaphanous draperies and butterfly wings could have come straight from illustrated story books. Doyle and Gardner worked hard, and unsuccessfully, to account for this. But Frances and Elsie were not folklorists or psychical researchers, concerned with recording truthfully and authentically real phenomena. They consciously used models from illustrated books and borrowed the idea of fairies at the bottom of the garden. They imagined the fairies, and then they photographed themselves imagining them.

It is not easy initially to see why this is so, partly because the interpretation of the photographs as documentary snapshots has been so powerful. However, it is also to do with the way the first and most famous photograph, 'Frances and the Fairies', was doctored at Gardner's request. The photograph shows Frances gazing artlessly at the camera, apparently oblivious to the troop of fairies dancing in front of her. Frances's gaze at the camera was used as evidence both by believers and sceptics: either she was so used to the fairies that she looked at the camera, or she looked at the camera because there were no fairies. Both views assume that the picture is composed so as to resemble the casual recording of a momentary glimpse of the fairies. This is a misreading encouraged by the processes used to 'improve' the photograph by Arthur Snelling, the trick photographer to whom Gardner took the pictures for verification and 'cleaning up'.[62] Snelling reduced the size of Frances's head by 10 per cent and touched up the fairies; he then re-photographed the whole thing, producing an entirely new negative which has since been used instead of the original. These processes disguise the original composition by making the fairies the focal point. In the original picture, however, the centre and focal point of the composition was Frances's face, instead of what is actually a double focus in the 'official' version.

In compositional terms, the fairies are an addition to a portrait of Frances in which her face is the centre and focal point of the picture. Instead of using the conventions of the snapshot, Elsie had set the photograph up using the conventions of the portrait photograph. Instead of being the point of the picture, the fairies are decorative props, rather like the pillars, aspidistras, costumes and so on used in studio portraits. This is hardly surprising, given that Elsie worked for some time in a portrait photographer's studio in Bradford learning to tint photographs. That is where she learned to use grey chalk to make the fairies translucent, and she would have learned from her experience how to arrange a portrait photograph. All four of the photographs which show the two girls are in fact portraits. Even 'Frances and the Leaping Fairy', which seems to record Frances jerking her head back in surprise as she sees the fairy, is a posed portrait. The blurring was in fact caused when Frances moved her head from side to side as she corrected her pose in order to appear as if she were gazing at the fairy.[63] The Cottingley photographs, then, do not record fairies seen by girls; they are portraits of girls-who-see-fairies.

Apart from 'Elsie and the Gnome', all the photographs use close-up, which magnifies the size of the object pictured. Normally in close-up pictures, everything in the frame is magnified to the same degree, so that the relative dimensions of each element of the composition are unchanged. In these pictures, however, the diminutive fairies act as scale markers to emphasise the exaggeration in the girls' size. The gigantic girls tower over the tiny fairies who, fashionably attired and coiffured as they are, resemble miniature adults. Furthermore, the fairies appear to supplicate the girls' attention, offering flowers, dancing and leaping for them. In both these aspects of the images the relation between adults and children is turned upside down, the girls appearing as children perceive adults to be: huge, powerful, needing to be propitiated.

In all the pictures the girls' gaze is central to the image, but it is particularly important in 'Fairy Offering a Posy to Elsie'. Here Elsie gazes at the fairy but does not focus on her, since the focal point of her gaze is in fact beyond the frame. The intimacy of the close-up shot directs the viewer's eye away from the fairy and towards Elsie, focusing the viewer's attention on her unfocused gaze. This was caused by the impossibility of focusing on the cardboard edge of the fairy; its result, however, is to suggest that seeing fairies is not like seeing other objects. That Elsie's gaze does not focus on what she is apparently looking at suggests that the fairy is visible only to the camera or the viewer; or it suggests that this is the representation of a vision or fantasy which can only be seen by an inward gaze. Elsie's description of the photographs as 'pictures of figments of our imagination' was in fact an accurate and revealing statement. When they took the pictures, Frances and Elsie looked at themselves and each other, and recorded what they saw: girls-who-see-fairies, beings between childhood and adulthood, illusion and reality, playing with these distinctions as if they were imaginary.

The Cottingley photographs became so famous that they dogged Elsie Wright and Frances Griffiths throughout their lives. The images are so well known that they have become a byword for fakery, even though the two girls did not intend them thus. One of the more distant echoes of the affair occurs in George Orwell's *Coming up for Air* (1939), a deeply nostalgic, enraged lament for a vanished rural England irreparably damaged and cheapened by modernity. The meretriciousness of the present is borne in upon the hero, George Bowling, when he revisits his childhood home in Lower Binfield, and finds that his childhood paradise, the grounds of the Old Hall, has become a suburb inhabited by open-necked-shirt-and-sandal-wearing vegetarians. He meets one such, who tells him:

And Professor Woad, the psychic research worker. Such a poetic character! He goes wandering out into the woods and the family can't find him at meal times. He says he's walking amongst the fairies. Do you believe in fairies? I admit – te-hee! – I am just a wee bit sceptical. But his photographs are most convincing.[64]

For all their efforts, Doyle's and Gardner's dearest hopes ended up ridiculed. Though their claim to have proved the existence of fairies has had champions in connoisseurs of the paranormal, in reality the photographs killed off interest in fairies as an adult preoccupation and consigned them to the world of childhood. The fairies which fascinated adults in the nineteenth century were creatures of legend and superstition, numinous beings caught in a liminal twilight between imagination and reality. Fixed, seemingly categorically, in the photographic image, fairies made the bathetic descent to ridicule and parody, to the saccharine illustrations of the Flower Fairy books. For Orwell, doubtless, any man who was interested in fairies was a bit of a crackpot; photographing them probably made him a bit of a fairy himself. (In fact, 'fairy' only became widely used as a slang term for homosexual after the publication of the photographs.[65]) By chaining the photographs to the obligation to speak as evidence, Doyle and Gardner effectively destroyed their own case. The 'coming of the fairies' they proclaimed turned out to be their departure.

After World War One it gradually became impossible to find consolation for the depredations of modernity in dreaming of fairyland. The failure of the fairies was predicted, ironically enough, by H. G. Wells, who was in many ways a proponent of science, rationality and progress, in a short story called 'Mr Skelmersdale in Fairyland' (1903). This tells the tale of an ordinary man, a small shop-keeper, who accidentally falls asleep on a fairy hill and is taken underground for a stay in the world of the fairies. He tells his story to the narrator, who refuses to judge whether the story is true or not:

Whether it really happened, whether he imagined it or dreamt it, or fell upon it in some strange hallucinatory trance, I do not profess to say. But that he invented it I will not for one moment entertain. The man simply and honestly believes the thing happened as he says it happened; he is transparently incapable of any lie so elaborate and sustained, and in the belief of the simple, yet often keenly penetrating, rustic minds about him I find a very strong confirmation of his sincerity. He believes – and nobody can produce any positive fact to falsify his belief. As for me, with this much of endorsement, I transmit his story – I am a little old now to justify or explain.[66]

Is fairyland nothing more than a hallucination, nothing less than a dream? As the narrator implies, whether the story can be verified is irrelevant. Fairies enchant because they hover on the boundaries of reality: they are as real as the imagination, as material as a dream, as true as a metaphor. The enchantment of the fairies lies in their power to work a little magic on the world, to make it once more a wondrous place, to turn modernity into fairyland. But it is this small power of enchantment which, the story makes clear, is no longer possible. Mr Skelmersdale returns from his time in fairyland with a broken heart and a pocket full of ashes, and with the words 'Fairy love and fairy gold!' ringing in his ears.[67] He tries to return to fairyland, but cannot:

'I used to walk over the Knoll and round it and round it, calling for them to let me in. Shouting. Near blubbering I was at times. Daft I was and miserable. I kept saying it was all a mistake. And every Sunday afternoon I went up there, wet and fine, though I know as well as you do that it wasn't no good by day. And I've tried to go to sleep there . . . often and often. And, you know, I couldn't, sir – never. I've thought if I could go to sleep there, there might be something . . . But I've sat up there and laid there, and I couldn't, not for thinking and longing. It's the longing . . . I've tried –'[68]

This is a terribly sad story because it bears witness to the impossibility of return, and the hopelessness of longing to do so. The Victorians could put their longings in an enchanted form by dreaming of fairies, and could imagine themselves differently and in a different world by doing so but, as Wells shows, that would eventually become impossible. The pressure of modernity was in the end too great a weight for the figure of the fairy to bear.

No-one has characterised the hopes and disasters of the first quarter of the twentieth century more succinctly or movingly than Walter Benjamin. In 1926 he wrote of 'a generation that had gone to school on a horse-drawn streetcar [and who] now stood under open sky in a countryside in which nothing remained unchanged but the clouds, and beneath these clouds, in a field of force of destructive torrents and explosions, was the tiny, fragile human body'.[69] In a world of destructive torrents and explosions, the fairies could no longer work their small enchantments. They could no longer console broken hearts and pockets full of ashes: thenceforward, dreams and longings had to find a different form.

Notes

INTRODUCTION: SMALL ENCHANTMENTS

1 Carole Silver, *Strange and Secret Peoples: Fairies and Victorian Consciousness* (New York and Oxford: Oxford University Press, 1999).
2 Diane Purkiss, *Troublesome Things* (London: Penguin, 2000).
3 William Blake, *Selected Poetry*, ed. Michael Mason (Oxford University Press World's Classics, 1996), p. 130.
4 Cited in *Victorian Fairy Painting* (Exhibition Catalogue; London: Royal Academy of Arts, 1997), p. 76.
5 John Keats, *Selected Poems*, ed. Robert Gittings (London: Dent Everyman, 1974), p. 190.
6 Alfred Tennyson, *Poems and Plays* (London: Oxford University Press, 1975), p. 173.
7 Letitia Landon, *The Poetical Works of L. E. L.*, 4 vols. (London: Longman, Rees, Orme, Brown and Green, 1827), vol. III, pp. 229–31.
8 Michael Tanner, 'Sentimentality', *Proceedings of the Aristotelian Society*, n.s., vol. 77 (1977), 127–47; p. 141. I am grateful to Paul McGoay for recommending this article to me.
9 Ibid., p. 143.
10 Wendy Wheeler, *A New Modernity? Change in Science, Literature and Politics* (London: Lawrence and Wishart, 1999), pp. 7–35.
11 Thomas Carlyle, 'Signs of the Times' (1829), *Collected Works*, 13 vols., (London: Chapman and Hall, 1857), vol. III, p. 209.

FANCIES OF FAIRIES AND SPIRITS
AND NONSENSE

1 T. G. Wainewright, *Essays and Criticisms*, ed. W. C. Hazlitt (London: Reeves and Turner, 1880), p. 149.
2 Fuseli exhibited three paintings at the 1821 Royal Academy exhibition: *Jealousy: A Sketch*, *Prometheus Delivered by Hercules* and *Amphiarus*, none a fairy subject. Evidently Fuseli was sufficiently identified with fairies in the mind of the exhibition-going public that they thought of him as a fairy painter even when, as here, his subjects were classical and allegorical themes.

3 Christina Rossetti, *Poems and Prose*, ed. Jan Marsh (London: Dent Everyman, 1994), p. 164.

4 David Morrill, in '"Twilight is not Good for Maidens": Uncle Polidori and the Psychodynamics of Vampirism in *Goblin Market*' (*Victorian Poetry*, vol. 28 (1994), no. 1, 1–16), has persuasively argued that the goblins should be seen as vampiric rather than fairy-like: 'The goblins in Rossetti's poem are hardly the sprightly, mischievous elves of folklore ... They are darker, more mysterious, more powerful, more terrifying, and more human. Above all, their actions are vampiric: they dole out strange, exotic fruits to young women who become drained, languid, bloodless' (pp. 1–2).

5 Mary Elizabeth Braddon, *Lady Audley's Secret* (1863), ed. David Skilton (Oxford University Press World's Classics, 1998), pp. 29, 64, 296–7.

6 Thomas Keightley, *The Fairy Mythology* (1826; London: Bohn, 1850), pp. 2–3.

7 John Black, *The Falls of Clyde, or The Fairies* (Edinburgh: William Creech, 1806), p. 13.

8 Isaiah Berlin, 'The Counter-Enlightenment', *Against the Current: Essays in the History of Ideas* (Oxford University Press, 1981), pp. 1–24.

9 Ibid., p. 10.

10 Ibid., p. 12.

11 See, for example, the discussion of the eighteenth-century conflict between social theories grounded in paternity and fraternity in Carol Pateman, 'The Fraternal Social Contract', *Civil Society and the State*, ed. J. Keane (London: Verso, 1988), pp. 101–27.

12 Hans-Georg Gadamer, *Truth and Method* (London: Sheed and Ward, 1979), p. 242.

13 Ibid., p. 243.

14 Recent scholarship has shown that the Grimms' sources were often middle-class, rather than peasants, and that their stories came from literary as well as oral traditions. Most of their storytellers were, nevertheless, women. See Jack Zipes, *The Brothers Grimm: From Enchanted Forests to the Modern World* (New York and London: Routledge, 1988). For a discussion of the ways in which women have been figured as storytellers in European culture, see Marina Warner, *From the Beast to the Blonde: On Fairy Tales and their Tellers* (London: Chatto and Windus, 1994).

15 Petra Maisak, 'Henry Fuseli: "Shakespeare's Painter"', *The Boydell Shakespeare Gallery*, ed. Walter Pape and Frederick Burwick (Bottrop: Peter Pomp, 1996), pp. 57–74; pp. 72–3.

16 Cited in Winifred Friedman, *Boydell's Shakespeare Gallery* (New York and London: Garland Publishing, 1976), pp. 208, 205, 207.

17 Cited in Eudo C. Mason, *The Mind of Henry Fuseli* (London: Routledge and Kegan Paul, 1951), p. 289.

18 Fuseli's (spectacularly unsuccessful) Milton Gallery was mainly taken up with illustrations of scenes from *Paradise Lost*. However, the lines from 'L'Allegro' which describe 'Fairy Mab' and the 'Lubber Fiend' were illustrated in several pictures in the series.

19 Johann Gottfried Herder, 'On Shakespeare', *Eighteenth-Century German Criticism*, ed. Timothy Chamberlain (New York: Continuum, 1992), p. 158.

20 Titania's wand links her to Circe, another enchantress who is associated with beasts. Circe's identifying attribute is her wand, which she uses to turn men to beasts and half-beasts just as, so it is implied, Titania is doing here. See Marina Warner, 'The Enchantments of Circe', *Raritan*, vol. 17 (1997), no. 1, 1–23.

21 See John Barrell, *The Political Theory of Painting from Reynolds to Fuseli* (London and New Haven: Yale University Press, 1986), pp. 291–6.

22 Mason, *Mind of Henry Fuseli*, pp. 179–80.

23 See Barrell, *Political Theory*, pp. 258–62.

24 Ibid., p. 145. It was a truism for eighteenth-century commentators that the present age was one of unbridled luxury, and the debates about the meaning of luxury and its vitiating and feminising effects were extensive. See, for example, Christopher Berry, *The Idea of Luxury: A Conceptual and Historical Investigation* (Cambridge University Press, 1994).

25 Kenneth Clark, *The Nude* (London: John Murray, 1956), p. 207, where Scamozzi's Vitruvian Man is reproduced. See Carol Louise Hall, *Blake and Fuseli: A Study in the Transmission of Ideas* (New York and London: 1985), especially pp. 56–65, for a detailed discussion of the friendship and mutual influence of Fuseli and Blake.

26 Joshua Reynolds, *Discourses on Art* (1778), ed. R. Wark (London: Collier–Macmillan, 1966), p. 46.

27 Ibid., p. 111.

28 Ibid., p. 112.

29 Pape and Burwick, *Boydell's Shakespeare Gallery*, p. 210. William Shakespeare, *The Tempest*, Act V, scene i, line 275.

30 William Shakespeare, *A Midsummer Night's Dream*, Act II, scene iv, lines 175–6.

31 Henry Fuseli, *Lectures on Painting by the Royal Academicians Barry, Opie, and Fuseli*, ed. R. Wornum (London: Bohn, 1848), pp. 439–40.

32 Ibid. p. 440.

33 Ibid. pp. 439–40.

34 Ibid. pp. 410–11.

35 Ibid. p. 441.

36 Joseph Addison and Henry Steele, *The Spectator and the Tatler*, 3 vols. (London: Dent Everyman, 1945), vol. III, p. 299. Italics in the original.

37 Ibid., p. 300.

38 Ibid., p. 301.

39 Jochen Schulte-Sasse, 'Imagination and Modernity: or the Taming of the Human Mind', *Cultural Critique*, no. 5 (1986–7), 23–48. For a detailed survey of the semantic histories of 'imagination' and 'fancy' see James Engell, *The Creative Imagination: Enlightenment to Romanticism* (Cambridge, Mass.: Harvard University Press, 1981), pp. 172–83.

40 Alexander Gerard, *An Essay on Genius* (London: W. Strahan, 1774), pp. 71–2.

41 Ibid., p. 36.

42 Samuel Johnson, *Rasselas and Other Tales*, ed. G. J. Kolb (New Haven and London: Yale University Press, 1990), pp. 150–2.

43 Roger Lonsdale (ed.), *The New Oxford Book of Eighteenth-Century Verse* (Oxford University Press, 1984), p. 365.

44 Ibid., p. 384.

45 Mary Wollstonecraft, *A Vindication of the Rights of Woman* in *Political Writings*, ed. Janet Todd (Oxford University Press World's Classics, 1994), pp. 274, 296.

46 For recent discussions of debates over sensibility in the 1790s, particularly in relation to Wollstonecraft, see Geoffrey Barker-Benfield, *The Culture of Sensibility: Sex and Society in Eighteenth-Century Britain* (Chicago and London: University of Chicago Press, 1992), and Robert W. Jones, 'Ruled Passions: Reading the Culture of Sensibility', *Eighteenth-Century Studies*, vol. 32 (1999), 395–402.

47 Mary Wollstonecraft and Mary Shelley, *Mary, A Fiction; Maria, or the Wrongs of Woman; Matilda* (Harmondsworth: Penguin, 1992), p. 78.

48 Barbara Taylor, 'Mary Wollstonecraft and the Wild Wish of Early Feminism', *History Workshop Journal*, vol. 33 (1992), 197–219; pp. 212–17.

49 Mary Hays, *The Memoirs of Emma Courtney* (1796; London: Pandora, 1987), p. 20.

50 Mary Robinson, *Poems*, 2 vols. (London: G. Bell, 1791), vol. 1, pp. 1–3. I am grateful to Jenny Lewis for drawing my attention to this poem.

51 Hester Thrale Piozzi, *British Synonymy: Or, an Attempt at Regulating the Choice of Words in Familiar Conversation* (London: G. and J. Robinson, 1794), p. 221. Italics in the original.

QUEEN MAB AMONG THE STEAM ENGINES

1 Elizabeth Gaskell, *The Life of Charlotte Brontë* (1857; London: Dent Everyman, 1966), pp. 49–50.

2 Michael Aislabie Denham, *To All and Singular Ghosts, Hobgoblins and Phantasms of the United Kingdom of Great Britain and Ireland* (Durham: William Duncan and Son, 1851), unpaginated.

3 Hugh Miller, *The Old Red Sandstone* (1841; Edinburgh: John Johnstone, 1842), p. 251.

4 Ibid.

5 Ibid.

6 John Ruskin, *The Art of England* (1884), *The Complete Works of John Ruskin* (Library Edition), ed. E. T. Cook and Alexander Wedderburn, 39 vols. (London: George Allen, 1903–12, vol. XXXIII), pp. 327–49; pp. 346–7.

7 Ibid., p. 349.

8 In *Strange and Secret Peoples: Fairies and Victorian Consciousness* (New York and Oxford: Oxford University Press, 1999), Carole Silver discusses the ways in which the fairy beliefs collected by folklore continued to influence Victorian culture. She argues that there was a 'trickle up' of belief in fairies from working to middle class (p. 33).

9 Ibid., p. 31.
10 From a review in the *Athenaeum*, 6 August 1853, p. 943. The original pamphlet has proved impossible to locate.
11 Fanny Kemble, *Records of a Girlhood* (1878), cited in Humphrey Jennings (ed.), *Pandaemonium: The Coming of the Machine as Seen by Contemporary Observers* (London: Macmillan, 1995), p. 174. See also Michael Freeman, *Railways and the Victorian Imagination* (New Haven and London: Yale University Press, 1999), pp. 9–27, 215–40.
12 W. F. Axton, 'Victorian Landscape Painting: a Change in Outlook', *Nature and the Victorian Imagination*, ed. U. C. Knoepflmacher and G. B. Tennyson (Berkeley and London: University of California Press, 1977), pp. 281–308. Isobel Armstrong has recently argued that such fragmentation, what she calls 'doubleness', is the distinctive characteristic of Victorian poetry; the poetic of doubleness is an attempt to find a form for poetry in which modernity can be adequately represented. Isobel Armstrong, *Victorian Poetry: Poetry, Poetics and Politics* (London: Routledge, 1993), pp. 1–25.
13 Axton, 'Victorian Landscape Painting', p. 308.
14 Alexander Pope, *The Rape of the Lock* (London: F. J. Du Roveray, 1798).
15 Clara Erskine Clement, *Angels in Art* (London: David Nutt, 1899), p. 19.
16 John Ruskin, *Giotto and his Works in Padua* (1853–60), *Complete Works*, vol. XXIV, p. 72.
17 John Clare, 'Journey out of Essex' (1841, first published 1865), *Selected Poetry and Prose*, ed. Merryn and Raymond Williams (London: Methuen, 1986), pp. 181–2. Spelling and punctuation are as in the original.
18 Samuel Taylor Coleridge, entry for 27 November 1799, *Notebooks*, ed. Kathleen Coburn, 3 double vols. (London: Bollingen Series and Routledge, 1957–73), vol. I, p. 589, cited in Jennings, *Pandaemonium*, p. 112.
19 Anne D. Wallace, *Walking, Literature and English Culture* (Oxford: Clarendon Press, 1994), p. 81.
20 James Thomson, *'The Seasons' and 'The Castle of Indolence'*, ed. James Sambrook (Oxford: Clarendon Press, 1972), 'Summer', lines 192–8, p. 42.
21 Percy Bysshe Shelley, *Poetical Works*, ed. T. Hutchinson (London: Oxford University Press, 1967), p. 577.
22 See I. F. Clarke's discussion of early balloon literature in *The Pattern of Expectation 1664–2001* (London: Jonathan Cape, 1979), pp. 29–34.
23 Simon Schama, *Citizens: A Chronicle of the French Revolution* (London: Viking, 1989), pp. 125–6.
24 Ibid. See pp. 123–31 for a brief but illuminating discussion of ballooning as spectacle and imaginative phenomenon.
25 Robert Darnton, *Mesmerism and the End of the Enlightenment in France* (Cambridge, Mass. and London: Harvard University Press, 1968), p. 22.
26 Anon., *The Balloon* (London: Religious Tract Society, 1789).
27 Rev. R. S. Medley, *The Air Balloon Spiritualized* (London: L. I. Higham, 1823), pp. 5–7.

28 Robert Beavan, *A History of the Balloon from its Discovery to the Present Time* (London: M'Gowan and Co., 1839), p. 36.

29 Henry Mayhew and John Binney, *The Criminal Prisons of London* (1862; London: Frank Cass, 1968), p. 9. This account was originally published in the *Illustrated London News*, 18 September, 1852.

30 T. Forster, *Annals of some Remarkable Aerial and Alpine Voyages, Including those of the Author* (London: Keating and Brown, 1832), p. vii.

31 Ibid., pp. xiv–xv.

32 Beavan, *History of the Balloon*, p. 40.

33 Ibid., p. 43.

34 John Poole, *Crotchets in the Air: or, an (Un)Scientific Account of a Balloon Trip* (London: Henry Colburn, 1838), pp. 12–13.

35 George Darley, *Sylvia, or The May Queen* (London: John Taylor, 1827), p. 43.

36 Ibid., p. 178.

37 Beavan, *History of the Balloon*, p. 28.

38 For a rather different interpretation of accounts of Victorian balloonists, see Elaine Freedgood, 'Groundless Optimism: Regression in the Service of Egos, England and Empire in Victorian Ballooning Memoirs', *Nineteenth-Century Contexts*, vol. 20 (1997), 61–80. Freedgood discusses many of the same phenomena of ballooning considered here, but argues that the sense of freedom, peace and euphoria experienced by the balloonist should be understood in relation to the narratives of risk and danger generated by industrial capitalism. 'Balloons became (and indeed remain) an emblem of a kind of giddy insouciance, an insouciance the first industrial society needed to offset the effects of mechanization, uniformity and asceticism. They took egos to a realm where, unimpeded by the usual resistances of terrestrial life, they could rest, gather a sense of strength, and return to the earth rejuvenated, ready to serve both England and empire with a fresh supply of truly groundless optimism' (p. 76). Freedgood's account of the balloon treats its importance as entirely secular, and does not consider the theological implications of balloon flight.

39 William Bell Scott, *Memoir of David Scott R.S.A.* (Edinburgh: A. and C. Black, 1850), p. 193.

40 Ibid., p. 208.

41 Ibid., p. 250.

42 A study for this work is reproduced in Mungo Campbell, *David Scott 1806–1849* (Edinburgh: National Gallery of Scotland, 1990), p. 10.

43 This work is now known as *The Discoverer of the Passage to India Passing the Cape of Good Hope*.

44 William Bell Scott, *Memoir*, p. 264.

45 Ibid., pp. 248–9.

46 William Shakespeare, *A Midsummer Night's Dream*, Act II, scene iv, lines 175–6.

47 William Bell Scott, *Memoir*, p. 207.

48 William Shakespeare, *The Tempest*, ed. Frank Kermode (London: Methuen Arden Edition, 1962), p. 130; Act v, scene 1, lines 175–6.

49 According to C. Duncan Rice, by 1830 anti-slavery views were almost universal in 'respectable and literate' Scottish households, and active support for abolition movements actually increased after the abolition of slavery in British dominions in 1833. C. Duncan Rice, *The Scots Abolitionists 1833–1861* (Baton Rouge and London: Louisiana University Press, 1981).

50 William Blake, *Selected Poetry*, ed. Michael Mason (Oxford University Press World's Classics, 1996), p. 66.

51 Mayhew, *Criminal Prisons*, p. 7.

52 Ibid., pp. 9–10.

53 Andrew Ure, *The Philosophy of Manufactures* (London: Charles Knight, 1835), p. 15.

54 Peter Gaskell, *Artisans and Machinery* (London: John W. Parker, 1836), p. 7.

55 Ure, *The Philosophy of Manufactures*, p. 18.

56 Marina Benjamin, 'Sliding Scales: Microphotography and the Victorian Obsession with the Minuscule', *Cultural Babbage: Technology, Time and Invention*, ed. Francis Spufford and Jenny Uglow (London: Faber and Faber, 1996), pp. 99–122; p. 121.

57 Gaston Bachelard, *The Poetics of Space* (1958; Boston, Mass.: Beacon Press, 1969), pp. 171–2.

58 Lewis Carroll, *'Alice in Wonderland' and 'Alice Through the Looking-Glass'* (1865, 1871; Harmondsworth: Penguin, 1998), p. 41.

59 Phillip Henry Gosse, *The Romance of Natural History* (London: James Nisbet, 1860), p. 171.

60 John Milton, *Paradise Lost* (1667) Book I, lines 670–737, *The Complete Poems* (London: Dent Everyman, 1980), pp. 173–4.

61 Cited in Herbert Sussman, *Victorians and the Machine: The Literary Response to Technology* (Cambridge, Mass.: Harvard University Press, 1968), p. 25.

62 John Ruskin, 'The Storm Cloud of the Nineteenth Century' (1884), *Complete Works*, vol. XXXIV, p. 40.

63 Stephen Daniels, 'Loutherberg's Chemical Theatre: *Coalbrookedale by Night*', *Painting and the Politics of Culture: New Essays on British Art 1700–1850*, ed. John Barrell (Oxford University Press, 1992), pp. 195–230; pp. 212–16, 228–30.

64 Susan Stewart, *On Longing: Narratives of the Miniature, the Gigantic, the Souvenir, the Collection* (Durham, N. C. and London: Duke University Press, 1993), p. 112.

65 Ibid., pp. 116–17.

66 *Scene from 'Undine'* was not their only fairy painting. Henry Townshend's *Ariel* (1845), another of their purchases, is in the Royal Collection at Osborne House, the Isle of Wight.

67 See William Vaughan, *German Romanticism and British Art* (New Haven and London: Yale University Press, 1979), p. 117; for German influence on Maclise more generally see pp. 147–9.

68 J. Dafforne, *Pictures by Daniel Maclise R. A.: With Descriptions and a Biographical Sketch* (London: Virtue, Spalding and Daldry, 1873), p. 29.

69 See the introduction, especially pp. 21–5, to *Shakespeare in Production: A Midsummer Night's Dream*, ed. Trevor R. Griffiths (Cambridge University Press, 1996).

70 Michael R. Booth, *Victorian Spectacular Theatre 1850–1910* (London: Routledge and Kegan Paul, 1981), pp. 1–29.

71 Ibid., p. 8.

72 Ibid., p. 4.

73 Ibid., pp. 25–6.

74 Reproduced in *Victorian Fairy Painting* (Exhibition Catalogue; London: Royal Academy of Arts, 1997).

75 *Victorian Fairy Painting*, p. 104; Huskisson was present at a dinner given by Lord Northwick at Thirlstane Hall in 1846, according to W. P. Frith's *My Autobiography and Reminiscences* (3 vols., London: Richard Bentley, 1887), vol. I, pp. 148–9; the commission of a subject from *Comus* is the subject of a series of letters between Miller and Huskisson written between 1848 and 1850 (Miller Papers, Royal Academy of Art Archives).

76 Samuel Carter Hall, *Retrospect of a Long Life from 1815 to 1883* (2 vols.; London: Richard Bentley, 1883).

77 George Speaight, *The History of the English Toy Theatre* (London: Studio Vista, 1969), pp. 88–90.

78 'The Late Richard Dadd', *Art-Union*, 1843, p. 267.

79 See Patricia Allderidge, *The Late Richard Dadd 1817–1886* (Exhibition Catalogue; London: Tate Gallery, 1974), pp. 59–62, 64, 147–8 for a discussion of Dadd's influences and influence in relation to these pictures.

80 Dadd probably saw the engraving after the painting, for the face is very similar in both images. Sets of the Boydell prints were reissued several times during the first half of the nineteenth century.

81 *Art-Union*, April 1841, p. 68.

82 Charlotte Brontë, *Shirley* (1849; London: Dent Everyman, 1975), p. 511. Parenthesis '(fairy)' is in the original.

83 Charles Dickens, *Hard Times* (1854; London: Dent Everyman, 1994), p. 66.

84 Cited in Jennings, *Pandaemonium*, p. 171.

85 Thomas Keightley, *The Fairy Mythology* (1826; London: Bohn's Antiquarian Library, 1850), p. 362.

86 A. E. Waite (ed.), *Songs and Poems of Fairyland* (London: Walter Scott, 1888), pp. 202–3. First published in *The Mystic and Other Poems*, 1855.

87 John Ruskin, *Works*, vol. II, pp. 1–2; Joseph Noel Paton, *Poems by a Painter* (Edinburgh: William Blackwood, 1861), p. 40.

88 Gaskell, *Artisans and Machinery*, pp. 355, 357–8.

89 *The Times*, 19 November 1814, cited in Jennings, *Pandaemonium*, p. 135.

90 Robert Southey, *Journal of a Tour to Scotland in 1819* (1829), cited in Jennings, *Pandaemonium*, pp. 157–8.

91 Thomas Carlyle, 'Signs of the Times' (1829), *Collected Works*, 13 vols. (London: Chapman and Hall, 1857), vol. III, pp. 100–1.

92 Ibid., p. 209.

93 John Stuart Mill, *On Liberty and Other Essays*, ed. John Gray (Oxford University Press World's Classics, 1991), p. 66.

94 Dickens, *Hard Times*, pp. 258–9.

95 Charles Dickens, *The Speeches of Charles Dickens*, ed. K. J. Fielding (Hemel Hempstead: Harvester Wheatsheaf, 1988), p. 284.

96 Charles Dickens, 'Frauds on the Fairies', *Household Words*, 1 October 1853, vol. 8, 97–100; p. 97.

97 'A Case of Real Distress', *Household Words*, 14 January 1854, vol. 8, 457–60; p. 460.

98 'Fairyland in 'Fifty-Four', *Household Words*, 3 December 1853, vol. 8, 313–16; p. 313.

99 Charles Dickens to Henry Cole, 17 June 1854, *The Letters of Charles Dickens*, ed. Madeleine House, Graham Storey, Kathleen Tillotson and Angus Easson, 10 vols. (Oxford: Clarendon Press, 1965–98), vol. VII, p. 354.

100 Ure, *Philosophy of Manufactures*, p. 301.

101 Peter Gaskell, *Artisans and Machinery* (London: John W. Parker, 1836), p. 104.

102 *Victorian Fairy Painting*, p. 110.

103 Richard Schindler has unravelled the complex patterning of narrative in the two pictures through the use of symbolism, design, art-historical references and motifs derived from folklore. Schindler sees Paton's work as a transition between early Victorian history painting and the Pre-Raphaelites, among whom he was close to Millais. He comments: 'The flexibility of this fairy narrative, wedded to the intense naturalism of the setting, foreshadows the dual nature of Pre-Raphaelitism. Their unification of realistic technique with literary, social, and moral themes fulfils the process partially suggested by Paton's works. Paton bridges the gap between early Victorian literary history painting and the beginning of realist narrative painting' ('Joseph Noel Paton's Fairy Paintings: Fantasy Art as Victorian Narrative', *Scotia: An Interdisciplinary Journal of Scottish Studies*, vol. 14 (1990), 13–29; p. 28).

A FEW FRAGMENTS OF FAIRYOLOGY, SHEWING ITS
CONNECTION WITH NATURAL HISTORY

1 James Hinton, 'The Fairy Land of Science', *Cornhill Magazine*, vol. 5 (January 1862), 36–42; p. 36.

2 Ibid., pp. 36–7.

3 Ibid., p. 38.

4 'The popular realism, which regards objects as material "things in themselves", together with the popular idea of God as the creator of the world from nothing by successive acts, and its governor through secondary causes and miraculous interpositions, he treats as due to a certain "spiritual deadness", the intellectual analogue of sin, to which man is prone, and as

exploded by scientific materialism, which, however, in its turn is proved by philosophy to have but a relative validity.' Entry on James Hinton, *Dictionary of National Biography*, ed. L. Stephen and S. Lee, 28 vols., (London: Oxford University Press, 1921), vol. IX, p. 899.

5 Hinton, 'Fairy Land of Science', p. 37.

6 Hinton's interest in Kant was particularly marked in the early 1860s. In a letter dated September 1862 he records having compared the German and English versions of Kant's *Critique of Pure Reason* sentence by sentence. Ellice Hopkins, *Life and Letters of James Hinton* (London: Kegan Paul, 1878), p. 193. An expanded account of his ideas at this time is contained in *Life in Nature* (London: Smith, Elder, 1862), in which he links some of the most problematic areas in physiology, such as the nature of consciousness, to a Kantian metaphysics.

7 Andrew Cunningham and Nicholas Jardine (eds.), *Romanticism and the Sciences* (Cambridge University Press, 1990), p. 7.

8 See H. A. M. Snelders, 'Oersted's Discovery of Electromagnetism', ibid., pp. 228–40. S. R. Morgan's 'Schelling and the origins of his *Naturphilosophie*' (pp. 25–37 of the same volume) gives a clear account of Kant's *Metaphysical Foundations of Natural Science* (1786) and Schelling's development of *Naturphilosophie* from Kantian origins.

9 H. C. Oersted, *The Soul in Nature* (London: Bohn, 1852), pp. 323–4.

10 Hinton, 'Fairy Land of Science', p. 40.

11 Ibid., p. 38.

12 Ibid., p. 39.

13 George Levine, *Darwin Among the Novelists: Patterns of Science in Victorian Fiction* (Cambridge, Mass. and London: Harvard University Press, 1988), pp. 3–4.

14 Thomas Henry Huxley, *Method and Results: Essays* (London: Macmillan, 1894), p. 160.

15 Ibid.

16 Michael Aislabie Denham, *A Few Fragments of Fairyology, Shewing its Connection with Natural History* (Durham: William Duncan and Son, 1854), unpaginated.

17 Andrew Lang and May Kendall, *That Very Mab* (London: Longmans, Green, 1885), p. 43.

18 Ibid., p. 23.

19 Ibid., pp. 23, 14. This idea is given a very similar expression in another book written in the same year: 'But, good or bad, the question still remains, and I am sure numbers of children are still asking it, – "What has become of the fairies?" If you ask it of a philosopher, and he is not a very, very wise man, he will tell you that scientific investigation has disproved the existence of any reasoning beings, except men and women, in the world … If you ask *me*, I can only tell you that I do not know; but of one thing I am quite sure, that, if the whole world were full of fairies, these wise men, with all their bottles and microscopes, would no more be able to analyze one and find out what it was made of, than they are today to

explain why a duck does not come out of a hen's egg!' T. Preston Battersby, *Elf Island: A Fairy Tale* (London: Griffith, Farran, Okeden and Welsh, 1885), pp. 11–12.

20 Edmund Gosse, *Father and Son* (1907; Harmondsworth: Penguin, 1983), p. 124.

21 Ibid., p. 129.

22 Hugh Miller, *The Old Red Sandstone* (1841; Edinburgh: John Johnstone, 1842), p. 250.

23 Ibid.

24 For more about Miller see Michael Shortland (ed.), *Hugh Miller and the Controversies of Victorian Geology* (Oxford: Clarendon Press, 1996).

25 Charles Lyell, *Principles of Geology*, ed. James Secord (1830–3; London: Penguin, 1997), pp. 26–7.

26 Ibid., p. 32. Umbriel is one of the fairies in Pope's 'The Rape of the Lock' (1714), Canto IV, lines 13–17.

27 Greg Myers, 'Science for Women and Children: the Dialogue of Popular Science in the Nineteenth Century', *Nature Transfigured: Science and Literature 1700–1900*, ed. John Christie and Sally Shuttleworth (Manchester and New York: Manchester University Press, 1989), pp. 171–200. See also Roger Cooter and Stephen Pumfrey, 'Separate Spheres and Public Places: Reflections on the History of Science, Popularization and Science in Popular Culture', *History of Science*, 32 (1994), 237–67.

28 Arabella Buckley, *The Fairy-Land of Science* (London: Edward Stanford, 1879), pp. 1–2. Other examples of popular science books using the metaphor of fairyland or fairy tale include J. C. Brough, *The Fairy Tales of Science: A Book for Youth* (London: Griffith and Farran, 1859), X. B. Saintine, *The Fairy Tales of Science, being the Adventures of Three Sisters, Animalia, Vegetalia and Mineralia* (London: Ward Lock, 1886), H. W. S. Worsley-Benison, *Nature's Fairy-Land: Rambles by Woodland, Meadow, Stream and Shore* (London: Elliot Stock, 1888), Joseph F. Charles, *Where is Fairyland?* (London: Sampson, Low, Marston, 1892) and Rev. J. Gordon MacPherson, *The Fairyland Tales of Science* (London: Simpkin, Marshall, 1891).

29 Review of the British Institution annual exhibition, *Art Journal*, n.s. vol. 5 (1859), p. 82. John Anster Fitzgerald (1823–1906), of whom little is known, produced prolific quantities of genre scenes and portraits, but was chiefly known in his lifetime, as now, for his fairy subjects. Fitzgerald exhibited nearly sixty works at the Royal Academy and British Institution between 1845 and 1902. Many of Fitzgerald's works were exhibited with titles which give little indication of their subject (such as these), and have been variously retitled by sale rooms and collectors, so it is not possible to identify whether these two works are still in existence.

30 Review of the British Institution annual exhibition, *Art Journal*, n.s. vol. 6 (1860), p. 80.

31 None of these paintings can be securely dated, and they are usually ascribed to the late 1850s and 1860s. One of the implications of the argument

I pursue here is that the paintings belong to the 1860s, and that Fitzgerald is unlikely to have taken up the subject before 1861.

32 *Victorian Fairy Painting* (Exhibition Catalogue; London: Royal Academy of Arts, 1997), pp. 17–20, 68–70.

33 Review of the Royal Academy of Arts annual exhibition, *Art Journal*, vol. 12 (1850), p. 175.

34 'This is a *quattro-cento*, displaying a great amount of genius, but a greater degree of laborious effort, with a considerable vein of eccentricity.' Ibid.

35 'Who killed Cock Robin?' is, of course, the first line of a nursery rhyme. Leaving aside the question of whether nursery rhymes can be considered 'literary', neither the painting with this title, nor any of those in the 'Cock Robin' series directly illustrates the tale, which is purely avian.

36 Robert M. Young, *Darwin's Metaphor: Nature's Place in Victorian Culture* (Cambridge University Press, 1985), pp. 5–9.

37 Examples of the ubiquity of the miniature are the Victorian passions for dolls' houses, microphotography, microscopy, and alpine rock gardens sited on imitation mountains – some, as at Lamport Hall in Northamptonshire, complete with gnomes living in hollowed-out caverns.

38 Marcia Pointon, 'Geology and Landscape Painting in Nineteenth-Century England', *Images of the Earth: Essays in the History of the Environmental Sciences*, ed. L. Jordanova and R. Porter (Chalfont St Giles: British Society for the History of Science, 1979), pp. 84–108; pp. 103, 104. Apart from those publications referred to later, studies of the relations between science and visual art have tended, not unnaturally, to concentrate on questions of perception such as the history of optics, the development of perspective, colour vision, the invention of photography and so on: for example Martin Kemp, *The Science of Art: Optical Themes in Western Art from Brunelleschi to Seurat* (New Haven and London: Yale University Press, 1990), Jonathan Crary, *Techniques of the Observer: On Vision and Modernity in the Nineteenth Century* (Cambridge, Mass.: MIT, 1990); or they are illustrated surveys of natural history illustration such as S. Peter Dance, *The Art of Natural History* (London: Country Life Books, 1978).

39 Ursula Seibold-Bultmann, 'Monster Soup: the Microscope and Victorian Fantasy', *Interdisciplinary Science Reviews*, vol. 25 (2000), 211–19; p. 217.

40 In his *Hieronymus Bosch: An Annotated Bibliography* (Boston, Mass.: Hall Reference Publications in Art History, 1983), Walter S. Gibson dates the beginning of the revival of interest in Bosch to the mid to late nineteenth century. He cites several European authors who began to move away from the conventional assessment of Bosch as 'the Hogarth of the lower world' (James Stirling Maxwell, *Annals of the Artists of Spain*, 2nd edn, London: John Nimmo, 1891; vol. I, p. 136) towards a view of Bosch as a serious religious artist. The first monograph was M.-G. Gossart, *Jérôme Bosch: Le 'Faizeur de Dyables' de Bois-le-Duc* (Lille: Central du Nord, 1907). British writers on art

were much slower to become interested in this artist than their European counterparts.

41 Matthew Pilkington, *A General Dictionary of Painters*, ed. Allan Cunningham, 4th edn (London: William Tegg, 1857), p. 60.

42 Richard Ford's *Handbook for Travellers in Spain and Readers at Home* (London: John Murray, 1845) reports that cheap engravings after works in the Museo del Prado could be bought in Madrid (p. 745). It is possible that engravings after *The Garden of Earthly Delights* were available and were seen in London. Ford's guide to the Prado collection, the most comprehensive then available in English, mentions only three works by Bosch: '. . . a fine sunset in a Rocky scene, with cowherds; the passage of the Mountain, fine; a mountain and a woody scene'.This certainly suggests that this image, now so famous, was hardly known in the mid-nineteenth century.

43 This conception of the natural world derives ultimately from Aristotle, who saw form as the invariable and inherited *telos* of organisms, embodying both matter and spirit. Aristotelian biology formed the basis of Medieval science, and was incorporated, in a Christianised form, in natural theology, first formulated in the seventeenth century in such works as William Derham, *Physico-Theology or, Demonstration of the Being and Attributes of God from his Works of Creation* (1713). The most famous, culminating works of natural theology from the nineteenth century are, of course, William Paley, *Natural Theology: or Evidences of the Existence and Attributes of the Deity, Collected from the Appearances of Nature* (1802), and the *Bridgewater Treatises* by William Whewell, William Buckland and others (1833–6).

44 Gosse, *Father and Son*, p. 192. For a recent influential discussion of the relationship between Pre-Raphaelite landscape and natural history illustration, see Ann Bermingham, *Landscape and Ideology* (London: Thames and Hudson, 1987), 174–84. It is explored at somewhat greater length in Lynne Merrill, *The Romance of Victorian Natural History* (New York and Oxford: Oxford University Press, 1989), pp. 163–89.

45 The conventions of natural history illustration have developed, of course, in relation to changing paradigms of scientific knowledge. See Allan Ellenius (ed.), *The Natural Sciences and the Arts: Aspects of their Interaction from the Renaissance to the Twentieth Century* (Uppsala: Acta Universitas Uppsaliensis 22, Almqvist and Wiksell International, 1985), and Martin Kemp, 'Taking it on Trust: Form and Meaning in Naturalistic Representation', *Annals of Natural History* 17 (1990), 127–88. Alex Potts describes specific differences between eighteenth- and nineteenth-century natural history illustration in 'Natural Order and the Call of the Wild: the Politics of Animal Picturing', *Oxford Art Journal* 13 (1990), no. 1, 12–33.

46 Phillip Henry Gosse, *Actinologia Britannica: A History of British Sea Anemones and Corals* (London: Van Voorst, 1858–60).

47 John Ruskin, *Modern Painters*, vol. 1 (1843), *The Complete Works of John Ruskin*, ed. E. T. Cook and Alexander Wedderburn, vol. III (1903–12), p. 616; *Stones of Venice III* (1853), *Complete Works*, vol. X, p. 228. Ruskin had *Peach and Grapes*

by Hunt above his bedroom fireplace at Brantwood, and organised a show of Hunt's work in 1880.

48 David Elliston Allen, *The Naturalist in Britain: A Social History* (London: Allen Lane, 1976), pp. 83–157. See also David Elliston Allen, 'Tastes and Crazes', *The Cultures of Natural History*, ed. N. Jardine, J. Secord and E. Spary (Cambridge University Press, 1996), pp. 394–407.

49 Fitzgerald was probably familiar with Hunt's work from the exhibitions of the Old Water Colour society, and may also have attended the posthumous sale of Hunt's work in 1864. It is quite possible that he was influenced by Hunt's watercolour technique in his many essays in the medium. Hunt's innovation was to use body colour as a white ground over which pure watercolour was laid; this gave brilliant colour effects (also noticeable in Fitzgerald's work) and was widely imitated, especially by the Pre-Raphaelites and later Victorian watercolourists. See John Witt, *William Henry Hunt (1790–1864): Life and Work with a Catalogue* (London: Barrie and Jenkins, 1982).

50 John Ruskin, *Modern Painters III* (1856), *Complete Works*, vol. V, p. 209.

51 Miller, *The Old Red Sandstone*, p. 245.

52 Thomas Henry Huxley, 'On the Physical Basis of Life' (1868), *Method and Results*, p. 131.

53 'Who is there who does not sympathise with him in the simple love with which he dwells on the brightness and bloom of our summer fruit and flowers?' Ruskin, *Pre-Raphaelitism* (1851), *Complete Works*, vol. XII, p. 361.

54 Jules Michelet, *The Insect*, trans. W. H. D. Adams (1858; Edinburgh: T. Nelson, 1875), pp. 163, 243.

55 A. L. O. E. [C. M. Tucker], *Fairy Frisket, Or Peeps at the Insect Folk* (London: T. Nelson, 1874).

56 One of the very first fairy paintings, *Puck*, by Henry Fuseli (1790; whereabouts unknown) gives Puck bats' wings, and connects him iconographically with witches and black magic. However, this is the only instance of a fairy with bats' wings, probably because fairy painting became popular only after the publication of Polidori's *The Vampyre* (1819).

57 Acheta Domestica [L. M. Budgen], *Episodes of Insect Life*, vol. I (London: Reeve, Benham and Reeve, 1849–51), p. 14.

58 Ibid., pp. 152–3.

59 Susan Stewart, *On Longing: Narratives of the Miniature, the Gigantic, the Souvenir, the Collection* (1984; Durham, N. C. and London: Duke University Press, 1993), p. 65.

60 Ibid., p. 66.

61 Ernest Van Bruyssel, *The Population of an Old Pear Tree* (London: Macmillan, 1870), p. 6.

62 Ibid., p. 9.

63 Ibid.

64 Acheta Domestica, *Episodes of Insect Life*, p. 14.

65 Stewart, *On Longing*, p. 68.

66 See Allen, 'Tastes and Crazes', and Anne Larsen, 'Equipment for the Field', *The Cultures of Natural History*, ed. Jardine, Secord and Spary, pp. 358–77, for further discussion of the material culture associated with mid-nineteenth-century natural history.

67 C. Stoate, *Taxidermy: The Revival of a Natural Art* (London: The Sportsman's Press, 1987), pp. 1–21.

68 Cited in C. H. Gibbs-Smith, *The Great Exhibition of 1851* (London: HMSO, 1964), p. 137.

69 *The Comical Creatures from Wurtemberg, Including the Story of Reynard the Fox with Twenty Illustrations drawn from the Stuffed Animals Contributed by Herrman Plouquet of Stuttgart to the Great Exhibition* (London: David Bogue, 1851).

70 For more information about Potter see Christopher Frost, *A History of British Taxidermy* (Long Melford: Privately Printed, 1987), pp. 80–1, and the brochure produced by Walter Potter's Museum of Curiosities, Cornwall, where his cases are now displayed.

71 Charles Darwin, *On the Origin of Species by Means of Natural Selection* (1859), ed. Gillian Beer (Oxford University Press World's Classics, 1996), pp. 395–6.

72 The emphasis in pre-nineteenth century natural history on the classification of specimens and species was motivated in great part by the belief that all life forms were related parts of the great divine plan, and linked by a natural classification it was the task of naturalists to discover. This was underpinned by natural theology, for example William Derham (1713) *Physico-Theology*, which argued that observation of the created world would lead to knowledge of the deity. Prior to the early nineteenth century, and later in Britain, natural history was principally concerned not with the relationships of life forms to each other and to the environment, but with their place in the natural classification of the divine order. 'By gathering together and comparing representatives of as many species as they could, some naturalists hoped to discover the natural classification system that related all living things to each other' (Larsen, 'Equipment for the Field', *The Cultures of Natural History*, ed. Jardine, Secord and Spary, p. 358).

73 Even before Darwin's formulation of the laws of evolution by natural selection, the entangled bank was, arguably, a key metaphor through which the workings of the natural world were conceptualised. Compare, for example, these instances from the *Journal of Researches*: 'On every side were lying irregular masses of rock and torn-up trees; other trees, though still erect, were decayed to the heart and ready to fall. The entangled mass of the thriving and the fallen reminded me of the forests within the tropics . . . The number of living creatures of all Orders, whose existence intimately depends on the kelp, is wonderful. A great volume might be written, describing the inhabitants of one of these beds of sea-weed. Almost all the leaves, excepting those that float on the surface, are so thickly incrusted with corallines as to be of a white colour. We find exquisitely delicate structures, some inhabited by simple hydra-like polypi, others by more organized kinds, and beautiful

compound Ascidiae. On the leaves, also, various patelliform shells, Trochi, uncovered molluscs, and some bivalves are attached. On shaking the great entangled roots, a pile of small fish, shells, cuttle-fish, crabs of all orders, sea-eggs, starfish, beautiful Holuthruiae, Planariae, and crawling nereidous animals of a multitude of forms, all fall out together . . . I can only compare these great aquatic forests of the southern hemisphere, with the terrestrial ones in the inter-tropical regions' (Charles Darwin, *Journal of Researches into the Geology and Natural History of Various Countries Visited During the Voyage of the Beagle* (1839; London: Dent, 1906), pp. 199–200, 228–9). The recurrence of the word 'entangled' here in the context of the multitudinousness and interdependence of life forms suggests that, even at this stage, Darwin saw entanglement as the underlying order of the natural world.

74 Gillian Beer, *Darwin's Plots* (London: Ark Paperbacks, 1985), p. 81.
75 Robert Browning, *The Poems*, ed. John Pettigrew, 2 vols. (Harmondsworth: Penguin, vol. I, 1981), p. 419.
76 Carol Christ, *The Finer Optic: The Aesthetic of Particularity in Victorian Poetry* (New Haven and London: Yale University Press, 1975), p. 68.
77 Ibid., p. 71.
78 Walter Bagehot, 'Wordsworth, Tennyson and Browning: or Pure, Ornate and Grotesque Art in Poetry', *Literary Studies*, 2 vols. (London: Longmans, 1879), vol. I, p. 375.
79 See Jonathan Lear, *Aristotle: The Desire to Understand* (Cambridge University Press, 1988), pp. 15–54, for an account of Aristotle's theory of form, which Lear summarises as follows: '. . . we should conceive the end as being the (*fully actualized*) form. For the form is and has been its nature throughout its development. The form is *both* that toward which the process is directed – 'that for the sake of which' the process occurs – *and* that which is directing the process. It is an immature organism's nature simply to be a member of that species in the fullest, most active sense. This, for Aristotle, is one and the same nature: the active, dynamic form which, at varying levels of potentiality and actuality, is at work in the appropriate matter' (pp. 19–20). For Aristotle, understanding the forms of organisms is the key to understanding the rationality of the natural world, and the constancy of forms from generation to generation embodies these rational structures. 'Animals, therefore, strive for immortality in the only way open to them: by reproducing their kind. In this way the species exists eternally. Now, while the parents may pass on family resemblance between one generation and the next, what primarily remains through the continuing change of generations is the formal, intelligible structure of each species. It is the intelligibility of each species that is truly eternal' (p. 54).
80 Lisbet Koerner notes that Carl Linnaeus' system of classification was derived ultimately from Aristotelian principles, whilst he also subscribed to the doctrines of natural theology, themselves a Christian interpretation of Aristotelian biology. 'Carl Linnaeus in his Time and Place', *The Cultures of Natural History*, ed. Jardine, Secord and Spary, pp. 145–62.

81 For a rather different discussion of Bagehot's conception of the grotesque, see Isobel Armstrong, *Victorian Poetry: Poetry, Poetics and Politics* (London: Routledge, 1993), pp. 284–6. Armstrong relates Bagehot's grotesque to religious typology: 'in attempting to establish the pure, fixed, universal theological Type against the Grotesque, Bagehot, even though using the Type metaphorically, exploits its conservative propensities' (p. 285). Armstrong also suggests, but does not develop the suggestion, that the Type is also 'evolutionary'.

82 Bagehot wrote of 'Caliban Upon Setebos' that 'Mr Browning has undertaken to describe what may be called *mind in difficulties* – mind set to make out the universe under the worst and hardest circumstances. He takes "Caliban", not perhaps exactly Shakespeare's Caliban, but an analogous and worse creature; a strong thinking power, but a nasty creature – a gross animal, uncontrolled and unelevated by any feeling of religion or duty. The delineation of him will show that Mr Browning does not wish to take undue advantage of his readers by choice of nice subjects' (*Literary Essays*, pp. 377–88).

83 Browning read *Origin of Species* on its publication, and followed the debate which ensued. In December 1859 Browning met an American Unitarian, Theodore Parker, who was also an amateur biologist. His *Discourse of Matters Pertaining to Religion* is another text Browning may well have had in mind when writing the poem. Compare, for example: 'A man rude in spirit must have a rude conception of God. He thinks the deity like himself. If a buffalo had a religion, his conception of the deity would probably be a buffalo' (cited in Browning, *The Poems*, vol. 1, p. 1158). Phillip Drew implies that Browning's reading of *Origin of Species* must have been a superficial one, and that he failed 'to notice that Darwin had added quite a lot to the idea of evolution which had been current in the 1830s' (Phillip Drew, 'Browning and Philosophy', *Writers and their Background: Robert Browning*, ed. Isobel Armstrong (London: G. Bell, 1974, pp. 104–41), p. 147). Whether Browning immediately and consciously grasped all the implications of Darwin's work, it is hard to believe that he would not have responded to an image of such power and vibrancy as the entangled bank.

84 Paley, *Natural Theology*, p. 42.

85 Browning, *The Poems*, vol. 1, p. 805, lines 1–11.

86 Jeff Karr, 'Caliban and Paley: Two Natural Theologians', *Studies in Browning and his Circle*, 13 (1985), 37–46; p. 39.

87 Browning, *The Poems*, vol. 1, pp. 806–7, lines 46–56, 99–109.

88 Beer, *Darwin's Plots*, p. 81.

89 Karr, 'Caliban and Paley', p. 45. See also Gillian Beer, *Darwin's Plots*, pp. 49–76, for an account of Darwin's own struggles against anthropomorphism in *Origin of Species*.

90 Beer, quoting Freud, describes Darwin's work as the 'second blow' to man's narcissism: the first being the Copernican revolution and the third being, of course, the discovery of the Unconscious. See Beer, *Darwin's Plots*,

pp. 12–18 for a discussion of the effects of this 'blow' on Victorian culture and mentality.

91 Walter Bagehot, 'Wordsworth, Tennyson and Browning', p. 375.

92 For a full account of Dadd's life, see Patricia Allderidge, *The Late Richard Dadd 1817–1886* (Exhibition Catalogue; London: Tate Gallery, 1974).

93 The two pictures clearly share some thematic concerns. The central figures in *Contradiction: Oberon and Titania* are framed by a tangle of plants and insects which push against the surface of the picture-plane. Dadd's rejection of reproduction, inheritance and generation which underlies his psychotic delusions, and which, I will argue, are central to understanding Dadd's representation of the natural world, is figured metonymically by the huge malachite egg supported by an extremely fragile pillar to the top right of the painting. Like the splitting of the nut in *The Fairy Feller's Master-Stroke*, the precarious poise of the egg, which could so easily fall and break, signifies the imminent destruction of the possibility of reproduction. And of course a malachite egg could not, in any case, ever be fertile.

94 Cited in Allderidge, *Richard Dadd*, pp. 22–4.

95 Ibid., p. 39.

96 Ibid. A much more detailed discussion of the origins of Dadd's belief in Osiris can be found in Louise Lippincott, 'Murder and the Fine Arts or, a Reassessment of Richard Dadd', *The John Paul Getty Museum Journal* 16 (1988), 75–94; pp. 79–81. Lippincott argues that Dadd's conviction of the priority of Osiris leads him to reverse conventional typological relationships, which see non-Christian religions as versions of the Christian type. Thus she reads *Mercy: David Spareth Saul's Life* (1854), a subject which has the conventional typological meaning of a prefiguration by David of Christ, as a representation of Osiris staying the sacrifice of human captives, a subject Dadd had seen repeatedly pictured on the walls of the temples he had visited.

97 Robert Chambers, *Vestiges of the Natural History of Creation and Other Evolutionary Writings* (1844), ed. James A. Secord (University of Chicago Press, 1994), pp. 272–3.

98 Patricia Allderidge contends that after his confinement Dadd 'produced only variations, increasingly idiosyncratic, on the themes which he was already handling; and his own development, marked by a progressive drive back into his inner resources to replace the ever receding stimuli of the world from which he had been cut off, proceeded, as it were, within a vacuum' (*Richard Dadd*, p. 41). This implies that the later pictures should be interpreted in purely formal terms, or that they should be regarded as 'pure fantasy', unmediated by any discursive or pictorial context. She also remarks that 'it would be misleading to single out insanity as having more effect on his painting than as part of his whole formative experience ... Delusional material – Osiris, devils and the like – does not intrude into his painting' (ibid., p. 43). My argument is that Dadd's insanity is derived at least in part from his 'whole formative experience', and that, on the

contrary, *The Fairy Feller's Master-Stroke* can only be properly understood if it is seen as containing 'delusional material', itself derived from the world from which he was isolated.

99 Dadd's method was to work the composition out in great detail in monochrome and then painstakingly to fill in the picture little by little in colour. There are several unfinished areas, the main ones being the 'floor' at the bottom of the picture and the Fairy Feller's axe at its centre.

100 Richard Dadd, 'Elimination of a Picture Called the Feller's Master-Stroke' lines 577–90. Cited in Allderidge, *Richard Dadd*, pp. 127–9.

101 Beer, *Darwin's Plots*, pp. 83–4.

102 Dadd, 'Elimination of a Picture', lines 117–36.

103 Interestingly, this echoes Aristotle's dictum 'For what is cannot come to be (because it *is* already) and from what is not nothing could have come to be . . .' (*Physics*, 1.8, emphasis in the original), which Jonathan Lear glosses thus: '. . . from nothing nothing could come to be. But nor can something come to be from something, for something already exists and thus cannot come to be' (*Aristotle: The Desire to Understand*, p. 55). Dadd's poem, which is to 'eliminate' his picture, returns to echo the Aristotelian conceptions of form and generation which underpinned the religious ideas which both he and Darwin, in very different ways, rejected.

104 William Shakespeare, *King Lear* (London: Penguin, 1996), Act I, scene i, line 90, p. 64.

A BROKEN HEART AND A POCKET FULL OF ASHES

1 Carole Silver discusses the tradition of the fairies' farewell in *Strange and Secret Peoples: Fairies and Victorian Consciousness* (New York and Oxford: Oxford University Press, 1999), pp. 193–203. Silver incorporates a wide range of accounts of the leaving of the fairies in a discussion which takes a rather different view of the cultural significance of this tradition from mine. See also Katherine Briggs, *The Vanishing People: Fairy Lore and Legends* (New York: Pantheon, 1978), pp. 7–9.

2 Rosamund Marriot Watson, *Poems* (London: John Lane The Bodley Head, 1912), pp. 141–3. First published in Graham R. Tomson (pseud. R. M. Watson), *A Summer Night and Other Poems* (1891).

3 Gillian Beer, *Arguing with the Past* (London: Routledge, 1989), pp. 30–1.

4 See Glyn Daniels, *The Idea of Prehistory* (Harmondsworth: Penguin, 1964), pp. 31–68, for an account of changing nineteenth-century attitudes to pre-history and pre-historic man.

5 Quoted in John Lubbock (Lord Avebury), *Prehistoric Times as Illustrated by Ancient Remains and the Manners and Customs of Ancient Savages* (London: Williams and Norgate, 1865), p. 1.

6 Silver, *Strange and Secret Peoples*, pp. 33–58. The origins of the fairies are also discussed in Briggs, *The Vanishing People*, pp. 27–38.

7 This term was coined by E. B. Tylor in *Primitive Culture* (1873) to describe remnants of obsolete rituals and customs that persist even though the original religion or culture to which they belonged has died out.

8 Cited in Silver, *Strange and Secret Peoples*, p. 46.

9 Ibid., pp. 43–50.

10 Alfred Noyes (ed.), *The Magic Casement: An Anthology of Fairy Poetry* (London: Chapman and Hall, 1908), p. xiv.

11 Ibid., pp. 35–6. The poem was first published in *The Wild Knight* (1900).

12 G. K. Chesterton, *Orthodoxy* (London: John Lane the Bodley Head, 1909), p. 92. Italics in the original.

13 Ibid., p. 14.

14 I have greatly simplified the complexity of Chesterton's thought in order to summarise. See John Coates, *Chesterton and the Edwardian Cultural Crisis* (Hull University Press, 1984), for a very full account of Chesterton's ideas and their contemporary context.

15 Alfred Noyes, *The Elfin Artist and Other Poems* (Edinburgh: Blackwood, 1920), p. 2.

16 Alfred Noyes, 'The Poet of Light', *Some Aspects of Modern Poetry* (London: Hodder and Stoughton, 1924), pp. 10–43; p. 12.

17 Watson, *Poems*, p. 52. First published in *The Bird Bride*, 1889.

18 Walter de la Mare, *Poems 1901 to 1918*, 2 vols. (London: Constable, 1920), vol. I, p. 113.

19 Walford Graham Robertson, *Time Was* (London: Hamish Hamilton, 1931), p. 321.

20 Walford Graham Robertson, *Pinkie and the Fairies* (London: William Heinemann, 1909), p. 100.

21 Robertson, *Time was*, pp. 311–13, 322–3.

22 *Peter Pan* was first produced in 1904, although Barrie did not publish the play until 1928. Jacqueline Rose examines Barrie's tortuous relationship with the play, its troubled emergence from his novel, *The Little White Bird* (1902) and his difficulties in asserting his authorship both of the play and of the novel, in *The Case of Peter Pan, or the Impossibility of Children's Fiction* (London: Macmillan, 1984), pp. 5–6, 20–41.

23 J. M. Barrie, *Peter Pan and Other Plays*, ed. Peter Hollindale (Oxford: Clarendon Press, 1995), pp. 136–7.

24 A. J. Ayer, *A Part of My Life* (London: Collins, 1977), p. 30, cited in Peter Lewis, 'A Note on Audience Participation and Psychical Distance', *British Journal of Aesthetics*, vol. 25 (1985), 273–7; p. 277.

25 Suzanne Langer, *Feeling and Form* (London: Routledge and Kegan Paul, 1953, p. 318), cited in Lewis, 'A Note on Audience Participation', p. 273.

26 Barrie, *Peter Pan*, p. 137.

27 Rose, *The Case of Peter Pan*, pp. 11, 137.

28 Kenneth Grahame, *The Golden Age* (1895), *The Penguin Kenneth Grahame*, ed. Naomi Lewis (Harmondsworth: Penguin, 1983), p. 5.

29 Ibid., pp. viii–x; Isobel Armstrong, Joseph Bristow and Katherine Sharrock (eds.), *Nineteenth-Century Women Poets* (Oxford: Clarendon Press, 1996), p. 746.
30 Malcolm Shaw and Christopher Chase, 'The Dimensions of Nostalgia', *The Imagined Past: History and Nostalgia,* ed. Christopher Chase and Malcolm Shaw (Manchester University Press, 1989), pp. 1–17, p. 4.
31 Ibid., p. 5.
32 Alfred Nutt, *The Fairy Mythology of Shakespeare* (London: David Nutt, 1900), pp. 26–7.
33 Ann C. Colley, *Nostalgia and Recollection in Victorian Culture* (London: Macmillan, 1998), p. 32.
34 See for an example, *The Stuff That Dreams are Made Of* (Exhibition Catalogue; London: Maas Gallery, 1996), p. 47.
35 Katherine Briggs, *An Encyclopaedia of Fairies* (New York: Pantheon Books, 1976), p. 246.
36 The legend of the Kelpie was well known: for example, Walter Scott's poem 'The Kelpy', which dramatises the tale in a medieval setting, was included in Noyes's anthology, *The Enchanted Island* (1908); 'The Kelpie of Corrieveckan' by Charles MacKay was included in Dora Owen (ed.), *The Book of Fairy Poetry* (London: Longmans, Green, 1920). It is entirely possible that Draper and the other painters who depicted Kelpies (especially Thomas Millie Dow, who was Scottish) knowingly changed the Kelpie's nature and sex.
37 Paul Connerton, *The Tragedy of Enlightenment: An Essay on the Frankfurt School* (Cambridge University Press, 1980), p. 119.
38 Max Weber, *Max Weber's 'Science as a Vocation'*, ed. Peter Lassman and Irving Velody (London: Unwin Hyman, 1989), p. 13.
39 Ibid., pp. 13–14. Italics in the original.
40 Ibid., p. 30.
41 Zygmunt Bauman, *Intimations of Postmodernity* (London: Routledge, 1992), p. x. Italics in the original.
42 Ibid., p. xi.
43 Vera Brittain, *Testament of Youth* (1933), cited in Adrian Caesar, *Taking it Like a Man: Suffering, Sexuality and the War Poets Brooke, Sassoon, Owen, Graves* (Manchester University Press, 1993), p. 3.
44 John Brophy and Eric Partridge (eds.), *Songs and Slang of the British Soldier: 1914–1918* (1930), cited in Allyson Booth, *Postcards from the Trenches: Negotiating the Space Between Modernism and the First World War* (New York and Oxford: Oxford University Press, 1996), p. 30. Italics in the original.
45 *Victorian Fairy Painting* (Exhibition Catalogue; London: Royal Academy of Arts, 1997), pp. 151–3; Estella Canziani, *Round About Three Palace Green* (London: Methuen, 1937), p. 205.
46 Robert Graves, *Fairies and Fusiliers* (London: Heinemann, 1917), p. 80.
47 Ibid., pp. 14–15.
48 Ibid., p. 50.
49 Caesar, *Taking it Like a Man*, p. 207.
50 Graves, *Fairies and Fusiliers*, p. 2. Adrian Caesar argues that this sense of the 'common bond' was troubled for Graves, because it both screened and

expressed homoerotic feelings that were intensely painful for him. Thus he asserts that the fairy poems 'evince a Romantic nostalgia, wherein childhood is viewed as a time of sexual "innocence", and it is this which is appealing to Graves. He was anxious to assert his heterosexual manliness, but also expresses his ambivalence about this, and the poems about fairies constitute a part of that ambivalence; they express a Puritanical longing to retreat from the adult world of the sexual altogether' (*Taking it Like a Man*, p. 207). It may well be that the fairy poems partake of Graves's sexual ambivalence; however, the nostalgia to which they give voice has other sources, and these are my interest.

51 Rose Fyleman, *Fairies and Chimneys* (London: Methuen, 1918), p. 41. First published in *Punch*, 4 July 1917.

52 Ibid., p. 19.

53 The titles were Gardner's and Doyle's.

54 For a full account of the making of the pictures see Geoffrey Crawley's investigation, 'That Astonishing Affair of the Cottingley Fairies', *British Journal of Photography*, December–April 1982–3, May 1985 and July 1986. Crawley proved definitively that the photographs were 'faked', and interviewed Elsie Hill (née Wright) and Frances Griffiths.

55 See Alex Owen, 'Borderland Forms: Arthur Conan Doyle, Albion's Daughters and the Politics of the Cottingley Fairies', *History Workshop Journal*, 38 (1994), 48–85, for a discussion of the ways contemporary spiritualist and mediumistic practices informed the affair.

56 Edward Gardner to Arthur Conan Doyle, 25 June 1920 (letter in the Cottingley archive in the Brotherton Collection, University of Leeds Library).

57 In my article, 'There are Fairies at the Bottom of Our Garden: Fairies, Fantasy and Photography', *Textual Practice*, vol. 10 (1996), no. 1, 57–82, I explore in some detail the ways in which anxieties about the boundary between childhood and adulthood shaped the Cottingley affair.

58 Cited in Arthur Conan Doyle, *The Coming of the Fairies* (London: Hodder and Stoughton, 1922), p. 57.

59 Cited in Crawley, 'That Astonishing Affair' (April 1983), p. 336.

60 See Joe Cooper, *The Case of the Cottingley Fairies* (London: Robert Hale, 1990), p. 132.

61 Fyleman, *Fairies and Chimneys*, pp. 9–10.

62 See Crawley, 'That Astonishing Affair' (February 1983), p. 144, for a full account of Snelling's expertise and the processes he used on the picture.

63 See Crawley, 'That Astonishing Affair' (January 1983), p. 68.

64 George Orwell, *Coming up for Air* (London: Victor Gollancz, 1939), p. 263.

65 Geoffrey Hughes, *Swearing* (Oxford: Blackwell, 1991), p. 229.

66 H. G. Wells, 'Mr Skelmersdale in Fairyland', *Twelve Stories and a Dream* (London: Macmillan, 1903), pp. 110–11.

67 Ibid., p. 122.

68 Ibid., pp. 125–6.

69 Walter Benjamin, 'The Storyteller' (1926), *Illuminations* (1955), ed. Hannah Arendt (London: Fontana, 1992), p. 84.

Bibliography

PRIMARY SOURCES

Acheta Domestica [Budgen, L. M.], *Episodes of Insect Life*, 3 vols., London: Reeve, Benham and Reeve, 1849–51.

Addison, Joseph, and Steele, Henry, *The Spectator and the Tatler* (1712–14), 3 vols., London: Dent Everyman, 1945.

Allingham, William, *Poems*, London: Chapman and Hall, 1850.

A. L. O. E. [Tucker, C. M.], *Fairy Know-A-Bit, or a Nutshell of Knowledge*, London: T. Nelson, 1866.

Fairy Frisket, or Peeps at the Insect Folk, London: T. Nelson, 1874.

Anon., *The Balloon*, London: Religious Tract Society, 1789.

Lessons Derived from the Animal World, London: Society for Promoting Christian Knowledge, 1851.

The Comical Creatures from Wurtemburg, Including the Story of Reynard the Fox with Twenty Illustrations drawn from the Stuffed Animals Contributed by Herrman Plouquet of Stuttgart to the Great Exhibition, London: David Bogue, 1851.

Bagehot, Walter, 'Wordsworth, Tennyson and Browning: or Pure, Ornate and Grotesque Art in Poetry', *Literary Studies*, 2 vols., vol. I, London: Longmans, 1879.

Barrie, J. M., *Peter Pan and Other Plays*, ed. Peter Hollindale, Oxford: Clarendon Press, 1995.

Battersby, T. Preston, *Elf Island: A Fairy Tale*, London: Griffith, Farran, Okeden and Welsh, 1885.

Beavan, Robert, *A History of the Balloon from its Discovery to the Present Time*, London: M'Gowan, 1839.

Black, John, *The Falls of Clyde, or The Fairies*, Edinburgh: William Creech, 1806.

Blake, William, *Selected Poetry*, ed. Michael Mason, Oxford University Press World's Classics, 1996.

Braddon, Mary Elizabeth, *Lady Audley's Secret* (1863), ed. David Skilton, Oxford University Press World's Classics, 1998.

Brontë, Charlotte, *Shirley* (1849), London: Dent Everyman, 1975.

Brough, J. C., *The Fairy Tales of Science: A Book for Youth*, London: Griffith and Farran, 1859.

Browning, Robert, *The Poems, Volume One*, ed. John Pettigrew, Harmondsworth: Penguin, 1981.

Buckley, Arabella, *The Fairy-Land of Science*, London: Edward Stanford, 1879.

Carlyle, Thomas, *Collected Works*, 13 vols., London: Chapman and Hall, 1857.

Carroll, Lewis, *'Alice in Wonderland' and 'Alice Through the Looking-Glass'* (1865, 1871), Harmondsworth: Penguin, 1998.

Chamberlain, Timothy (ed.), *Eighteenth-Century German Criticism*, New York: Continuum, 1992.

Chambers, Robert, *Vestiges of the Natural History of Creation and Other Evolutionary Writings* (1844), ed. James A. Secord, University of Chicago Press, 1994.

Charles, Joseph F., *Where is Fairyland?*, London: Sampson, Low, Marston, 1892.

Chesterton, G. K., *The Wild Knight and Other Poems*, London: Grant Richards, 1900.

Orthodoxy, London: John Lane The Bodley Head, 1909.

Clare, John, *Selected Poetry and Prose*, ed. Merryn and Raymond Williams, London: Methuen, 1986.

Clement, Clara Erskine, *Angels in Art*, London: David Nutt, 1899.

Coleridge, Samuel Taylor, *Notebooks*, ed. Kathleen Coburn, 3 double vols., London: Bollingen Series and Routledge, 1957–73.

Dafforne, J., *Pictures by Daniel Maclise R. A.: With Descriptions and a Biographical Sketch*, London: Virtue, Spalding and Daldry, 1873.

Darley, George, *Sylvia, or The May Queen*, London: John Taylor, 1827.

Darwin, Charles, *The Journal of Researches into the Geology and Natural History of Various Countries Visited During the Voyage of the Beagle* (1839), London: Dent, 1906.

On the Origin of Species by Means of Natural Selection (1859), ed. Gillian Beer, Oxford University Press World's Classics, 1996.

De la Mare, Walter, *Poems 1901 to 1918*, 2 vols., London: Constable, 1920.

Denham, Michael Aislabie, *To All and Singular Ghosts, Hobgoblins and Phantasms of the United Kingdom of Great Britain and Ireland*, Durham: William Duncan and Son, 1851.

A Few Fragments of Fairyology, Shewing its Connection with Natural History, Durham: William Duncan and Son, 1854.

Derham, William, *Physico-Theology or, Demonstration of the Being and Attributes of God from his Works of Creation*, London: 1713.

Dickens, Charles, *Hard Times* (1854), London: Dent Everyman, 1994.

'Frauds on the Fairies', *Household Words*, vol. 8 (October 1853), pp. 97–100.

The Letters of Charles Dickens, ed. Madeline House, Graham Storey, Kathleen Tillotson and Angus Easson, 10 vols., Oxford: Clarendon Press, 1965–98.

The Speeches of Charles Dickens, ed. K. J. Fielding, Hemel Hempstead: Harvester Wheatsheaf, 1988.

Doyle, Arthur Conan, *The Coming of the Fairies*, London: Hodder and Stoughton, 1922.

Ford, Richard, *Handbook for Travellers in Spain and Readers at Home*, London: John Murray, 1845.

Forster, Thomas, *Annals of some Remarkable Aeriel and Alpine Voyages, Including those of the Author*, London: Keating and Brown, 1832.

Frith, W. P., *My Autobiography and Reminiscences*, 3 vols., London: Richard Bentley, 1887.

Fuseli, Henry, et al., *Lectures on Painting by the Royal Academicians Barry, Opie, and Fuseli*, ed. R. Wornum, London: Bohn, 1848.

Fyleman, Rose, *Fairies and Chimneys*, London: Methuen, 1918.

Gaskell, Elizabeth, *The Life of Charlotte Brontë* (1857), London: Dent Everyman, 1966.

Gaskell, Peter, *Artisans and Machinery*, London: John W. Parker, 1836.

Gerard, Alexander, *An Essay on Genius*, London: W. Strahan, 1774.

Gosse, Edmund, *Father and Son* (1907), Harmondsworth: Penguin, 1983.

Gosse, Phillip Henry, *Actinologia Britannica: A History of British Sea Anemones and Corals*, 2 vols., London: Van Voorst, 1858–60.

The Romance of Natural History, London: James Nisbet, 1860.

Grahame, Kenneth, *The Golden Age* (1895), *The Penguin Kenneth Grahame*, ed. Naomi Lewis, Harmondsworth: Penguin, 1983.

Graves, Robert, *Fairies and Fusiliers*, London: Heinemann, 1917.

Grimm, J. C. and W. C., *German Popular Stories*, ed. Edgar Taylor, 2 vols., London: C. Baldwin, 1824–6.

Hall, Samuel Carter, *Retrospect of a Long Life from 1815 to 1883*, 2 vols., London: Richard Bentley, 1883.

Hays, Mary, *The Memoirs of Emma Courtney* (1796), London: Pandora, 1987.

Herder, Johann Gottfried, 'On Shakespeare', *Eighteenth-Century German Criticism*, ed. Timothy Chamberlain, New York: Continuum, 1992.

Hinton, James, 'The Fairy Land of Science', *Cornhill Magazine*, vol. 5 (January 1852), 36–42.

Life in Nature, London: Smith, Elder, 1862.

Hopkins, Ellice, *Life and Letters of James Hinton*, London: Kegan Paul, 1878.

Huxley, Thomas Henry, *Method and Results: Essays*, London: Macmillan, 1894.

Jennings, Humphrey, *Pandaemonium: The Coming of the Machine as seen by Contemporary Observers*, London: Macmillan, 1995.

Johnson, Samuel, *Rasselas and Other Tales*, ed. G. J. Kolb, New Haven and London: Yale University Press, 1990.

Keats, John, *Selected Poems*, ed. Robert Gittings, London: Dent Everyman, 1974.

Keightley, Thomas, *The Fairy Mythology* (1826), London: Bohn, 1850.

Landon, Letitia, *The Poetical Works of L. E. L.*, 2 vols., London: Longman, Rees, Orme, Brown and Green, 1827.

Lang, Andrew, and Kendall, May, *That Very Mab*, London: Longmans, Green, 1885.

Lonsdale, Roger (ed.), *The New Oxford Book of Eighteenth-Century Verse*, Oxford University Press, 1984.

Lubbock, John (Lord Avebury), *Prehistoric Times as Illustrated by Ancient Remains and the Manners and Customs of Ancient Savages*, London: Williams and Norgate, 1865.

Lyell, Charles, *Principles of Geology* (1830–3), ed. James A. Secord, London: Penguin, 1997.

MacPherson, Rev. J. Gordon, *The Fairyland Tales of Science*, London: Simpkin, Marshall, 1891.

Mayhew, Henry, and Binney, John, *The Criminal Prisons of London* (1862), London: Frank Cass, 1968.

Maxwell, James Stirling, *Annals of the Artists of Spain*, 2nd edn, London: John Nimmo, 1891.

Medley, Rev. R. S., *The Air Balloon Spiritualized*, London: L. I. Higham, 1823.

Michelet, Jules, *The Insect* (1858), trans. W. H. D. Adams, Edinburgh: T. Nelson, 1875.

Mill, John Stuart, *On Liberty and Other Essays*, ed. John Gray, Oxford University Press World's Classics, 1991.

Miller, Hugh, *The Old Red Sandstone, or New Walks in an Old Field* (1841), Edinburgh: John Johnstone, 1842.

Milton, John, *The Complete Poems*, London: Dent Everyman, 1980.

Noyes, Alfred, *The Enchanted Island and Other Poems*, Edinburgh: William Blackwood, 1909.

  The Elfin Artist and Other Poems, Edinburgh: Blackwood, 1920.

  Some Aspects of Modern Poetry, London: Hodder and Stoughton, 1924.

Noyes, Alfred (ed.), *The Magic Casement: An Anthology of Fairy Poetry*, London: Chapman and Hall, 1908.

Nutt, Alfred, *The Fairy Mythology of Shakespeare*, London: David Nutt, 1900.

Oersted, H. C., *The Soul in Nature*, London: Bohn, 1852.

Orwell, George, *Coming up for Air*, London: Victor Gollancz, 1939.

Owen, Dora (ed.), *The Book of Fairy Poetry*, London: Longmans, Green, 1920.

Paley, William, *Natural Theology: or Evidences of the Existence and Attributes of the Deity, Collected from the Appearances of Nature*, London: R. Faulder, 1802.

Pilkington, Matthew, *A General Dictionary of Painters*, ed. Allan Cunningham (4th edn), London: William Tegg, 1857.

Piozzi, Hester Thrale, *British Synonymy: Or, an Attempt at Regulating the Choice of Words in Familiar Conversation*, London: G. and J. Robinson, 1794.

Poole, John, *Crotchets in the Air: or, an (Un)Scientific Account of a Balloon Trip*, London: Henry Colburn, 1838.

Pope, Alexander, *The Rape of the Lock*, London: F. J. Du Roveray, 1798.

Reynolds, Joshua, *Discourses on Art* (1778), ed. R. Wark, London: Collier–Macmillan, 1966.

Robertson, Walford Graham, *Time Was*, London: Hamish Hamilton, 1931.

  Pinkie and the Fairies, London: William Heinemann, 1909.

Robinson, Mary, *Poems*, 2 vols., London: G. Bell, 1791.

Rossetti, Christina, *Poems and Prose*, ed. Jan Marsh, London: Dent Everyman, 1994.

Ruskin, John, *The Complete Works of John Ruskin* (Library Edition), ed. E. T. Cook and Alexander Wedderburn, 39 vols., London: George Allen, 1903–12.

Saintine, X. B., *The Fairy Tales of Science, being the Adventures of Three Sisters, Animalia, Vegetalia and Mineralia*, London: Ward Lock, 1886.

Scott, William Bell, *Memoir of David Scott R. S. A.*, Edinburgh: A. and C. Black, 1850.

Shakespeare, William, *King Lear*, London: Penguin, 1966.

    A Midsummer Night's Dream, Shakespeare in Production, ed. Trevor R. Griffiths, Cambridge University Press, 1996.

    The Tempest, ed. Frank Kermode, London: Methuen Arden Editions, 1962.

Shelley, Percy Bysshe, *Poetical Works*, ed. T. Hutchinson, London: Oxford University Press, 1967.

Tennyson, Alfred, *Poems and Plays*, London: Oxford University Press, 1975.

Thomson, James, *'The Seasons' and 'The Castle of Indolence'*, ed. James Sambrook, Oxford: Clarendon Press, 1972.

Tylor, Edward, *Primitive Culture*, London: John Murray, 1873.

Ure, Andrew, *The Philosophy of Manufactures*, London: Charles Knight, 1835.

Van Bruyssel, Ernest, *The Population of an Old Pear Tree*, London: Macmillan, 1870.

Wainewright, T. G., *Essays and Criticisms*, ed. W. C. Hazlitt, London: Reeves and Turner, 1880.

Waite, A. E. (ed.), *Songs and Poems of Fairyland*, London: Walter Scott, 1888.

Watson, Rosamund Marriott, *Poems*, London: John Lane The Bodley Head, 1912.

Wells, H. G., *Twelve Stories and a Dream*, London: Macmillan, 1903.

Whewell, William, *Astronomy and General Physics considered with reference to Natural Theology*, London: William Pickering, 1833.

Wollstonecraft, Mary, *Political Writings*, ed. Janet Todd, Oxford University Press World's Classics, 1994.

Wollstonecraft, Mary, and Shelley, Mary, *Mary, A Fiction; Maria, or the Wrongs of Woman; Matilda*, Harmondsworth: Penguin, 1992.

Worsley-Benison, H. W. S., *Nature's Fairy-Land: Rambles by Woodland, Meadow, Stream and Shore*, London: Elliot Stock, 1888.

SECONDARY SOURCES

Allderidge, Patricia, *The Late Richard Dadd: 1817–1886*, Exhibition Catalogue; London: Tate Gallery, 1974.

Allen, David Elliston, *The Naturalist in Britain: A Social History*, London: Allen Lane, 1976.

    'Tastes and Crazes', *The Cultures of Natural History*, ed. N. Jardine, J. Secord and E. Spary, Cambridge University Press, 1996.

Armstrong, Isobel, *Victorian Poetry: Poetry, Poetics and Politics*, London: Routledge, 1993.

Armstrong, Isobel (ed.), *Writers and their Background: Robert Browning*, London: G. Bell, 1974.

Armstrong, Isobel, Bristow, Joseph, and Sharrock, Katherine (eds.), *Nineteenth-Century Women Poets*, Oxford: Clarendon Press, 1996.

Axton, W. F., 'Victorian Landscape Painting: a Change in Outlook', *Nature and the Victorian Imagination*, ed. U. C. Knoepflmacher and G. B. Tennyson, Berkeley and London: University of California Press, 1977, pp. 281–308.

Bachelard, Gaston, *The Poetics of Space* (1958), Boston, Mass.: Beacon Press, 1969.

Barker-Benfield, Geoffrey, *The Culture of Sensibility: Sex and Society in Eighteenth-Century Britain*, Chicago and London: University of Chicago Press, 1992.

Barrell, John, *The Political Theory of Painting from Reynolds to Fuseli*, London and New Haven: Yale University Press, 1986.

Barrell, John (ed.), *Painting and the Politics of Culture: New Essays on British Art 1700–1850*, Oxford University Press, 1992.

Bauman, Zygmunt, *Intimations of Postmodernity*, London: Routledge, 1992.

Beer, Gillian, *Darwin's Plots: Evolutionary Narrative in Darwin, George Eliot and Nineteenth-Century Fiction* (1983), London: Ark Paperbacks, 1985.
Arguing with the Past, London: Routledge, 1989.

Benjamin, Marina, 'Sliding Scales: Microphotography and the Victorian Obsession with the Minuscule', *Cultural Babbage: Technology, Time and Invention*, ed. Francis Spufford and Jenny Uglow, London: Faber and Faber, 1996, pp. 99–122.

Benjamin, Walter, 'The Storyteller' (1926), *Illuminations* (1955), ed. Hannah Arendt, London: Fontana, 1992.

Berlin, Isaiah, *Against the Current: Essays in the History of Ideas*, Oxford University Press, 1981.

Bermingham, Ann, *Landscape and Ideology*, London: Thames and Hudson, 1987.

Berry, Christopher, *The Idea of Luxury: A Conceptual and Historical Investigation*, Cambridge University Press, 1994.

Booth, Allyson, *Postcards from the Trenches: Negotiating the Space Between Modernism and the First World War*, New York and Oxford: Oxford University Press, 1996.

Booth, Michael R., *Victorian Spectacular Theatre 1850–1910*, London: Routledge and Kegan Paul, 1981.

Bown, Nicola, 'There are Fairies at the Bottom of our Garden: Fairies, Fantasy and Photography', *Textual Practice*, vol. 10 (1996), no. 1, 57–82.

Briggs, Katherine, *An Encylopaedia of Fairies*, New York: Pantheon Books, 1976.
The Vanishing People: Fairy Lore and Legends, New York: Pantheon Books, 1978.

Caesar, Adrian, *Taking it Like a Man: Suffering, Sexuality and the War Poets Brooke, Sassoon, Owen, Graves*, Manchester University Press, 1993.

Campbell, Mungo, *David Scott 1806–1849*, Edinburgh: National Gallery of Scotland, 1990.

Canziani, Estella, *Round About Three Palace Green*, London: Methuen, 1937.

Castle, Terry, *The Female Thermometer: Eighteenth-Century Culture and the Invention of the Uncanny*, New York and Oxford: Oxford University Press, 1995.

Chase, Christopher, and Shaw, Malcolm, *The Imagined Past: History and Nostalgia*, Manchester University Press, 1989.

Christ, Carol, *The Finer Optic: The Aesthetic of Particularity in Victorian Poetry*, New Haven and London: Yale University Press, 1975.

Christie, John, and Shuttleworth, Sally (eds.), *Nature Transfigured: Science and Literature 1700–1900*, Manchester and New York: Manchester University Press, 1989.

Clark, Kenneth, *The Nude*, London: John Murray, 1956.

Clarke, I. F., *The Pattern of Expectation 1664–2001*, London: Jonathan Cape, 1979.

Clery, E. J., *The Rise of Supernatural Fiction 1762–1800*, Cambridge University Press, 1995.

Coates, John, *Chesterton and the Edwardian Cultural Crisis*, Hull University Press, 1984.

Colley, Ann C., *Nostalgia and Recollection in Victorian Culture*, London: Macmillan, 1998.

Connerton, Paul, *The Tragedy of Enlightenment: An Essay on the Frankfurt School*, Cambridge University Press, 1980.

Cooper, Joe, *The Case of the Cottingley Fairies*, London: Robert Hale, 1990.

Cooter, Roger, and Pumfrey, Stephen, 'Separate Spheres and Public Places: Reflections on the History of Science, Population and Science in Popular Culture', *History of Science*, 32 (1994), 237–67.

Crary, Jonathan, *Techniques of the Observer: On Vision and Modernity in the Nineteenth Century*, Cambridge, Mass.: MIT Press, 1990.

Crawley, Geoffrey, 'That Astonishing Affair of the Cottingley Fairies', *British Journal of Photography*, December–April 1982–3, May 1985, July 1986.

Cunningham, Andrew, and Jardine, Nicholas (eds.), *Romanticism and the Sciences*, Cambridge University Press, 1990.

Dance, S. Peter, *The Art of Natural History*, London: Country Life Books, 1978.

Daniels, Glyn, *The Idea of Prehistory*, Harmondsworth: Penguin, 1964.

Daniels, Stephen, 'Loutherberg's Chemical Theatre: *Coalbrookedale by Night*', *Painting and the Politics of Culture: New Essays on British Art 1700–1850*, ed. John Barrell, Oxford University Press, 1992, pp. 195–230.

Darnton, Robert, *Mesmerism and the End of the Enlightenment in France*, Cambridge, Mass. and London: Harvard University Press, 1968.

Dorson, Richard, *The British Folklorists*, London: Routledge, 1968.

Drew, Phillip, 'Browning and Philosophy', *Writers and their Background: Robert Browning*, ed. Isobel Armstrong, London: G. Bell, 1974.

Ellenius, Allan (ed.), *The Natural Sciences and the Arts: Aspects of their Interaction from the Renaissance to the Twentieth Century*, Uppsala: Acta Universitas Uppsaliensis 22, Almkqvist and Wiksell International, 1985.

Engell, James, *The Creative Imagination: Enlightenment to Romanticism*, Cambridge, Mass.: Harvard University Press, 1981.

Freedgood, Elaine, 'Groundless Optimism: Regression in the Service of Egos, England and Empire in Victorian Ballooning Memoirs', *Nineteenth-Century Contexts*, vol. 20 (1997), 61–80.

Freeman, Michael, *Railways and the Victorian Imagination*, New Haven and London: Yale University Press, 1999.

Friedman, Winifred, *Boydell's Shakespeare Gallery*, New York and London: Garland Publishing, 1976.

Frost, Christopher, *A History of British Taxidermy*, Long Melford: Privately Printed, 1987.

Gadamer, Hans-Georg, *Truth and Method* (1965), London: Sheed and Ward, 1979.

Gibbs-Smith, C. H., *The Great Exhibition of 1851*, London: HMSO, 1964.

Gibson, Walter S., *Hieronymus Bosch: An Annotated Bibliography*, Boston, Mass.: Hall, Reference Publications in Art History, 1983.

Hall, Carol Louise, *Blake and Fuseli: A Study in the Transmission of Ideas*, New York and London: 1985.

Hughes, Geoffrey, *Swearing*, Oxford: Blackwell, 1991.

Jardine, N., Secord, J. and Spary, E., *The Cultures of Natural History*, Cambridge University Press, 1996.

Jones, Robert W., 'Ruled Passions: Reading the Culture of Sensibility', *Eighteenth-Century Studies*, vol. 32 (1999), 395–402.

Jordanova, Ludmilla, and Porter, Roy (eds.), *Images of the Earth: Essays in the History of the Environmental Sciences*, Chalfont St Giles: British Society for the History of Science, 1979.

Karr, Jeff, 'Caliban and Paley: Two Natural Theologians', *Studies in Browning and his Circle*, 13 (1985), 37–46.

Kemp, Martin, 'Taking it on Trust: Form and Meaning in Naturalistic Representation', *Annals of Natural History*, vol. 17 (1990), 128–88.

The Science of Art: Optical Themes in Western Art from Brunelleschi to Seurat, New Haven and London: Yale University Press, 1990.

Koerner, Lisbet, 'Carl Linnaeus in his Time and Place', *The Cultures of Natural History*, ed. N. Jardine, J. Secord and E. Spary, Cambridge University Press, 1996, pp. 145–62.

Larsen, Anne, 'Equipment for the Field', *The Cultures of Natural History*, ed. N. Jardine, J. Secord and E. Spary, Cambridge University Press, 1996.

Lear, Jonathan, *Aristotle: The Desire to Understand*, Cambridge University Press, 1988.

Levine, George, *Darwin Among the Novelists: Patterns of Science in Victorian Fiction*, Cambridge, Mass. and London: Harvard University Press, 1988.

Lewis, Peter, 'A Note on Audience Participation and Psychical Distance', *British Journal of Aesthetics*, vol. 25 (1985), 273–7.

Lippincott, Louise, 'Murder and the Fine Arts or, a Reassessment of Richard Dadd', *The John Paul Getty Museum Journal*, vol. 16 (1988), 75–94.

Maisak, Petra, 'Henry Fuseli: "Shakespeare's Painter"', *The Boydell Shakespeare Gallery*, ed. Walter Pape and Frederick Burwick, Bottrop: Peter Pomp, 1996, pp. 57–74.

Mason, Eudo C., *The Mind of Henry Fuseli*, London: Routledge and Kegan Paul, 1951.

Merrill, Lynne, *The Romance of Victorian Natural History*, New York and Oxford: Oxford University Press, 1989.

Morgan, S. R., 'Schelling and the Origins of his *Naturphilosophie*', *Romanticism and the Sciences*, ed. Andrew Cunningham and Nicholas Jardine, Cambridge University Press, 1990, pp. 25–37.

Morrill, David, '"Twilight is not Good for Maidens": Uncle Polidori and the Psychodynamics of Vampirism in *Goblin Market*', *Victorian Poetry*, vol. 28 (1994), no. 1, 1–16.

Myers, Greg, 'Science for Women and Children: the Dialogue of Popular Science in the Nineteenth Century', *Nature Transfigured: Science and Literature 1700–1900*, ed. John Christie and Sally Shuttleworth, Manchester and New York: Manchester University Press, 1989, pp. 171–200.

Owen, Alex, 'Borderland Forms: Arthur Conan Doyle, Albion's Daughters and the Politics of the Cottingley Fairies', *History Workshop Journal*, no. 38 (1994), 48–85.

Pateman, Carol, 'The Fraternal Social Contract', *Civil Society and the State*, ed. J. Keane, London: Verso, 1988, pp. 101–27.

Philpotts, Beatrice, *Fairy Painting*, London: Ash and Grant, 1978.

Pointon, Marcia, 'Geology and Landscape Painting in Nineteenth-Century England', *Images of the Earth: Essays in the History of the Environmental Sciences*, ed. L. Jordanova and R. Porter, Chalfont St Giles: British Society for the History of Science, 1979, pp. 84–108.

Potts, Alex, 'Natural Order and the Call of the Wild: the Politics of Animal Picturing', *Oxford Art Journal*, vol. 13 (1990), no. 1, 12–33.

Purkiss, Diane, *Troublesome Things*, London: Penguin, 2000.

Rice, C. Duncan, *The Scots Abolitionists 1833–1861*, Baton Rouge and London: Louisiana University Press, 1981.

Rose, Jacqueline, *The Case of Peter Pan, or the Impossibility of Children's Fiction*, London: Macmillan, 1984.

Schama, Simon, *Citizens: A Chronicle of the French Revolution*, London: Viking, 1989.

Schindler, Richard, 'Joseph Noel Paton's Fairy Paintings: Fantasy Art as Victorian Narrative', *Scotia: An Interdisciplinary Journal of Scottish Studies*, vol. 14 (1990), 13–29.

Schulte-Sasse, Jochen, 'Imagination and Modernity: or the Taming of the Human Mind', *Cultural Critique*, no. 5 (1986–7), 23–48.

Seibold-Bultmann, Ursula, 'Monster Soup: the Microscope and Victorian Fantasy', *Interdisciplinary Science Reviews*, vol. 25 (2000), 211–19.

Shaw, Malcolm, and Chase, Christopher, 'The Dimensions of Nostalgia', *The Imagined Past: History and Nostalgia*, ed. Christopher Chase and Malcolm Shaw, Manchester University Press, 1989, pp. 1–17.

Shortland, Michael (ed.), *Hugh Miller and the Controversies of Victorian Geology*, Oxford: Clarendon Press, 1996.

Silver, Carole, *Strange and Secret Peoples: Fairies and Victorian Consciousness*, New York and Oxford: Oxford University Press, 1999.

'On the Origin of Fairies: Victorians, Romantics, and Folk Belief', *Browning Institute Studies*, vol. 14 (1986), pp. 141–56.

Snelders, H. A. M., 'Oersted's Discovery of Electromagnetism', *Romanticism and the Sciences*, ed. Andrew Cunningham and Nicholas Jardine, Cambridge University Press, 1990, pp. 228–40.

Speaight, George, *The History of the English Toy Theatre*, London: Studio Vista, 1969.

Stephen, L., and Lee, S. (eds.), *Dictionary of National Biography*, 28 vols., London: Oxford University Press, 1921.

Stewart, Susan, *On Longing: Narratives of the Miniature, the Gigantic, the Souvenir, the Collection*, Durham, N. C. and London: Duke University Press, 1993.

Stoate, C., *Taxidermy: The Revival of a Natural Art*, London: The Sportsman's Press, 1987.

The Stuff That Dreams are Made Of, Exhibition Catalogue: London, Maas Gallery, 1997.

Sussman, Herbert, *Victorians and the Machine: The Literary Response to Technology*, Cambridge, Mass.: Harvard University Press, 1968.

Tanner, Michael, 'Sentimentality', *Proceedings of the Aristotelian Society*, n.s., vol. 77 (1977), 127–47.

Taylor, Barbara, 'Mary Wollstonecraft and the Wild Wish of Early Feminism', *History Workshop Journal*, vol. 33 (1992), 197–219.

Vaughan, William, *German Romanticism and British Art*, New Haven and London: Yale University Press, 1979.

Victorian Fairy Painting, Exhibition Catalogue, London: Royal Academy of Arts, 1997.

Wallace, Anne D., *Walking, Literature and English Culture*, Oxford: Clarendon Press, 1994.

Warner, Marina, *From the Beast to the Blonde: On Fairy Tales and their Tellers*, London: Chatto and Windus, 1994.

'The Enchantments of Circe', *Raritan*, vol. 17 (1997), no. 1, 1–23.

Weber, Max, *Max Weber's 'Science as a Vocation'*, ed. Peter Lassman and Irving Velody, London: Unwin Hyman, 1989.

Wheeler, Wendy, *A New Modernity? Change in Science, Literature and Politics*, London: Lawrence and Wishart, 1999.

Witt, John, *William Henry Hunt (1790–1864): Life and Work with a Catalogue*, London: Barrie and Jenkins, 1982.

Young, Robert M., *Darwin's Metaphor: Nature's Place in Victorian Culture*, Cambridge University Press, 1985.

Zipes, Jack, *The Brothers Grimm: From Enchanted Forests to the Modern World*, New York and London: Routledge, 1988.

Index

Page numbers in *italics* refer to illustrations

'Acheta Domestica'
  see Budgen, L. M.
Addison, Joseph
  'Pleasures of the Imagination', 32–3, 34
Alcock, Mary, 51
Allen, David, 122
angels, 47–8
anthropomorphism, 117, 125–31
Ariel, 59–63, *61*, 110, *111*
Aristotle's theory of form, 144, 211 n. 43,
  214 n. 79, 217 n. 103
Arkwright, Joseph, 65, 68
Armstrong, Isobel, 203 n. 12, 215 n. 81
Axton, W. F., 44
Ayer, A. J., 172

Bachelard, Gaston, 66
Bagehot, Walter
  'Pure, Ornate and Grotesque Art in
    Poetry', 143–6, 148–9, 215 n. 82
Bailey, Phillip James, 85
ballet see theatre
balloons, hot-air, 48, 50–6, 67
  see also flight/flying
Barrie, J. M.
  Peter Pan, 172–3
Battersby, T. Preston, 208 n. 19
Bauman, Zygmunt, 182
Beavan, Robert, 54
Beer, Gillian, 142, 149, 158–9, 164,
  166, 174
Benjamin, Marina, 66
Benjamin, Walter, 181, 197
Berlin, Isaiah, 16
Black, John, 15

Blake, William, 56, 66
  Albion Rose, 26
  Europe: A Prophecy, 6
  'The Little Black Boy', 62
Bodmer, J. J., 21
Booth, Michael, 74
Bosch, Hieronymus
  The Garden of Earthly Delights, 117–19
Boydell, Josiah
  Boydell's Shakespeare Gallery, 6, 19, 20, 24
Braddon, Mary
  Lady Audley's Secret, 14
Brickdale, Eleanor Fortescue, 13
Briggs, Katherine, 177
Brittain, Vera, 183
Brontë, Charlotte, 13, 39
  Shirley, 82
Brophy, John, 183
Brown, Ford Madox, 86
Brown, Samuel, 57, 82
Browning, Robert, 142–4, 146, 148–9, 158,
  161–2, 215 n. 83
  'Caliban upon Setebos', 146–50
  'Sibrandus Schnafnaburgensis', 143–4
Brunel, Isambard Kingdom, 63–4, 65, 70
Buckley, Arabella
  The Fairy Land of Science, 107–8
Budgen, L. M. ('Acheta Domestica'), 125
  Episodes of Insect Life, 127–30, *30*
Burne-Jones, Edward, 48
Burnett, Frances Hodgson, 184

Caesar, Adrian, 183
Caliban, 57, *60–3*, 61, 156–60, *149*,
  158

Canziani, Estella
  The Piper of Dreams, 184, *185*, 187
Carlyle, Thomas, 68
  'Signs of the Times', 11, 87–8,
    142
Carroll, Lewis
  Alice in Wonderland, 66
Castle, Terry, 13
celtic revival, 166
Chambers, Robert
  Vestiges of the Natural History of Creation, 142,
    154
Chase, Malcolm, 174, 180
Chesterton, G. K.
  'Modern Elfland', 167–8
  Orthodoxy, 168–9
Christ, Carol, 144
Clare, John, 49
Clery, E. J., 13
Coleridge, Samuel Taylor, 49
Colley, Ann, 176
Collins, Charles Alston, 124
Collins, William
  'Ode on Popular Superstitions', 34–5
Connerton, Paul, 181
Constable, John, 43
Cruikshank, George, 89

Dadd, Richard, 75, 78–82, 109, 142–3,
    150–62
  cult of Osiris, 153–4
  madness, 78, 150, 152–5, 160, 216 n. 98
  Come unto these Yellow Sands, 80–2, *81*
  Contradiction: Oberon and Titania, 150,
    216 n. 93
  'Elimination of a Picture', 152, 156–7,
    160–1
  The Fairy Feller's Master-Stroke, 150–2, *151*,
    155–62
  Puck, 78–80, *79*
  Songe de la Fantaisie, *152*, 156
  Titania Sleeping, 78
Danby, Francis, 75
Darley, George
  Sylvia, or the May Queen, 54–5
Darnton, Robert, 52
Darwin, Charles, 67–8, 101, 115, 125, 135,
    141–2, 145, 155, 158, 161–2
  Journal of Researches, 213–14 n. 73

On the Origin of Species, 108–9, 132, 146,
    149–50
  see also natural selection
de la Mare, Walter
  'Martha', 170–1
Denham, Michael Aislabie, 39–40, 102–3
Dickens, Charles, 83, 88–9
  'Frauds on the Fairies', 89
  Hard Times, 83, 88–9
  Household Words, 88–90
  Letter to Henry Cole, 90
disenchantment and enchantment, 180–1
  and modernity, 1, 182–3, 197
  and science, 98, 100–1
Dow, Thomas Millie, 177
Doyle, Arthur Conan, 188, 191–3
Draper, Herbert
  The Kelpie, 177, *178*, 179–80
dreams, 91, 95
  see also flight/flying
Duncan, John, 166

Eliot, T. S., 10
Enlightenment and counter-Enlightenment,
    15–18, 23–4
Eroticism, 31–2, 90–1, 95–6
Etty, William, 77
evolution *see* natural selection

Fairies
  and race, 27, 62
  as causes of natural phenomena, 102–3
  as consolatory figures, 1, 11, 45, 70, 82, 84,
    96–7, 140, 150, 197
  as subject for poetry, 34–5
  belief in, 2, 15, 41, 166, 173, 175, 191
  constant presence in nineteenth century,
    1–2, 45
  departure of, 39–41, 163–5, 170
  different respose of men and women to, 4,
    12–14, 17, 18, 36–7
  like insects, 125–31, 135
  like humans, 69–70, 116, 179, 180
  photographs, 187–95, *188–91*
  study of, 5–6, 15–16, 166
  wings, 27, 45–9, 125
fairyland, 88–91
  and childhood, 90, 171–2, 184–7
  as Arcadian landscape, 85–7, 91–7

fairyland (*cont.*)
  depictions, 168
  nostalgic representations, 85–6, 169
  passage of time in, 13, 175
  wartime interest in, 183–7
feminism, 18, 36
Fitzgerald, John Anster, 109–20, 122, 130–3,
    135–6, 139–40
  contemporary significance, 109–10
  The Captive Robin, 118
  Cock Robin Defending his Nest, 112, 129, 139
  Fairies Sleeping in a Bird's Nest, 114, 139
  Who Killed Cock Robin?, 113, 118, 131, 140
flight/flying, 48, 50–6
  dreams, 49, 55, 59
  new perspective on earth, 53–4
  versus walking, 49, 50, 55
folklore, collecting, 5–6, 15–16, 41,
    165–7
Forbes, Elizabeth Stanhope, 177
Fouque, Friedrich de la Motte, 72
Freedgood, Elaine, 204 n. 38
Frith, William Powell, 74
Fuseli, Henry, 12, 18, 19–28, 37–8, 47,
    56, 70
  lectures at Royal Academy, 28–31
  Puck, 25, 26–8
  Titania and Bottom, 19, 19–23
Fyleman, Rose, 187
  'Fairies', 192–3

Gadamer, Hans-Georg, 17
Gardner, Edward, 188, 191–4
Gaskell, Elizabeth
  Life of Charlotte Brontë, 39
Gaskell, Peter, 65
  Artisans and Machinery, 86–7, 90
Gerard, Alexander, 33–4
Gere, Charlotte, 110
Goethe, J. W. von, 21
Gosse, Edmund
  Father and Son, 104–5, 120
Gosse, Phillip Henry, 104, 120, 121
  Actinologia Britannica, 121
  Romance of Natural History, 67
Grahame, Kenneth
  The Golden Age, 173, 176
Graves, Robert
  Fairies and Fusiliers, 184, 186–7
Gray, Thomas
  'The Bard', 34

Grieve, John and family, 73, 74
Griffiths, Frances, 188–95
  Fairies Offering a Posy to Elsie, 190, 195
  see also Wright, Elsie
Grimm, J. C. and W. C.
  Kinder und Hausmärchen, 16, 18, 200 n. 14
Grimshaw, John Atkinson
  Iris, 177
grotesqueness and the grotesque, 27–8, 119,
    142–9, 158, 161

Haddon, A. C., 166
Hall, S. C., 75, 76, 95
Hall-Edwards, Major, 191–2
Hays, Mary, 36
Hemans, Felicia, 13
Henley, T. E., 172
Herder, Johann Gottfried, 16, 24, 181
  'Shakespeare', 21
Hinton, James
  'The Fairy Land of Science', 98–102
Hopkins, Ellice, 142
Hopley, Edward, 41
  Puck and a Moth, 42, 43–5
Howard, Henry, 70
Howlett, Robert
  Photograph of Brunel, 63–4, 65
human form, 26
  dwarfed by machinery, 64–5, 68–9, 82
  fairies as miniature humans, 69–70, 72–3
  materiality of, 57–63
  size relative of fairies, 69–70
  size relative to God, 67–70, 115, 119
  viewed from the air, 63, 67
  see also scale
Hunt, William Henry, 117
  Primroses and a Bird's Nest, 121–2
Hunt, William Holman, 120, 124
Huskisson, Robert, 75
  Come unto these Yellow Sands, 76
  The Midsummer Night's Fairies, 75–7, 76
Huxley, Thomas Henry
  'On the Physical Basis of Life', 101–2, 123

ideal, theory of, 26–31, 69, 70
imagination and fancy, 20–1, 31, 32–7, 192,
    193–4
  women's denigration of, 35–7
Inchbold, Elizabeth, 51
industrialisation, 17, 64–5, 68, 83–91,
    168, 180

caused departure of fairies, 39–41, 83–4
  images of, 68–9
  railways, 43
  spiritual effects of, 86–90
insects, 117, 125–35, *130*
Ireland
  legends, 166
  nationalism, 4
  see also celtic revival

Johnson, Samuel
  Rasselas, 34

Kant, Immanuel, 99–101
Karr, Jeff, 149
Keats, John, 8
Keightley, Thomas, 38
  The Fairy Mythology, 14–15, 85
Kemble, Fanny, 43
Kendall, May
  That Very Mab, 103
King Lear, 160–1
Klopstock, F. G., 21

Landon, Letitia (L. E. L.), 13
  'Fantasies', 9
Landon, Paul
  Daedalus and Icarus, 56
Landseer, Edwin
  Titania and Bottom, 70
Lang, Andrew
  That Very Mab, 103
Langer, Suzanne, 172
Lavater, J. K., 21
Levine, George, 101
Linnaeus, 144, 145
Loutherberg, Phillip de
  Coalbrookedale by Night, 68
Lyell, Charles, 101
  Principles of Geology, 106–7, 142, 154

Mass, Jeremy, 109–10
MacCulloch, David, 166
Maclise, Daniel
  Scene from 'Undine', 70–3, *71*, 77
Maeterlinck, Maurice, 171
Maisak, Petra, 19–20
Martin, John
  The Last Judgement, 69
Mason, Eudo C., 14
Mayhew, Henry, 53, 63

Medley, Rev. R. S., 52
memory, 164–7
  see also nostalgia
Mendelssohn-Bartholdy, Felix, 73
Michelangelo, 23, 56
Michelet, Jules, 125
  'Insects at work', *126*
Midsummer Night's Dream, A, 6, 38
  illustrations of, 31, 19–28, 31, 91–6, *19, 25, 79, 92, 93*
  productions of, 73–4
  see also Puck
Mill, John Stuart, 88
Millais, John Everett
  Ferdinand Lured by Ariel, 44, 110–11, *111*, 114
Miller, Hugh, 40, 105–6, 123
Milton, John, 21, 68
miniatures, 115–16
  miniaturisation, 70, 127, 131–3, 136
  microphotography, 66
  microscopy, 67, 103
modernism, 10, 169–70, 179
modernity, 45, 167
  see also disenchantment and enchantment
Montgolfier brothers, 50–2

Nasmyth, James, 84
natural selection, 68, 104, 117, 132, 135, 141–3, 161–2, 164
  see also Darwin, Charles
natural theology, 115, 129, 147
nostalgia
  and fairies, 85, 174, 176–7
  conditions for, 173–4, 180
  for childhood, 171–2, 183–7
  images of, 176, 184
  see also fairyland
Noyes, Alfred, 176
  'The Elfin Artist', 169–70
Nutt, Alfred, 175

Oersted, Hans Christian, 99
Orwell, George
  Coming up for Air, 195–6
Owen, Robert, 87

Paintings
  allegory in, 29–31, 119
  scale in, 74–5, 77–80, 82, 119, 157–8
  sources of fairy paintings, 23, 26, 94, 115–17

Paintings (*cont.*)
styles, 110
see also Pre-Raphaelitism
Paley, William, 146–7, 158–9, 161
Palgrave, Francis, 165
Partridge, Eric, 183
Paton, Joseph Noel, 86, 91–7
The Fairy Raid, 177
The Quarrel of Oberon and Titania, 91, *92*, 94–7
The Reconciliation of Oberon and Titania, 91, *93*,
94–7, 110
photography
see fairies, photographs of
Piozzi, Hester Thrale, 37
Planché, J. R., 73
Plouquet, Herrman, 137
The Comical Creatures from Wurtemberg, 137,
138
point-of-view, 119–20, 122
Pointon, Marcia, 116
Pope, Alexander
The Rape of the Lock, 45–7, *46*
Potter, Walter, 137, 139
The Death of Cock Robin, *139*
Pre-Raphaelitism, 41, 43–4, 110, 113–14,
120–1, 124
Puck, 24–8, *25*, 41–5, *59*, 59–60, 79–80, *79*

Queen Victoria, 72, 137

Raphael, 23
religious doubt, 2, 120, 150, 154
Reynolds, Joshua, 19, 26–7
Robertson, Walford Graham
Pinkie and the Fairies, 171–2
Robinson, Mary, 37
Romanticism, 6–8
Rose, Jacqueline, 173
Rossetti, Christina
Goblin Market, 13, 200 n. 4
Rossetti, Dante Gabriel, 48
Ruskin, John, 48, 68, 85–6, 116
'Fairyland', 40–1
Pathetic Fallacy, 121–4

Sawyer, Amy, 13
scale, 63–73, 132–3
instability of, 66, 67, 69, 72–3, 77–82,
115–16, 133–5, 137, 157–8, 180, 195

paradoxes of, 64–5
size of fairies, 22–3, 74–5,
69, 116
see also human form, miniaturisation,
paintings
Scamozzi
Vitruvian Man, 26–7
Schama, Simon, 52
Schindler, Richard, 207 n. 103
Schulte-Sasse, Jochen, 33
science
and fairyland, 98–101
and visual art, 108, 116–17
attitudes to embodied in the gaze, 122–32,
135
attitudes to symbolised by fairies,
102–8
illustrations, 120–2, 129
see also natural selection, natural
theology
Scott, David, 48, 56–64
The Agony of Discord, 57
Ariel and Caliban, *61*, 60–4
Philoctetes, 57
Puck Fleeing before the Dawn, *59*,
59–60
The Rime of the Ancient Mariner, 58
The Spirit of the Cape, 58
Scott, Walter
Scott, William Bell, 56–7, 60
sentimentality, 10–11
Shakespeare, William, 19–21
see also Ariel, Boydell's Shakespeare
Gallery; Browning, Robert; Dadd,
Richard; Fuseli, Henry; *King Lear;*
Millais, John Everett;
A Midsummer Night's Dream; Paton,
Joseph Noel; Puck; Scott, David;
The Tempest
Shaw, Christopher, 174, 180
Shelley, Percy Bysshe
Queen Mab, 6
'Ode to the West Wind', 50–1
Siebold-Bultmann, Ursula, 117
Silver, Carole, 4, 41, 165–6
slavery, 62
Smith, Adam, 13
Snelling, Arthur, 194
Solomon, Simeon, 48

Southey, Robert, 87
Stainton, Charles Prosper, 177
Stevenson, Robert Louis, 173
Stewart, Susan, 69, 131, 140
Stothard, Thomas
  The Rape of the Lock, 46

Taglioni, Marie, 73
Tanner, Michael, 10
taxidermy, 136–40
  anthropomorphic, 137, 140
Taylor, Barbara, 36
Tempest, The, 6
  illustrations of, 27, 44, 59–62, 76, 80–2,
    59, 61, 81
Tennyson, Alfred
  'Bugle Song', 8
theatre, 73–5
  ballet, 73
  fairy extravaganzas, 73
  'fairy plays', 171
  influence on fairy painting, 75–82,
    94–5
  toy theatres, 77
Thomson, James, 50
traditional stories
  see folklore, collecting
Tucker, C. M. ('A. L. O. E.'), 125
Turner, J. M. W., 70, 124
  Queen Mab's Cave, 7–8, 7

Ure, Andrew
  The Philosophy of Manufactures, 64–5, 85,
    90, 96

Van Bruyssel, Ernest
  The Population of an Old Pear Tree, 132–5, *134*
Vestris, Madame, 73–4, 94

Wainewright, T. G., 12
Wallace, Anne D., 50
Watson, Rosamund Marriot, 13
  'The Fairies' Valediction', 170, 174,
  'The Last Fairy', 163–4
Weber, Max
  Science as a Vocation, 180–1
  see also disenchantment and enchantment
Wells, H. G.
  'Mr Skelmersdale goes to Fairyland', 196
Wheeler, Wendy, 10
Wilkinson, John Gardner, 153
wings
  angels', 47–8
  bats', 28
  fairies', 27, 45–9
  insects', 47, 125
Wollstonecraft, Mary, 32, 38
  dismissive of fairies, 18
  Mary, a Fiction, 36
  A Vindication of the Rights of Woman, 18,
    35–6
World War One, 183–7
Wright, Elsie, 187–95
  Frances and the Fairies, 188, 194
  Frances and the Leaping Fairy, 189, 194
  see also Griffiths, Frances
Wright of Derby, Joseph, 68

Young, Robert, 115

CAMBRIDGE STUDIES IN NINETEENTH-CENTURY
LITERATURE AND CULTURE

General editor
Gillian Beer, *University of Cambridge*

Titles published

1 The Sickroom in Victorian Fiction: The Art of Being Ill
   by Miriam Bailin, *Washington University*

2 Muscular Christianity: Embodying the Victorian Age
   edited by Donald E. Hall, *California State University, Northridge*

3 Victorian Masculinities: Manhood and Masculine Poetics in Early
   Victorian Literature and Art
   by Herbert Sussman, *Northeastern University*

4 Byron and the Victorians
   by Andrew Elfenbein, *University of Minnesota*

5 Literature in the Marketplace: Nineteenth-Century British
   Publishing and the Circulation of Books
   edited by John O. Jordan, *University of California, Santa Cruz*
   and Robert L. Patten, *Rice University*

6 Victorian Photography, Painting and Poetry
   by Lindsay Smith, *University of Sussex*

7 Charlotte Brontë and Victorian Psychology
   by Sally Shuttleworth, *University of Sheffield*

8 The Gothic Body: Sexuality, Materialism and Degeneration at the
   Fin de Siècle
   by Kelly Hurley, *University of Colorado at Boulder*

9 Rereading Walter Pater
   by William F. Shuter, *Eastern Michigan University*

10 Remaking Queen Victoria
   edited by Margaret Homans, *Yale University*
   and Adrienne Munich, *State University of New York, Stony Brook*

11 Disease, Desire, and the Body in Victorian Women's
   Popular Novels
   by Pamela K. Gilbert, *University of Florida*

1 2 Realism, Representation, and the Arts in Nineteenth-Century
Literature
by Alison Byerly, *Middlebury College, Vermont*

1 3 Literary Culture and the Pacific
by Vanessa Smith, *King's College, Cambridge*

1 4 Professional Domesticity in the Victorian Novel: Women,
Work and Home
by Monica F. Cohen

1 5 Victorian Renovations of the Novel: Narrative Annexes
and the Boundaries of Representation
by Suzanne Keen, *Washington and Lee University*

1 6 Actresses on the Victorian Stage: Feminine Performance
and the Galatea Myth
by Gail Marshall, *University of Leeds*

1 7 Death and the Mother from Dickens to Freud: Victorian Fiction
and the Anxiety of Origin
by Carolyn Dever, *Vanderbilt University*

1 8 Ancestry and Narrative in Nineteenth-Century British Literature:
Blood Relations from Edgeworth to Hardy
by Sophie Gilmartin, *Royal Holloway, University of London*

1 9 Dickens, Novel Reading, and the Victorian Popular Theatre
by Deborah Vlock

20 After Dickens: Reading, Adaptation and Performance
by John Glavin, *Georgetown University*

21 Victorian Women Writers and the Woman Question
edited by Nicola Diane Thompson, *Kingston University, London*

22 Rhythm, and Will in Victorian Poetry
by Matthew Campbell, *University of Sheffield*

23 Gender, Race, and the Writing of Empire: Public Discourse
and the Boer War
by Paula M. Krebs, *Wheaton College, Massachusetts*

24 Ruskin's God
by Michael Wheeler, *University of Southampton*

25 Dickens and the Daughter of the House
by Hilary M. Schor, *University of Southern California*

26 Detective Fiction and the Rise of Forensic Science
by Ronald R. Thomas, *Trinity College, Hartford*

27 Testimony and Advocacy in Victorian Law, Literature, and Theology
   by Jan-Melissa Schramm, *Lucy Cavendish College, Cambridge*

28 Victorian Writing about Risk: Imagining a Safe England
   in a Dangerous World
   by Elaine Freedgood, *University of Pennsylvania*

29 Physiognomy and the Meaning of Expression
   in Nineteenth-Century Culture
   by Lucy Hartley, *University of Southampton*

30 The Victorian Parlour: A Cultural Study
   by Thad Logan, *Rice University, Houston*

31 Aestheticism and Sexual Parody, 1840–1940
   by Dennis Denisoff, *Ryerson University*

32 Literature, Technology and Magical Thinking, 1880–1920
   by Pamela Thurschwell, *University College London*

33 Fairies in Nineteenth-Century Art and Literature
   by Nicola Bown, *Birkbeck College, London*

Lightning Source UK Ltd.
Milton Keynes UK
26 January 2010

149146UK00001B/26/A